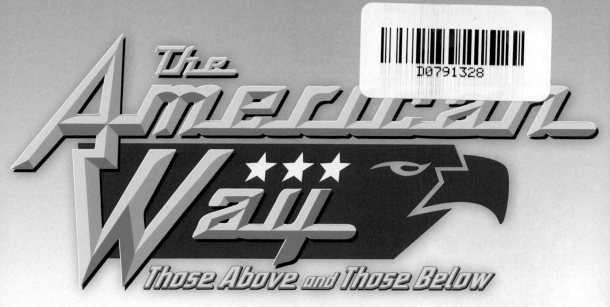

The American Way

Those Above and Those Below

Written by
JOHN RIDLEY

Pencils by
GEORGES JEANTY

Inks by
JOHN LIVESAY
DANNY MIKI
PAUL NEARY
LE BEAU UNDERWOOD

Colors by
NICK FILARDI

Letters by
TRAVIS LANHAM

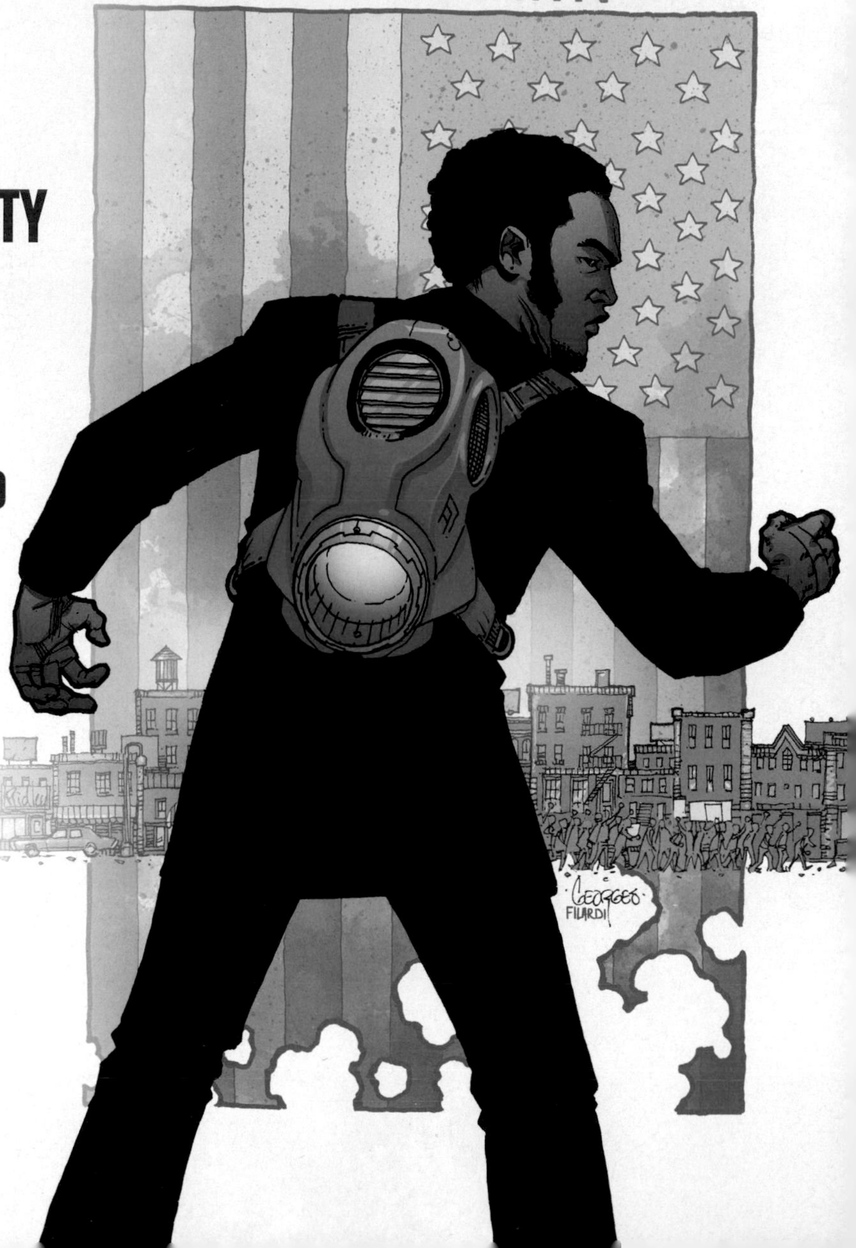
GEORGES
FILARDI

Cover Art and Original Series Covers by
GEORGES JEANTY
and **NICK FILARDI**

THE AMERICAN WAY
created by **JOHN RIDLEY**

JAMIE S. RICH
Editor - Original Series and Group Editor - Vertigo Comics
MAGGIE HOWELL
Assistant Editor - Original Series
JEB WOODARD
Group Editor - Collected Editions
SCOTT NYBAKKEN
Editor - Collected Edition
STEVE COOK
Design Director - Books
CURTIS KING JR.
Publication Design

BOB HARRAS
Senior VP - Editor-in-Chief, DC Comics
MARK DOYLE
Executive Editor, Vertigo

DIANE NELSON
President
DAN DiDIO
Publisher
JIM LEE
Publisher
GEOFF JOHNS
President & Chief Creative Officer
AMIT DESAI
Executive VP - Business & Marketing Strategy,
Direct to Consumer & Global Franchise Management
SAM ADES
Senior VP & General Manager, Digital Services
BOBBIE CHASE
VP & Executive Editor, Young Reader & Talent Development
MARK CHIARELLO
Senior VP - Art, Design & Collected Editions
JOHN CUNNINGHAM
Senior VP - Sales & Trade Marketing
ANNE DePIES
Senior VP - Business Strategy, Finance & Administration
DON FALLETTI
VP - Manufacturing Operations
LAWRENCE GANEM
VP - Editorial Administration & Talent Relations
ALISON GILL
Senior VP - Manufacturing & Operations
HANK KANALZ
Senior VP - Editorial Strategy & Administration
JAY KOGAN
VP - Legal Affairs
JACK MAHAN
VP - Business Affairs
NICK J. NAPOLITANO
VP - Manufacturing Administration
EDDIE SCANNELL
VP - Consumer Marketing
COURTNEY SIMMONS
Senior VP - Publicity & Communications
JIM (SKI) SOKOLOWSKI
VP - Comic Book Specialty Sales & Trade Marketing
NANCY SPEARS
VP - Mass, Book, Digital Sales & Trade Marketing
MICHELE R. WELLS
VP - Content Strategy

THE AMERICAN WAY: THOSE ABOVE AND THOSE BELOW

DC Comics, 2900 West Alameda Avenue, Burbank, CA 91505
LSC Communications, Kendallville, IN, USA. 3/16/18.
First Printing. ISBN: 978-1-4012-7835-9

Library of Congress Cataloging-in-Publication Data is available.

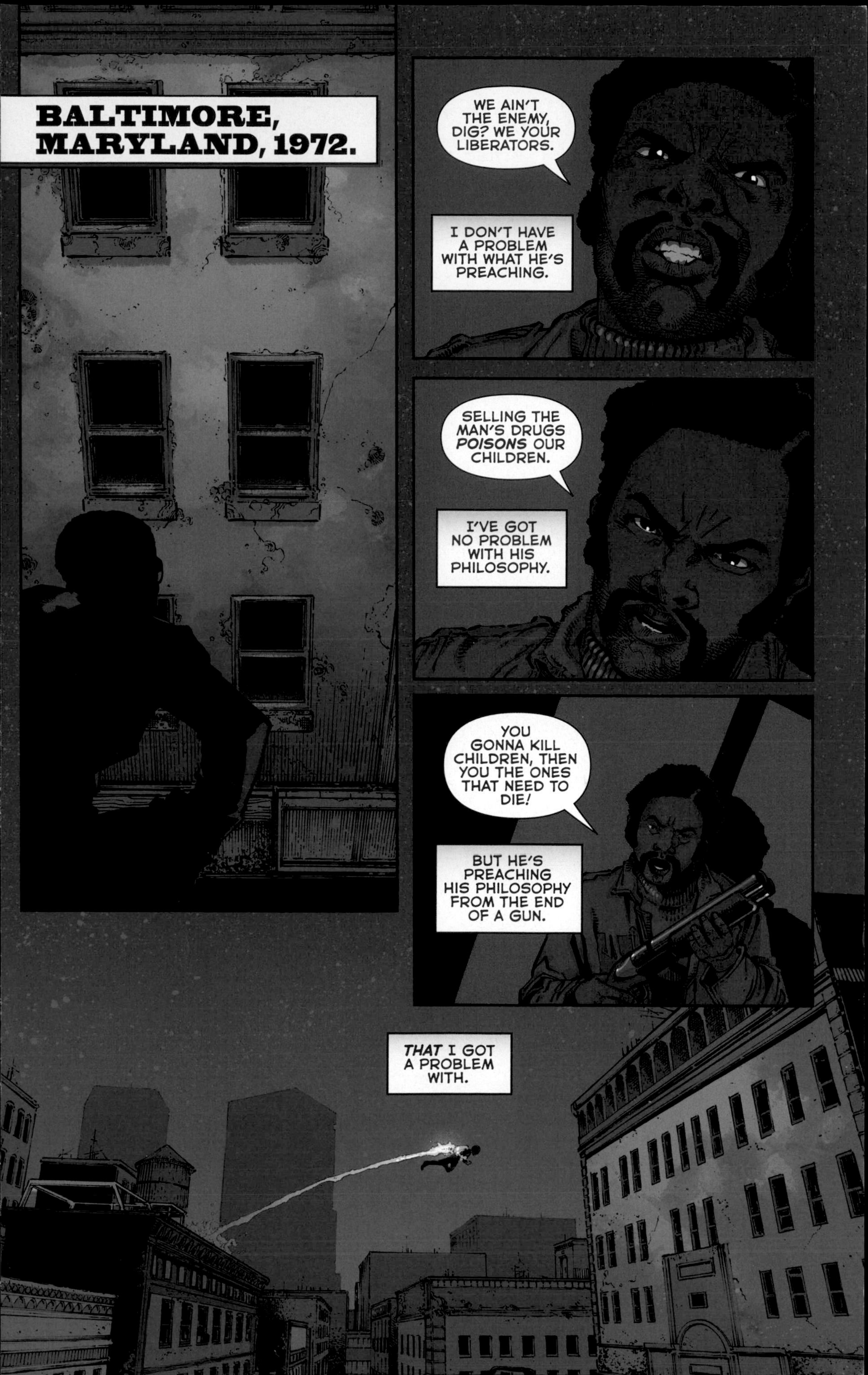
BALTIMORE, MARYLAND, 1972.
WE AIN'T THE ENEMY, DIG? WE YOUR LIBERATORS.
I DON'T HAVE A PROBLEM WITH WHAT HE'S PREACHING.
SELLING THE MAN'S DRUGS *POISONS* OUR CHILDREN.
I'VE GOT NO PROBLEM WITH HIS PHILOSOPHY.
YOU GONNA KILL CHILDREN, THEN YOU THE ONES THAT NEED TO DIE!
BUT HE'S PREACHING HIS PHILOSOPHY FROM THE END OF A GUN.
THAT I GOT A PROBLEM WITH.

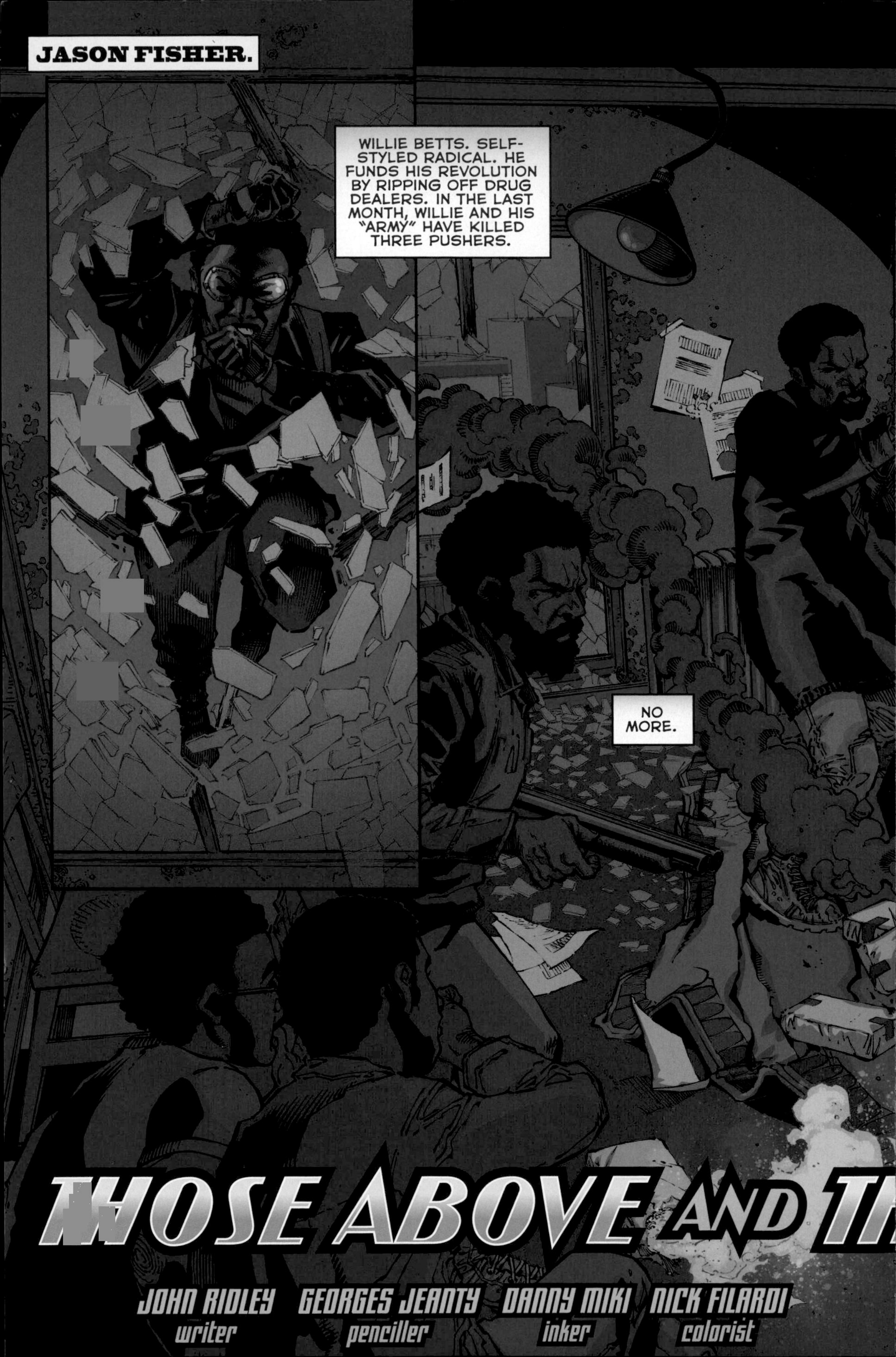
JASON FISHER.
WILLIE BETTS. SELF-STYLED RADICAL. HE FUNDS HIS REVOLUTION BY RIPPING OFF DRUG DEALERS. IN THE LAST MONTH, WILLIE AND HIS "ARMY" HAVE KILLED THREE PUSHERS.
NO MORE.
HOSE ABOVE AND
JOHN RIDLEY writer
GEORGES JEANTY penciller
DANNY MIKI inker
NICK FILARDI colorist

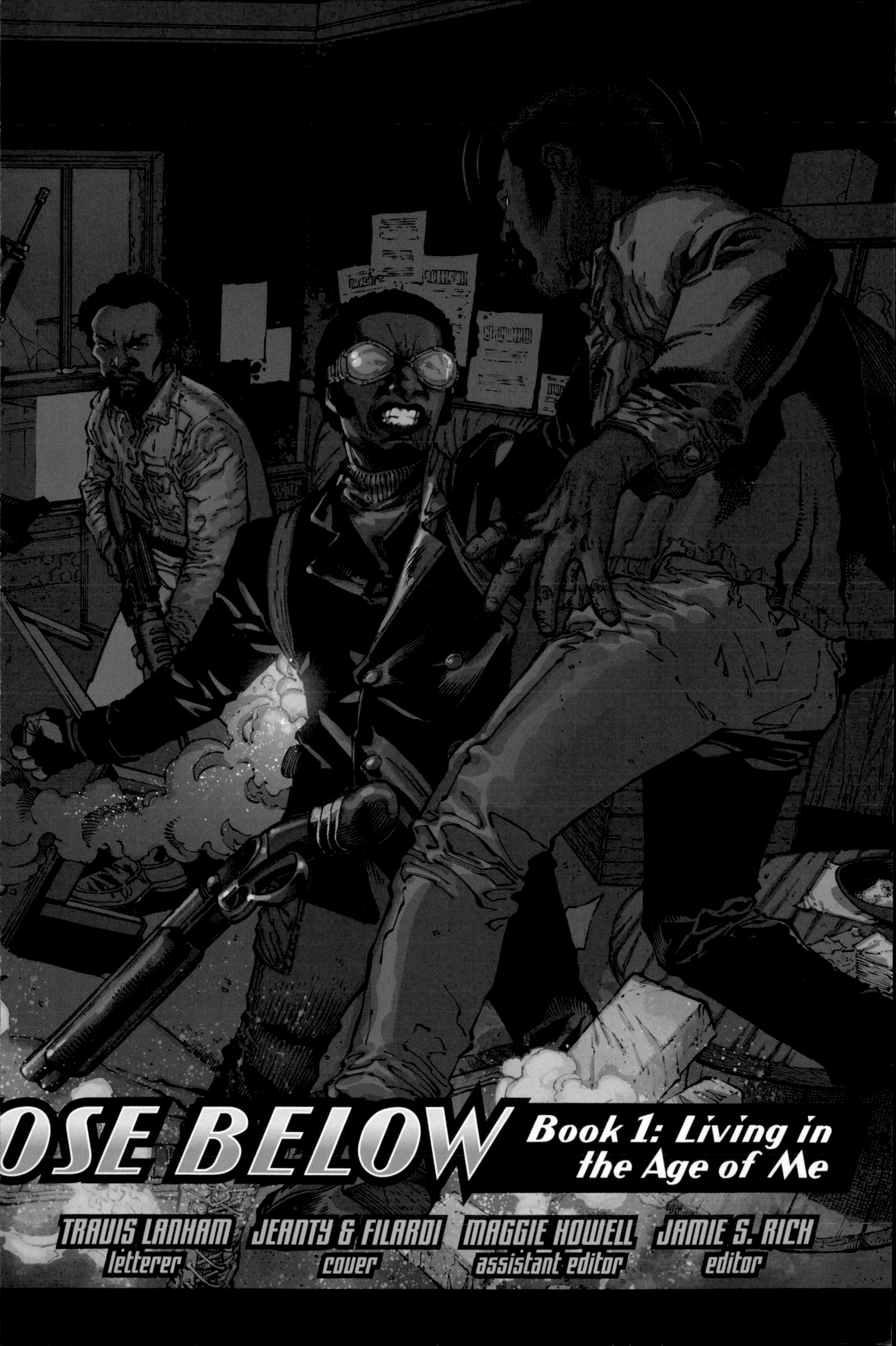

OSE BELOW
Book 1: Living in the Age of Me
TRAVIS LANHAM letterer
JEANTY & FILARDI cover
MAGGIE HOWELL assistant editor
JAMIE S. RICH editor

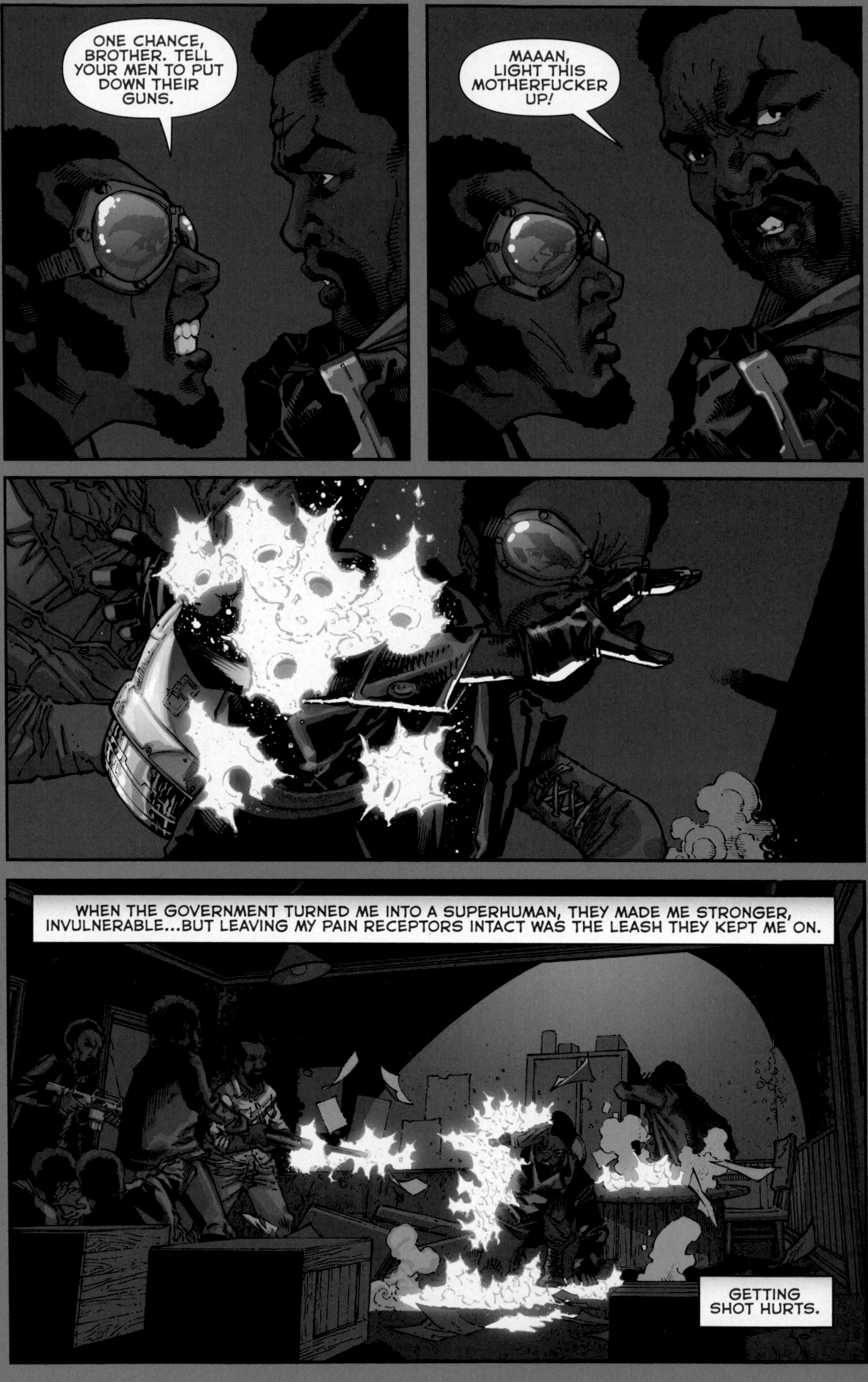
ONE CHANCE, BROTHER. TELL YOUR MEN TO PUT DOWN THEIR GUNS.
MAAAN, LIGHT THIS MOTHERFUCKER UP!
WHEN THE GOVERNMENT TURNED ME INTO A SUPERHUMAN, THEY MADE ME STRONGER, INVULNERABLE...BUT LEAVING MY PAIN RECEPTORS INTACT WAS THE LEASH THEY KEPT ME ON.
GETTING SHOT HURTS.

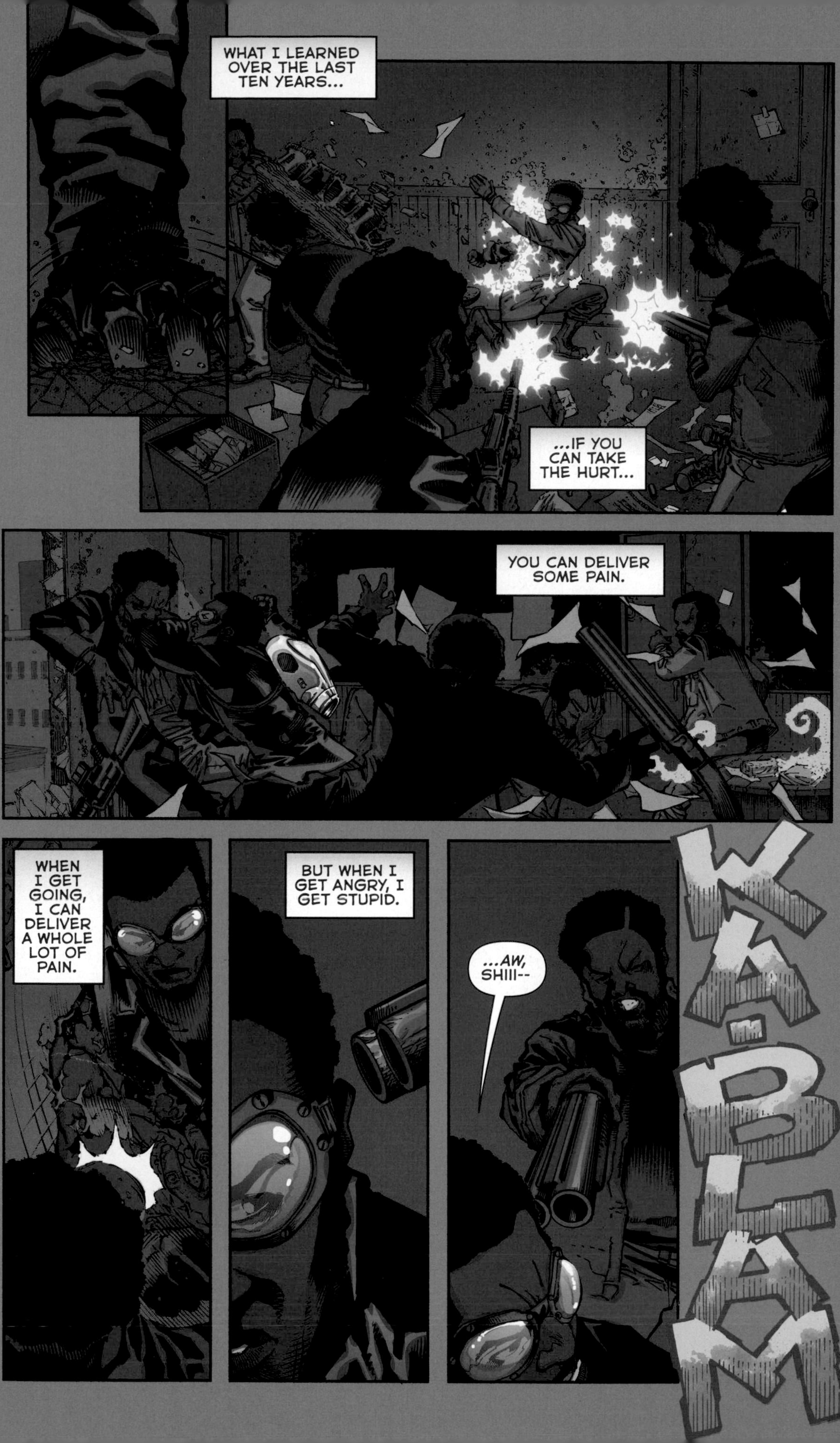
WHAT I LEARNED OVER THE LAST TEN YEARS...
...IF YOU CAN TAKE THE HURT...
YOU CAN DELIVER SOME PAIN.
WHEN I GET GOING, I CAN DELIVER A WHOLE LOT OF PAIN.
BUT WHEN I GET ANGRY, I GET STUPID.
...AW, SHIII--
KABLAM

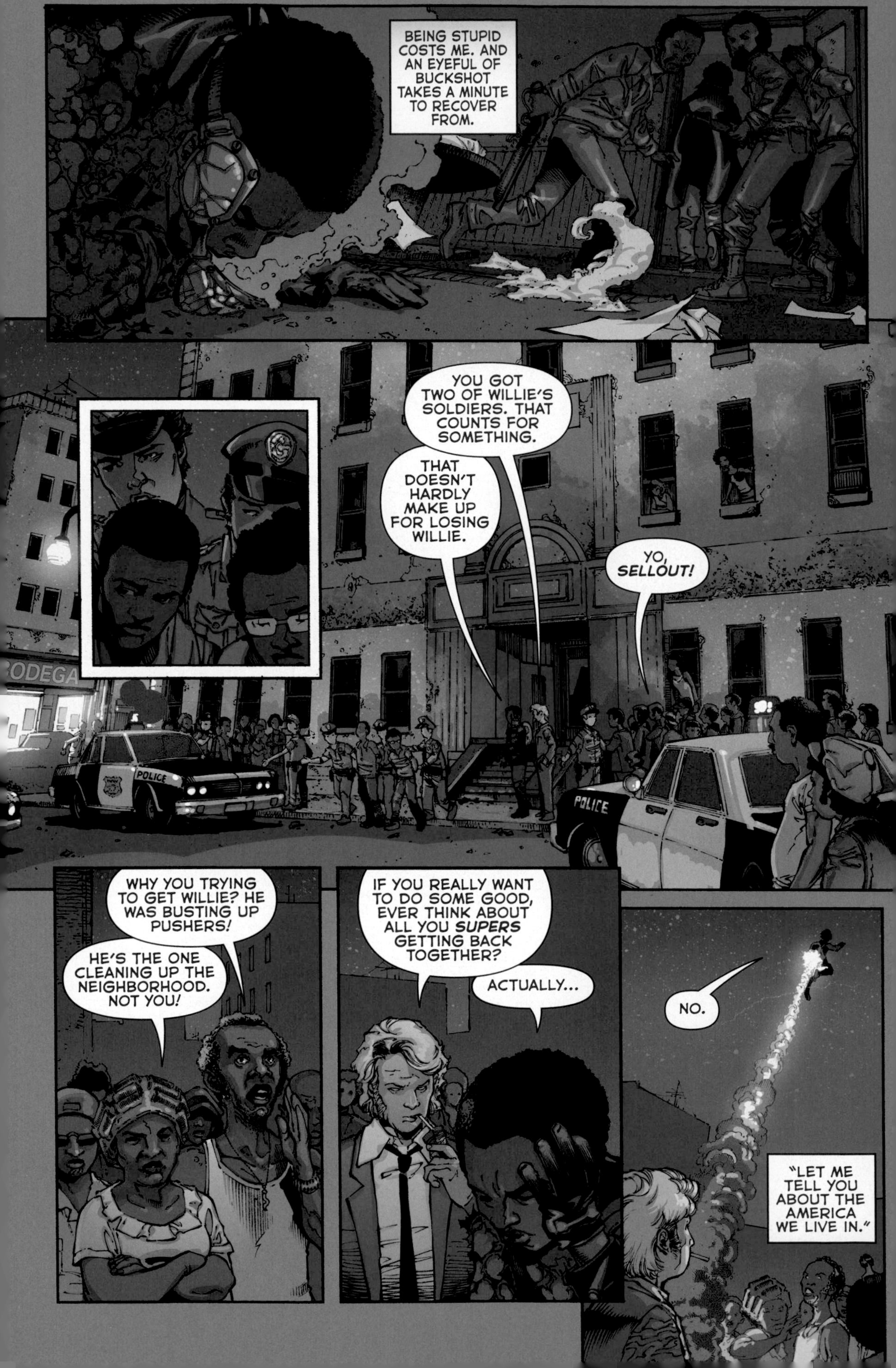
BEING STUPID COSTS ME. AND AN EYEFUL OF BUCKSHOT TAKES A MINUTE TO RECOVER FROM.
YOU GOT TWO OF WILLIE'S SOLDIERS. THAT COUNTS FOR SOMETHING.
THAT DOESN'T HARDLY MAKE UP FOR LOSING WILLIE.
YO, SELLOUT!
BODEGA
POLICE
POLICE
WHY YOU TRYING TO GET WILLIE? HE WAS BUSTING UP PUSHERS!
HE'S THE ONE CLEANING UP THE NEIGHBORHOOD. NOT YOU!
IF YOU REALLY WANT TO DO SOME GOOD, EVER THINK ABOUT ALL YOU SUPERS GETTING BACK TOGETHER?
ACTUALLY...
NO.
"LET ME TELL YOU ABOUT THE AMERICA WE LIVE IN."

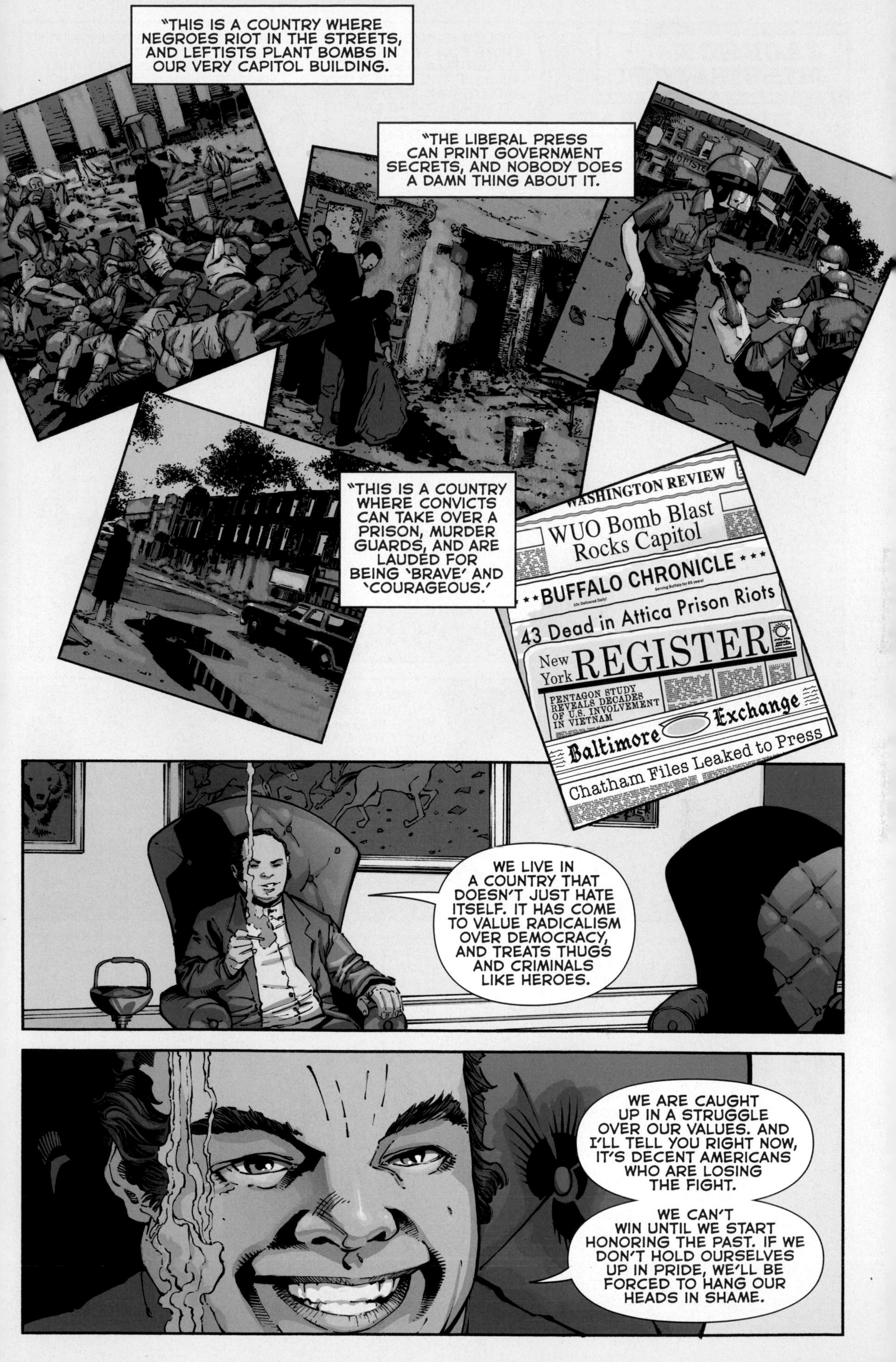
"THIS IS A COUNTRY WHERE NEGROES RIOT IN THE STREETS, AND LEFTISTS PLANT BOMBS IN OUR VERY CAPITOL BUILDING.
"THE LIBERAL PRESS CAN PRINT GOVERNMENT SECRETS, AND NOBODY DOES A DAMN THING ABOUT IT.
"THIS IS A COUNTRY WHERE CONVICTS CAN TAKE OVER A PRISON, MURDER GUARDS, AND ARE LAUDED FOR BEING 'BRAVE' AND 'COURAGEOUS.'
WASHINGTON REVIEW
WUO Bomb Blast Rocks Capitol
BUFFALO CHRONICLE
43 Dead in Attica Prison Riots
New York REGISTER
PENTAGON STUDY REVEALS DECADES OF U.S. INVOLVEMENT IN VIETNAM
Baltimore Exchange
Chatham Files Leaked to Press
WE LIVE IN A COUNTRY THAT DOESN'T JUST HATE ITSELF. IT HAS COME TO VALUE RADICALISM OVER DEMOCRACY, AND TREATS THUGS AND CRIMINALS LIKE HEROES.
WE ARE CAUGHT UP IN A STRUGGLE OVER OUR VALUES. AND I'LL TELL YOU RIGHT NOW, IT'S DECENT AMERICANS WHO ARE LOSING THE FIGHT.
WE CAN'T WIN UNTIL WE START HONORING THE PAST. IF WE DON'T HOLD OURSELVES UP IN PRIDE, WE'LL BE FORCED TO HANG OUR HEADS IN SHAME.

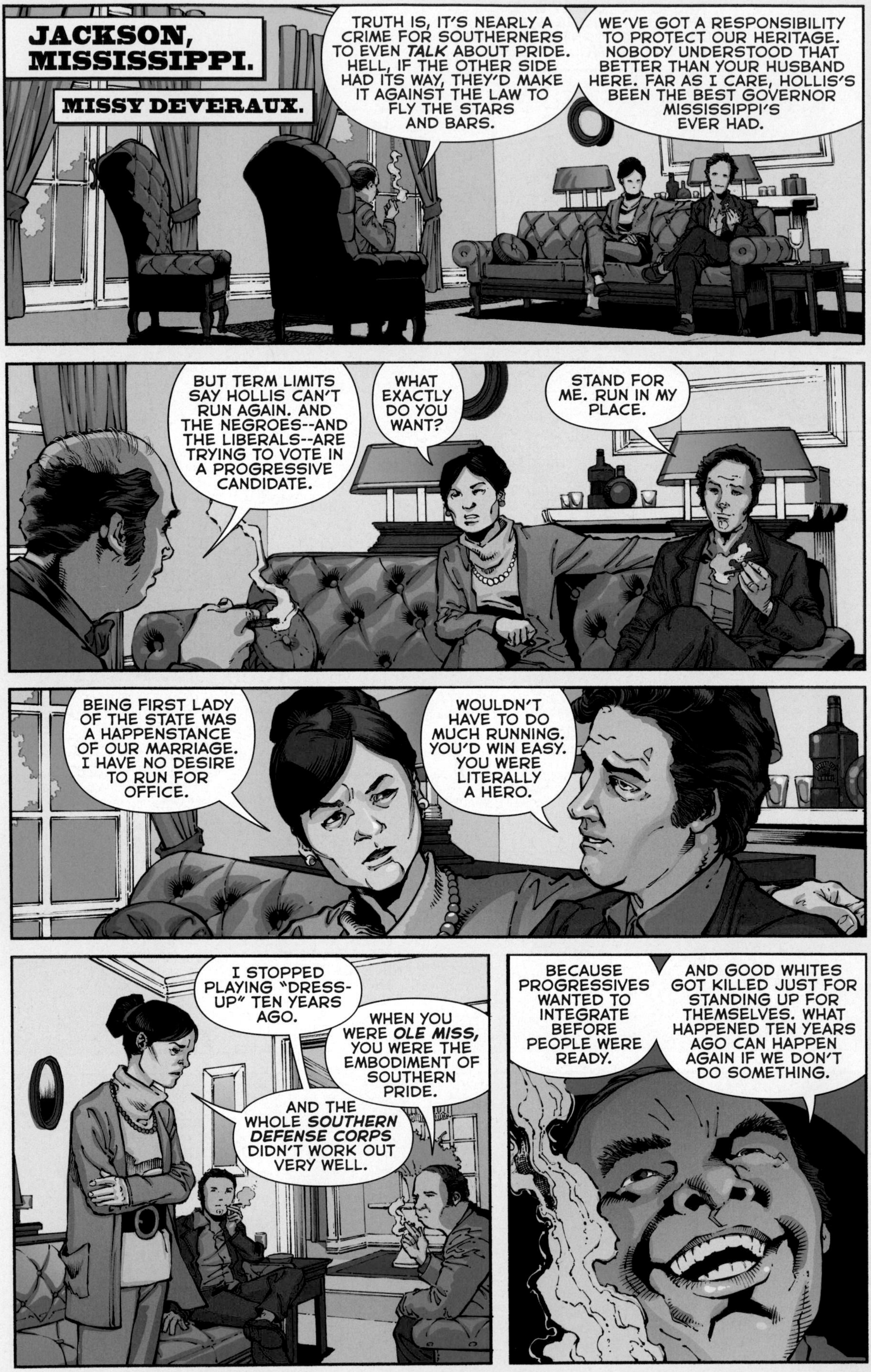
JACKSON, MISSISSIPPI.
MISSY DEVERAUX.
TRUTH IS, IT'S NEARLY A CRIME FOR SOUTHERNERS TO EVEN *TALK* ABOUT PRIDE. HELL, IF THE OTHER SIDE HAD ITS WAY, THEY'D MAKE IT AGAINST THE LAW TO FLY THE STARS AND BARS.
WE'VE GOT A RESPONSIBILITY TO PROTECT OUR HERITAGE. NOBODY UNDERSTOOD THAT BETTER THAN YOUR HUSBAND HERE. FAR AS I CARE, HOLLIS'S BEEN THE BEST GOVERNOR MISSISSIPPI'S EVER HAD.
BUT TERM LIMITS SAY HOLLIS CAN'T RUN AGAIN. AND THE NEGROES--AND THE LIBERALS--ARE TRYING TO VOTE IN A PROGRESSIVE CANDIDATE.
WHAT EXACTLY DO YOU WANT?
STAND FOR ME. RUN IN MY PLACE.
BEING FIRST LADY OF THE STATE WAS A HAPPENSTANCE OF OUR MARRIAGE. I HAVE NO DESIRE TO RUN FOR OFFICE.
WOULDN'T HAVE TO DO MUCH RUNNING. YOU'D WIN EASY. YOU WERE LITERALLY A HERO.
I STOPPED PLAYING "DRESS-UP" TEN YEARS AGO.
WHEN YOU WERE *OLE MISS,* YOU WERE THE EMBODIMENT OF SOUTHERN PRIDE.
AND THE WHOLE *SOUTHERN DEFENSE CORPS* DIDN'T WORK OUT VERY WELL.
BECAUSE PROGRESSIVES WANTED TO INTEGRATE BEFORE PEOPLE WERE READY.
AND GOOD WHITES GOT KILLED JUST FOR STANDING UP FOR THEMSELVES. WHAT HAPPENED TEN YEARS AGO CAN HAPPEN AGAIN IF WE DON'T DO SOMETHING.

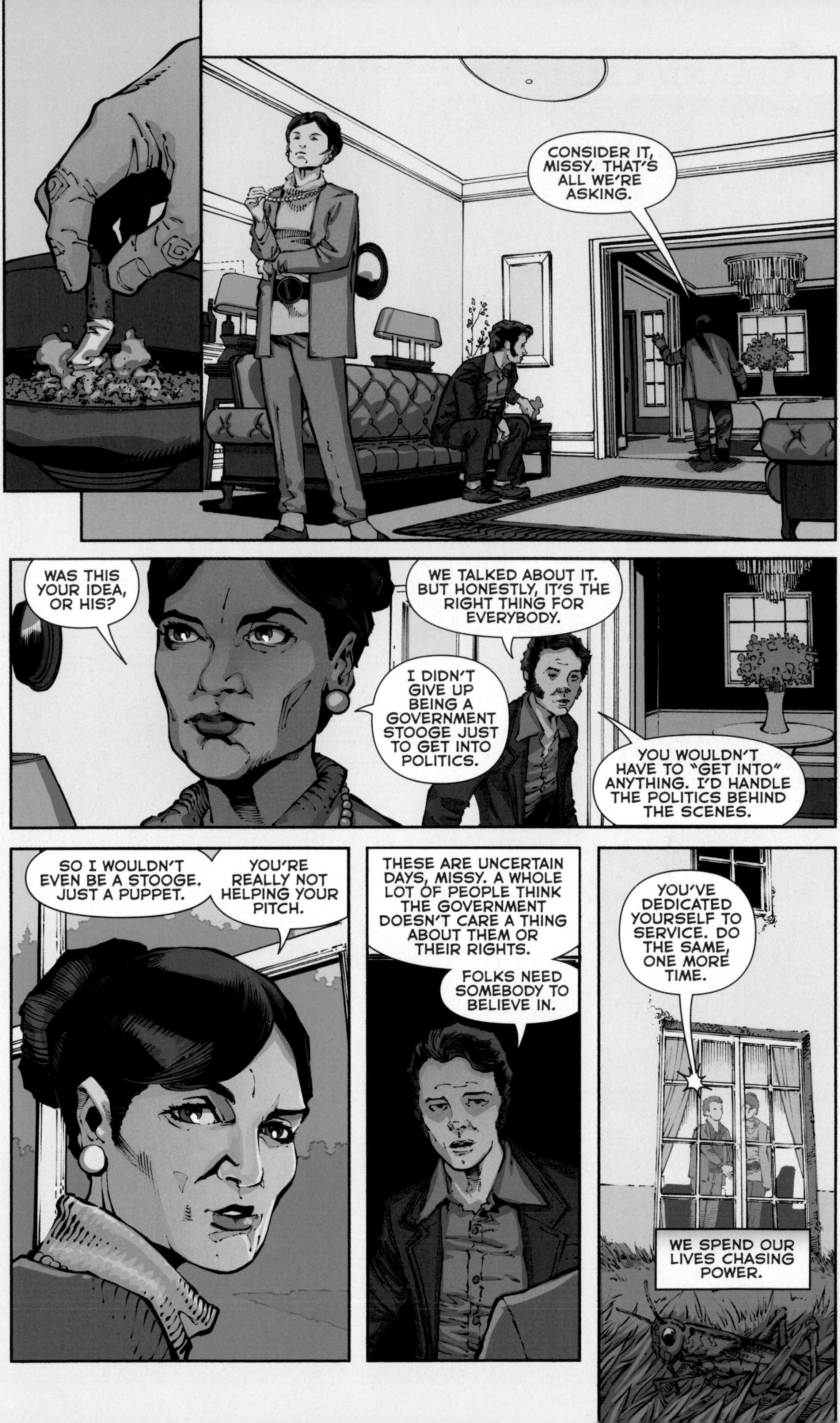
CONSIDER IT, MISSY. THAT'S ALL WE'RE ASKING.
WAS THIS YOUR IDEA, OR HIS?
WE TALKED ABOUT IT. BUT HONESTLY, IT'S THE RIGHT THING FOR EVERYBODY.
I DIDN'T GIVE UP BEING A GOVERNMENT STOOGE JUST TO GET INTO POLITICS.
YOU WOULDN'T HAVE TO "GET INTO" ANYTHING. I'D HANDLE THE POLITICS BEHIND THE SCENES.
SO I WOULDN'T EVEN BE A STOOGE. JUST A PUPPET.
YOU'RE REALLY NOT HELPING YOUR PITCH.
THESE ARE UNCERTAIN DAYS, MISSY. A WHOLE LOT OF PEOPLE THINK THE GOVERNMENT DOESN'T CARE A THING ABOUT THEM OR THEIR RIGHTS.
FOLKS NEED SOMEBODY TO BELIEVE IN.
YOU'VE DEDICATED YOURSELF TO SERVICE. DO THE SAME, ONE MORE TIME.
WE SPEND OUR LIVES CHASING POWER.

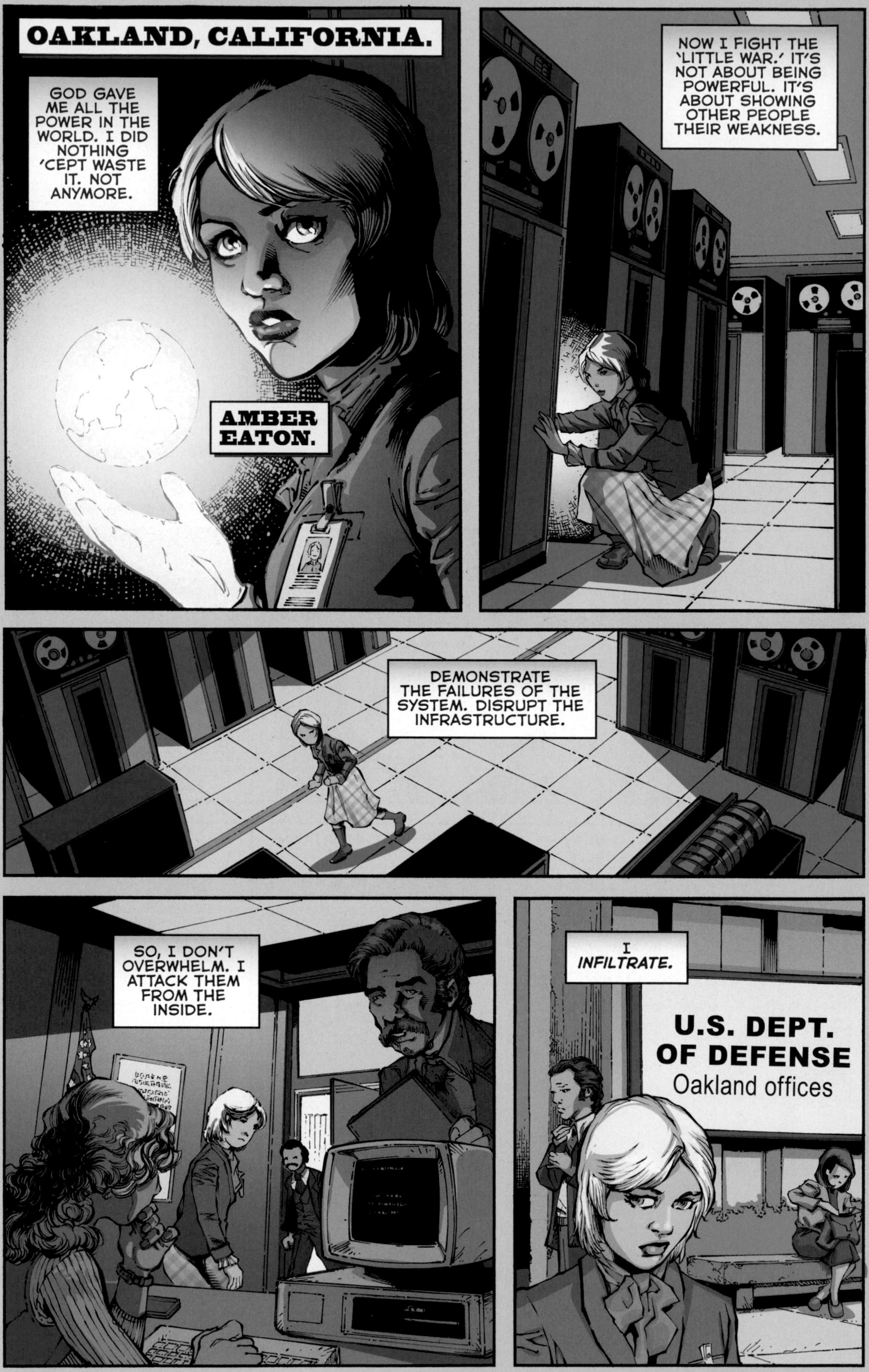
OAKLAND, CALIFORNIA.
GOD GAVE ME ALL THE POWER IN THE WORLD. I DID NOTHING 'CEPT WASTE IT. NOT ANYMORE.
AMBER EATON.
NOW I FIGHT THE 'LITTLE WAR.' IT'S NOT ABOUT BEING POWERFUL. IT'S ABOUT SHOWING OTHER PEOPLE THEIR WEAKNESS.
DEMONSTRATE THE FAILURES OF THE SYSTEM. DISRUPT THE INFRASTRUCTURE.
SO, I DON'T OVERWHELM. I ATTACK THEM FROM THE INSIDE.
I *INFILTRATE.*
U.S. DEPT. OF DEFENSE
Oakland offices

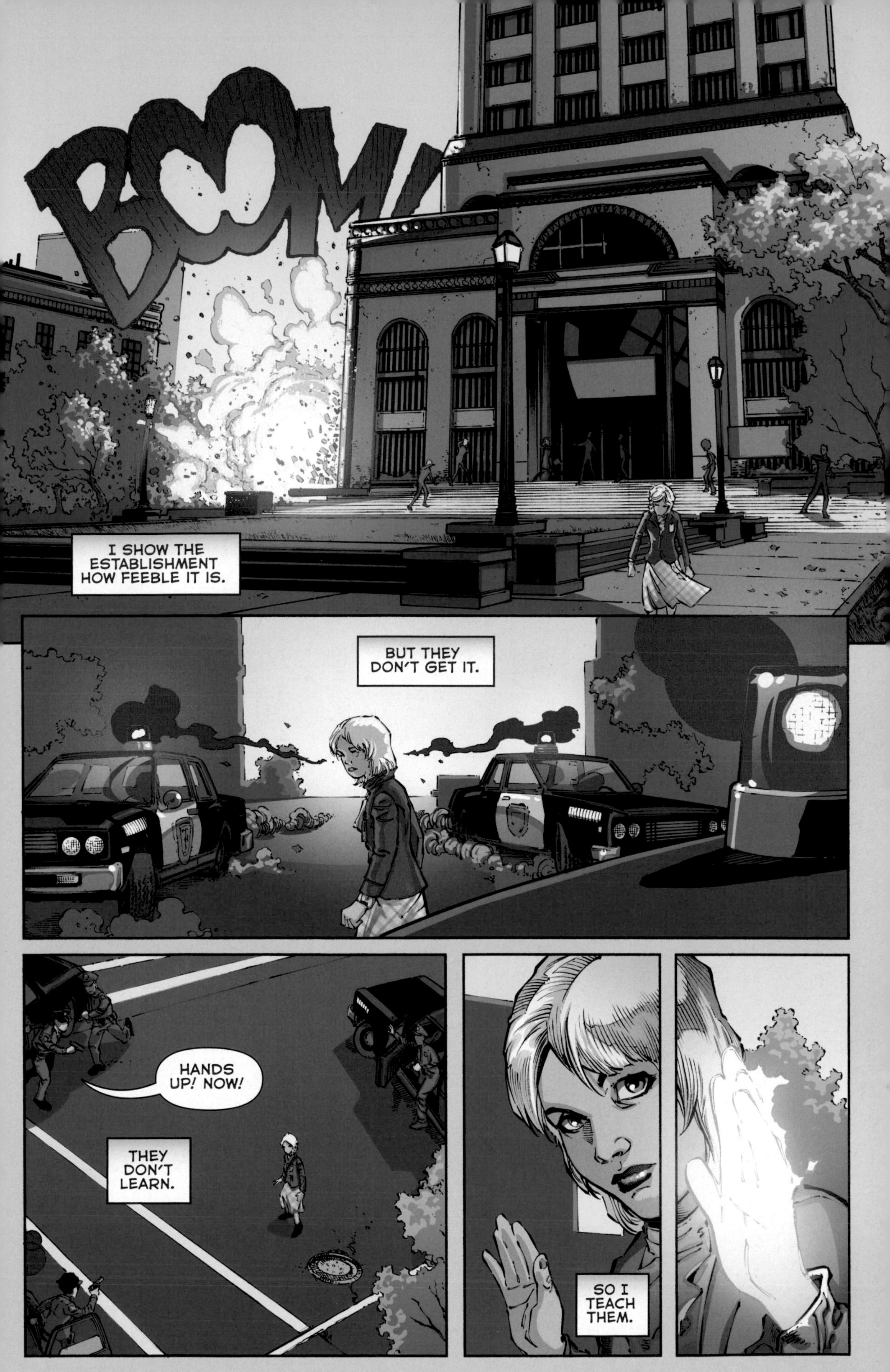
BOOM!
I SHOW THE ESTABLISHMENT HOW FEEBLE IT IS.
BUT THEY DON'T GET IT.
HANDS UP! NOW!
THEY DON'T LEARN.
SO I TEACH THEM.

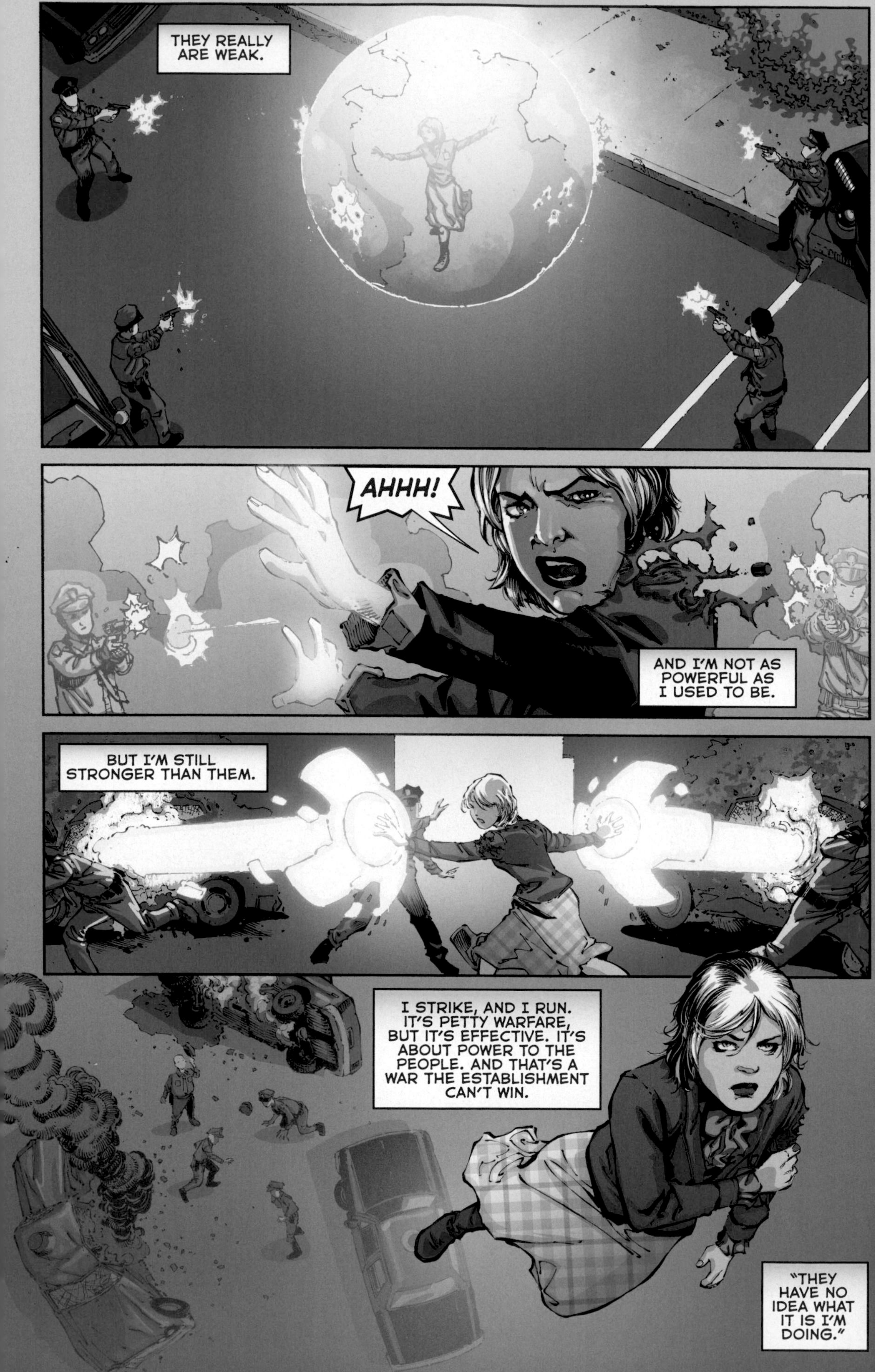
THEY REALLY ARE WEAK.
AHHH!
AND I'M NOT AS POWERFUL AS I USED TO BE.
BUT I'M STILL STRONGER THAN THEM.
I STRIKE, AND I RUN. IT'S PETTY WARFARE, BUT IT'S EFFECTIVE. IT'S ABOUT POWER TO THE PEOPLE. AND THAT'S A WAR THE ESTABLISHMENT CAN'T WIN.
"THEY HAVE NO IDEA WHAT IT IS I'M DOING."

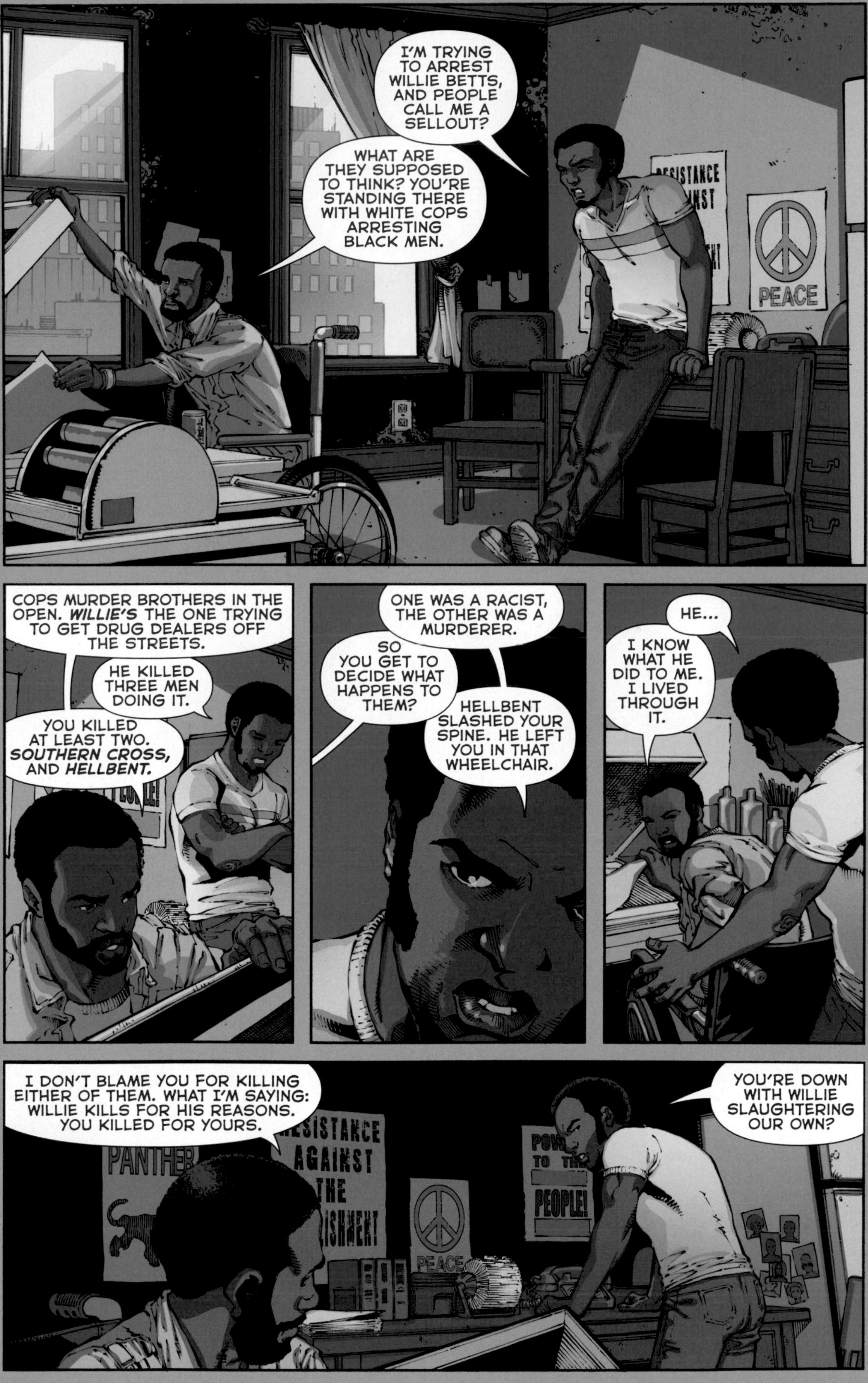
I'M TRYING TO ARREST WILLIE BETTS, AND PEOPLE CALL ME A SELLOUT?
WHAT ARE THEY SUPPOSED TO THINK? YOU'RE STANDING THERE WITH WHITE COPS ARRESTING BLACK MEN.
PEACE
COPS MURDER BROTHERS IN THE OPEN. WILLIE'S THE ONE TRYING TO GET DRUG DEALERS OFF THE STREETS.
HE KILLED THREE MEN DOING IT.
YOU KILLED AT LEAST TWO. SOUTHERN CROSS, AND HELLBENT.
ONE WAS A RACIST, THE OTHER WAS A MURDERER.
SO YOU GET TO DECIDE WHAT HAPPENS TO THEM?
HELLBENT SLASHED YOUR SPINE. HE LEFT YOU IN THAT WHEELCHAIR.
HE...
I KNOW WHAT HE DID TO ME. I LIVED THROUGH IT.
I DON'T BLAME YOU FOR KILLING EITHER OF THEM. WHAT I'M SAYING: WILLIE KILLS FOR HIS REASONS. YOU KILLED FOR YOURS.
YOU'RE DOWN WITH WILLIE SLAUGHTERING OUR OWN?
PANTHER
RESISTANCE AGAINST THE
PEACE
PEOPLE!

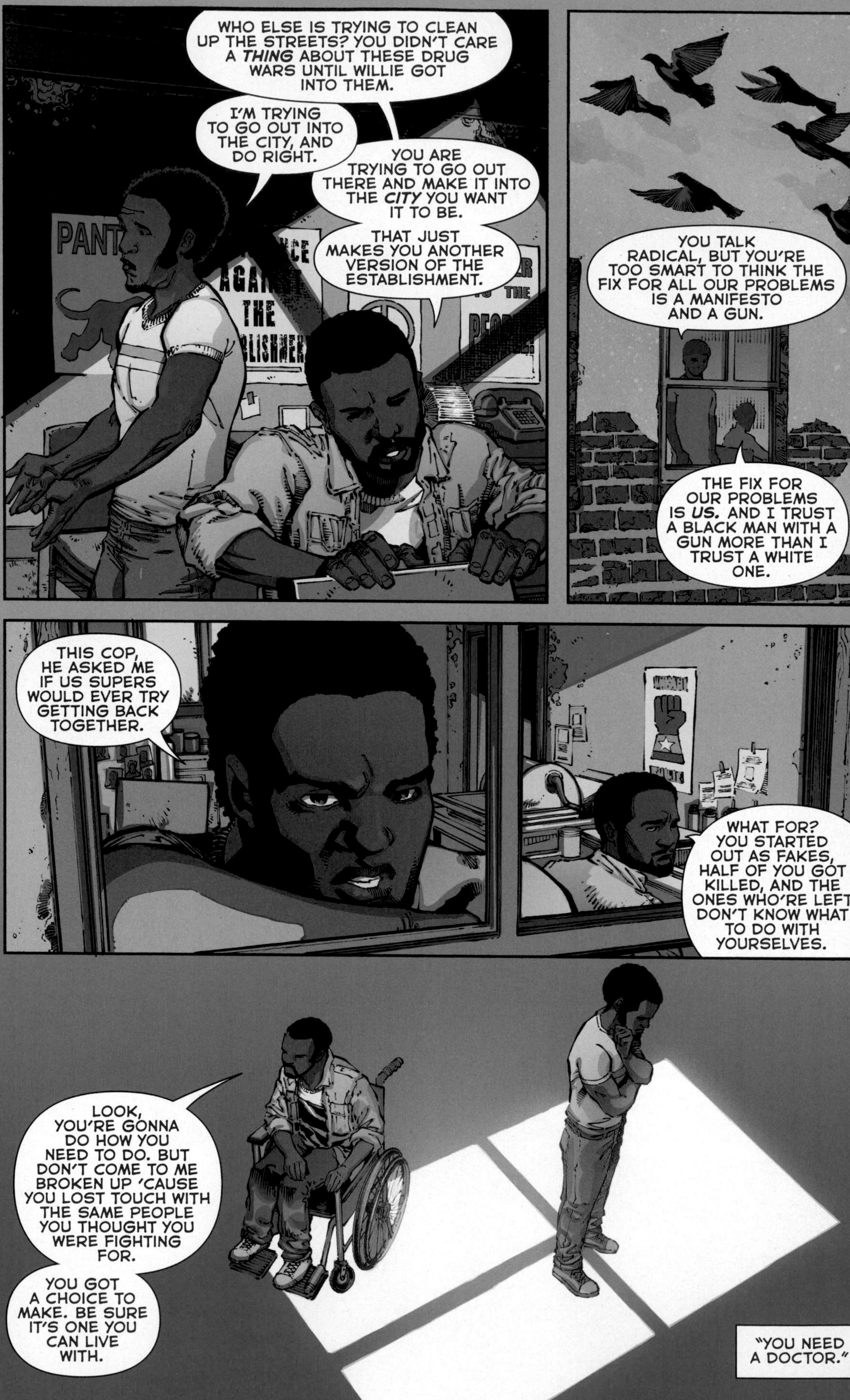
WHO ELSE IS TRYING TO CLEAN UP THE STREETS? YOU DIDN'T CARE A *THING* ABOUT THESE DRUG WARS UNTIL WILLIE GOT INTO THEM.
I'M TRYING TO GO OUT INTO THE CITY, AND DO RIGHT.
YOU ARE TRYING TO GO OUT THERE AND MAKE IT INTO THE *CITY* YOU WANT IT TO BE.
THAT JUST MAKES YOU ANOTHER VERSION OF THE ESTABLISHMENT.
YOU TALK RADICAL, BUT YOU'RE TOO SMART TO THINK THE FIX FOR ALL OUR PROBLEMS IS A MANIFESTO AND A GUN.
THE FIX FOR OUR PROBLEMS IS *US.* AND I TRUST A BLACK MAN WITH A GUN MORE THAN I TRUST A WHITE ONE.
THIS COP, HE ASKED ME IF US SUPERS WOULD EVER TRY GETTING BACK TOGETHER.
WHAT FOR? YOU STARTED OUT AS FAKES, HALF OF YOU GOT KILLED, AND THE ONES WHO'RE LEFT DON'T KNOW WHAT TO DO WITH YOURSELVES.
LOOK, YOU'RE GONNA DO HOW YOU NEED TO DO. BUT DON'T COME TO ME BROKEN UP 'CAUSE YOU LOST TOUCH WITH THE SAME PEOPLE YOU THOUGHT YOU WERE FIGHTING FOR.
YOU GOT A CHOICE TO MAKE. BE SURE IT'S ONE YOU CAN LIVE WITH.
"YOU NEED A DOCTOR."

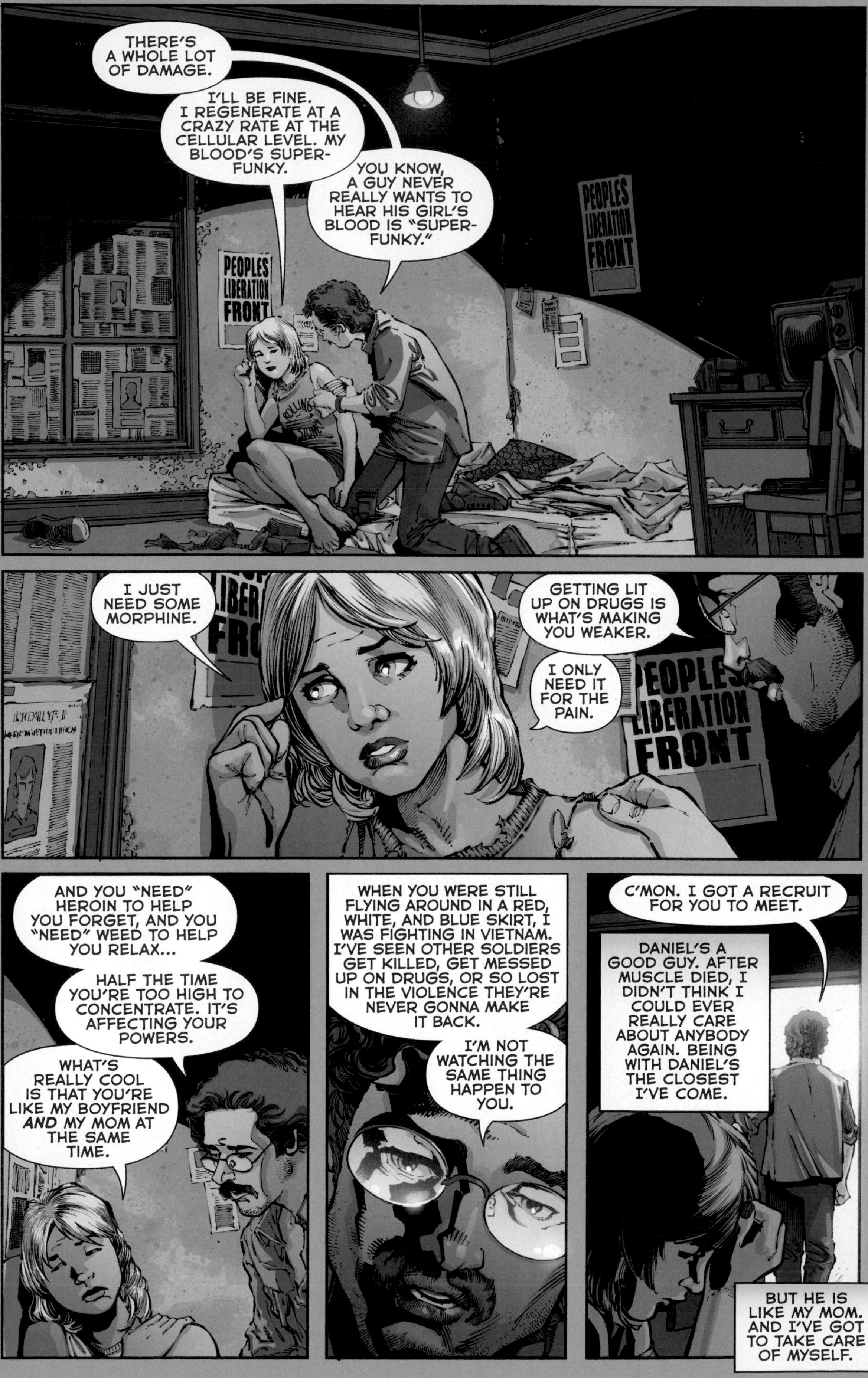

THERE'S A WHOLE LOT OF DAMAGE.
I'LL BE FINE. I REGENERATE AT A CRAZY RATE AT THE CELLULAR LEVEL. MY BLOOD'S SUPER-FUNKY.
YOU KNOW, A GUY NEVER REALLY WANTS TO HEAR HIS GIRL'S BLOOD IS "SUPER-FUNKY."
PEOPLES LIBERATION FRONT
PEOPLES LIBERATION FRONT
I JUST NEED SOME MORPHINE.
GETTING LIT UP ON DRUGS IS WHAT'S MAKING YOU WEAKER.
I ONLY NEED IT FOR THE PAIN.
PEOPLES LIBERATION FRONT
AND YOU "NEED" HEROIN TO HELP YOU FORGET, AND YOU "NEED" WEED TO HELP YOU RELAX...
HALF THE TIME YOU'RE TOO HIGH TO CONCENTRATE. IT'S AFFECTING YOUR POWERS.
WHAT'S REALLY COOL IS THAT YOU'RE LIKE MY BOYFRIEND *AND* MY MOM AT THE SAME TIME.
WHEN YOU WERE STILL FLYING AROUND IN A RED, WHITE, AND BLUE SKIRT, I WAS FIGHTING IN VIETNAM. I'VE SEEN OTHER SOLDIERS GET KILLED, GET MESSED UP ON DRUGS, OR SO LOST IN THE VIOLENCE THEY'RE NEVER GONNA MAKE IT BACK.
I'M NOT WATCHING THE SAME THING HAPPEN TO YOU.
C'MON. I GOT A RECRUIT FOR YOU TO MEET.
DANIEL'S A GOOD GUY. AFTER MUSCLE DIED, I DIDN'T THINK I COULD EVER REALLY CARE ABOUT ANYBODY AGAIN. BEING WITH DANIEL'S THE CLOSEST I'VE COME.
BUT HE IS LIKE MY MOM. AND I'VE GOT TO TAKE CARE OF MYSELF.

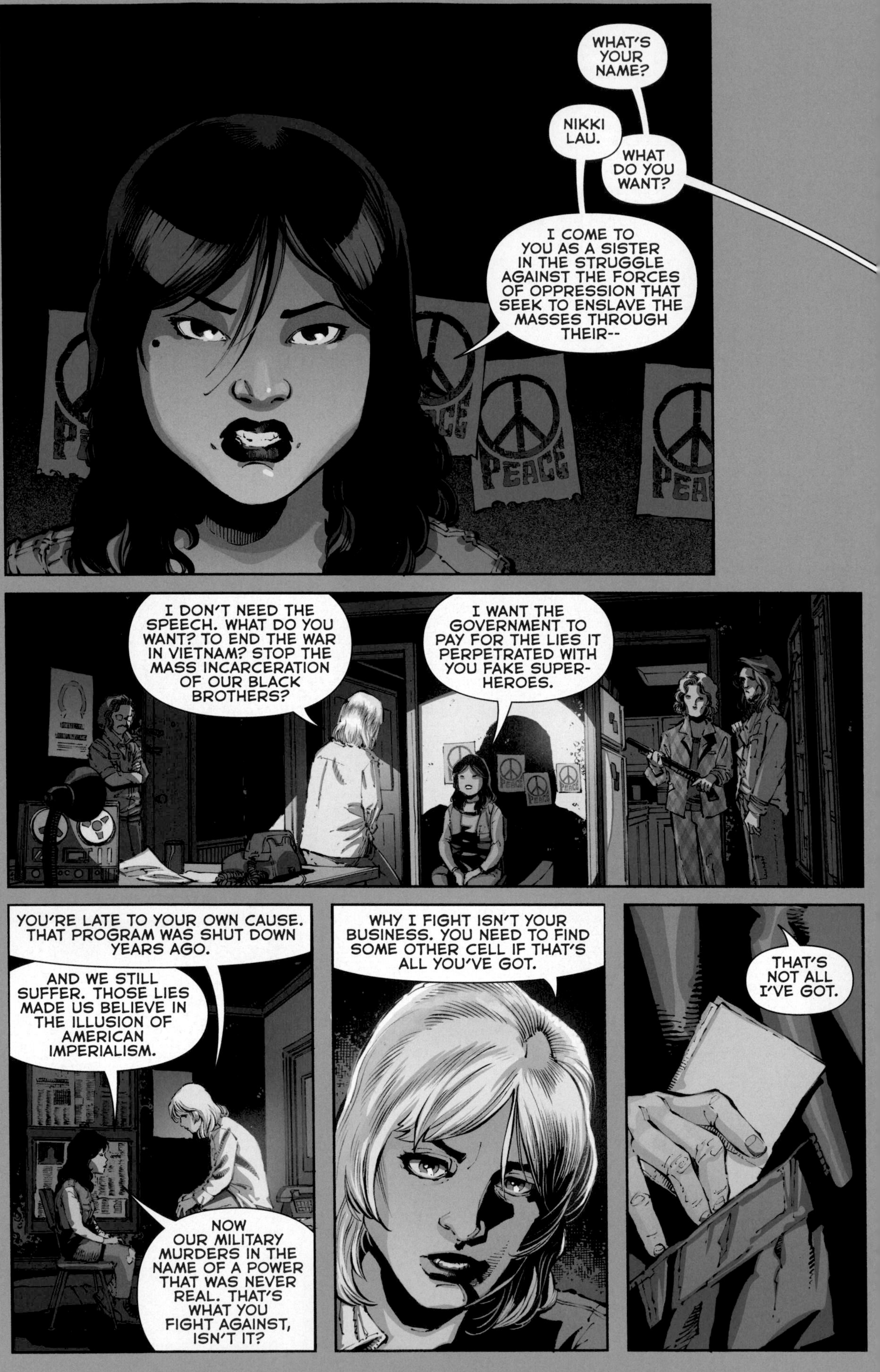
WHAT'S YOUR NAME?
NIKKI LAU.
WHAT DO YOU WANT?
I COME TO YOU AS A SISTER IN THE STRUGGLE AGAINST THE FORCES OF OPPRESSION THAT SEEK TO ENSLAVE THE MASSES THROUGH THEIR--
PEACE
PEACE
PEACE
I DON'T NEED THE SPEECH. WHAT DO YOU WANT? TO END THE WAR IN VIETNAM? STOP THE MASS INCARCERATION OF OUR BLACK BROTHERS?
I WANT THE GOVERNMENT TO PAY FOR THE LIES IT PERPETRATED WITH YOU FAKE SUPER-HEROES.
YOU'RE LATE TO YOUR OWN CAUSE. THAT PROGRAM WAS SHUT DOWN YEARS AGO.
AND WE STILL SUFFER. THOSE LIES MADE US BELIEVE IN THE ILLUSION OF AMERICAN IMPERIALISM.
NOW OUR MILITARY MURDERS IN THE NAME OF A POWER THAT WAS NEVER REAL. THAT'S WHAT YOU FIGHT AGAINST, ISN'T IT?
WHY I FIGHT ISN'T YOUR BUSINESS. YOU NEED TO FIND SOME OTHER CELL IF THAT'S ALL YOU'VE GOT.
THAT'S NOT ALL I'VE GOT.

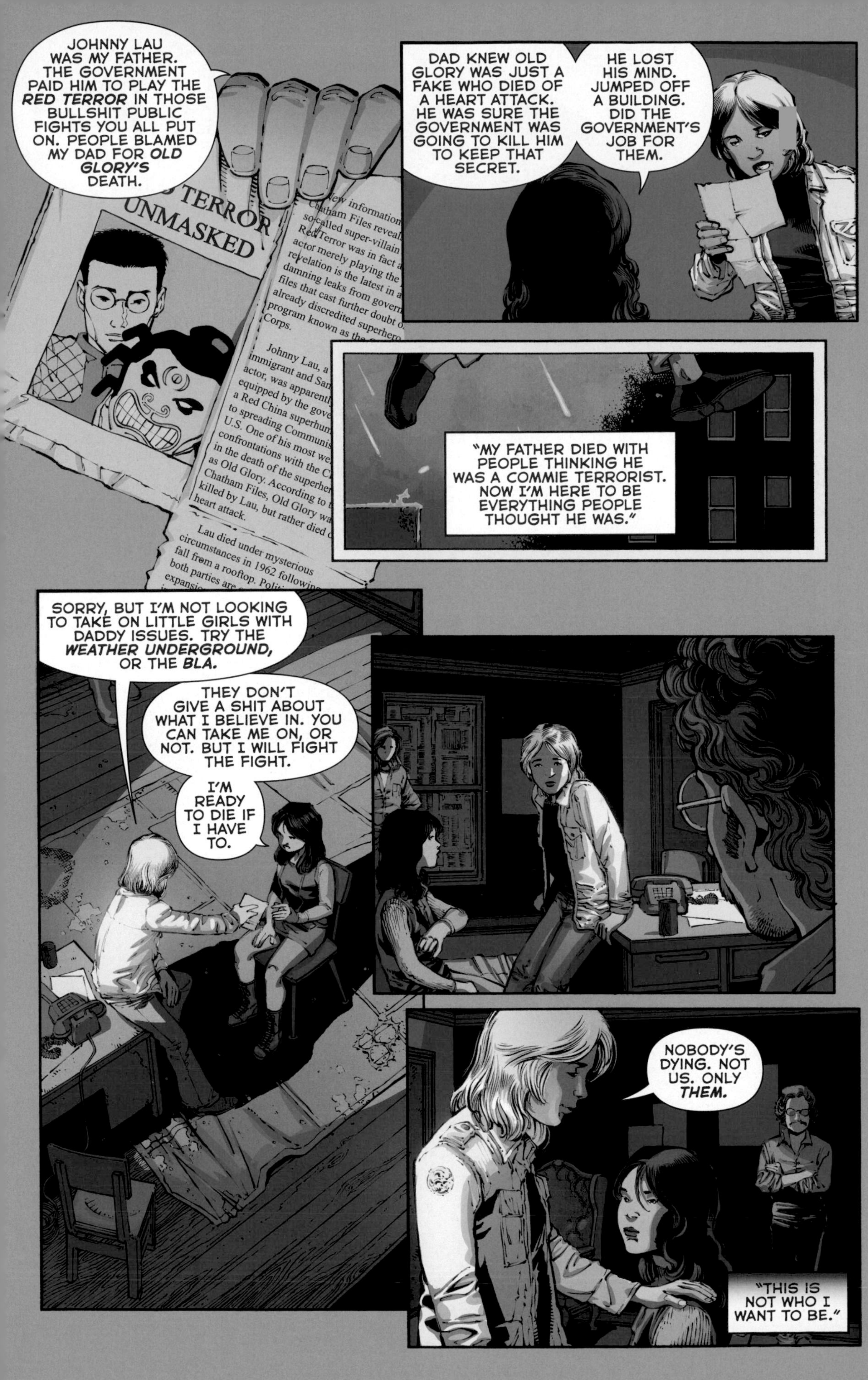

JOHNNY LAU WAS MY FATHER. THE GOVERNMENT PAID HIM TO PLAY THE *RED TERROR* IN THOSE BULLSHIT PUBLIC FIGHTS YOU ALL PUT ON. PEOPLE BLAMED MY DAD FOR *OLD GLORY'S* DEATH.
UNMASKED
DAD KNEW OLD GLORY WAS JUST A FAKE WHO DIED OF A HEART ATTACK. HE WAS SURE THE GOVERNMENT WAS GOING TO KILL HIM TO KEEP THAT SECRET.
HE LOST HIS MIND. JUMPED OFF A BUILDING. DID THE GOVERNMENT'S JOB FOR THEM.
"MY FATHER DIED WITH PEOPLE THINKING HE WAS A COMMIE TERRORIST. NOW I'M HERE TO BE EVERYTHING PEOPLE THOUGHT HE WAS."
SORRY, BUT I'M NOT LOOKING TO TAKE ON LITTLE GIRLS WITH DADDY ISSUES. TRY THE *WEATHER UNDERGROUND,* OR THE *BLA.*
THEY DON'T GIVE A SHIT ABOUT WHAT I BELIEVE IN. YOU CAN TAKE ME ON, OR NOT. BUT I WILL FIGHT THE FIGHT.
I'M READY TO DIE IF I HAVE TO.
NOBODY'S DYING. NOT US. ONLY *THEM.*
"THIS IS NOT WHO I WANT TO BE."

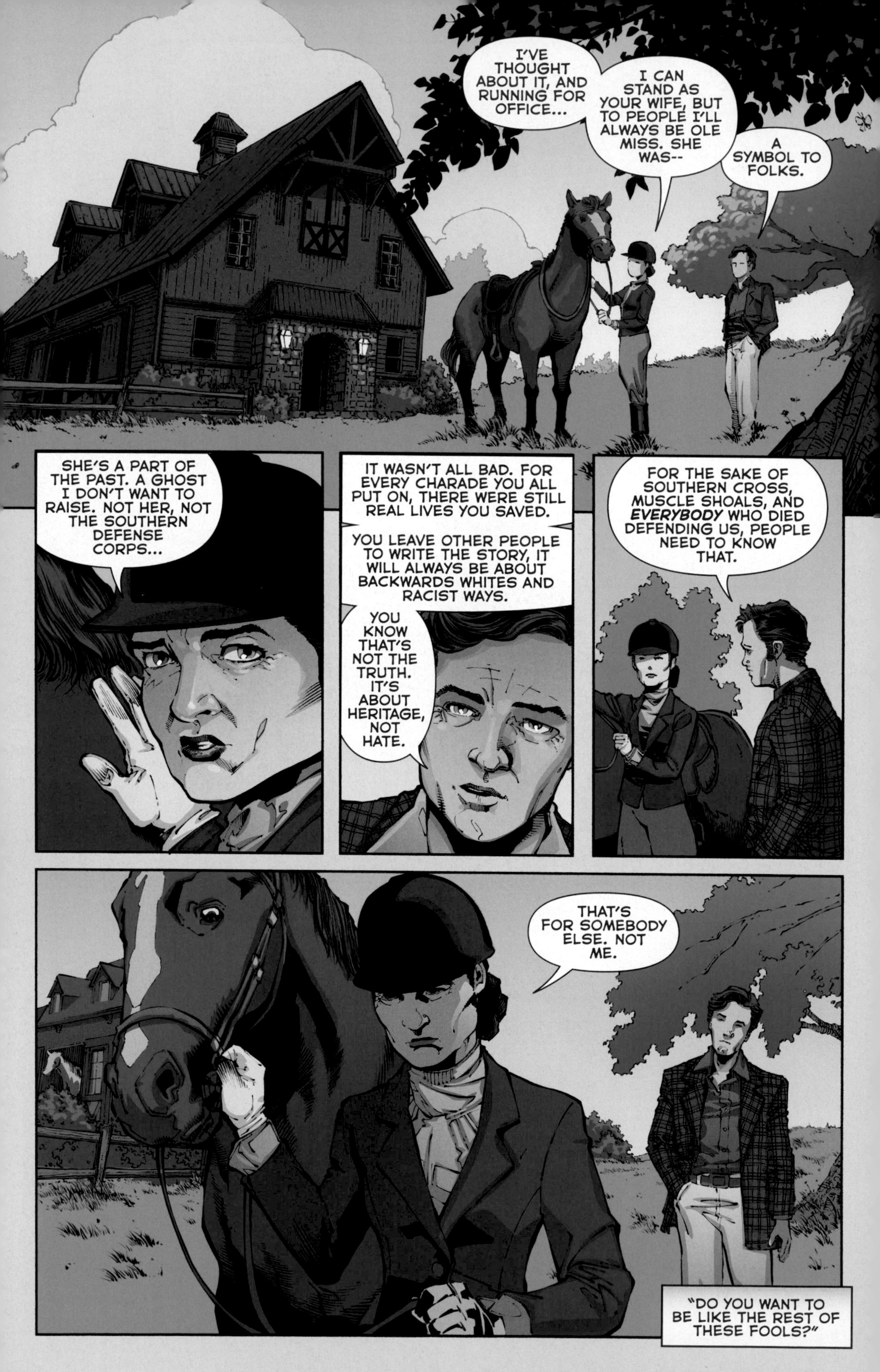
I'VE THOUGHT ABOUT IT, AND RUNNING FOR OFFICE...
I CAN STAND AS YOUR WIFE, BUT TO PEOPLE I'LL ALWAYS BE OLE MISS. SHE WAS--
A SYMBOL TO FOLKS.
SHE'S A PART OF THE PAST. A GHOST I DON'T WANT TO RAISE. NOT HER, NOT THE SOUTHERN DEFENSE CORPS...
IT WASN'T ALL BAD. FOR EVERY CHARADE YOU ALL PUT ON, THERE WERE STILL REAL LIVES YOU SAVED.
YOU LEAVE OTHER PEOPLE TO WRITE THE STORY, IT WILL ALWAYS BE ABOUT BACKWARDS WHITES AND RACIST WAYS.
YOU KNOW THAT'S NOT THE TRUTH. IT'S ABOUT HERITAGE, NOT HATE.
FOR THE SAKE OF SOUTHERN CROSS, MUSCLE SHOALS, AND EVERYBODY WHO DIED DEFENDING US, PEOPLE NEED TO KNOW THAT.
THAT'S FOR SOMEBODY ELSE. NOT ME.
"DO YOU WANT TO BE LIKE THE REST OF THESE FOOLS?"

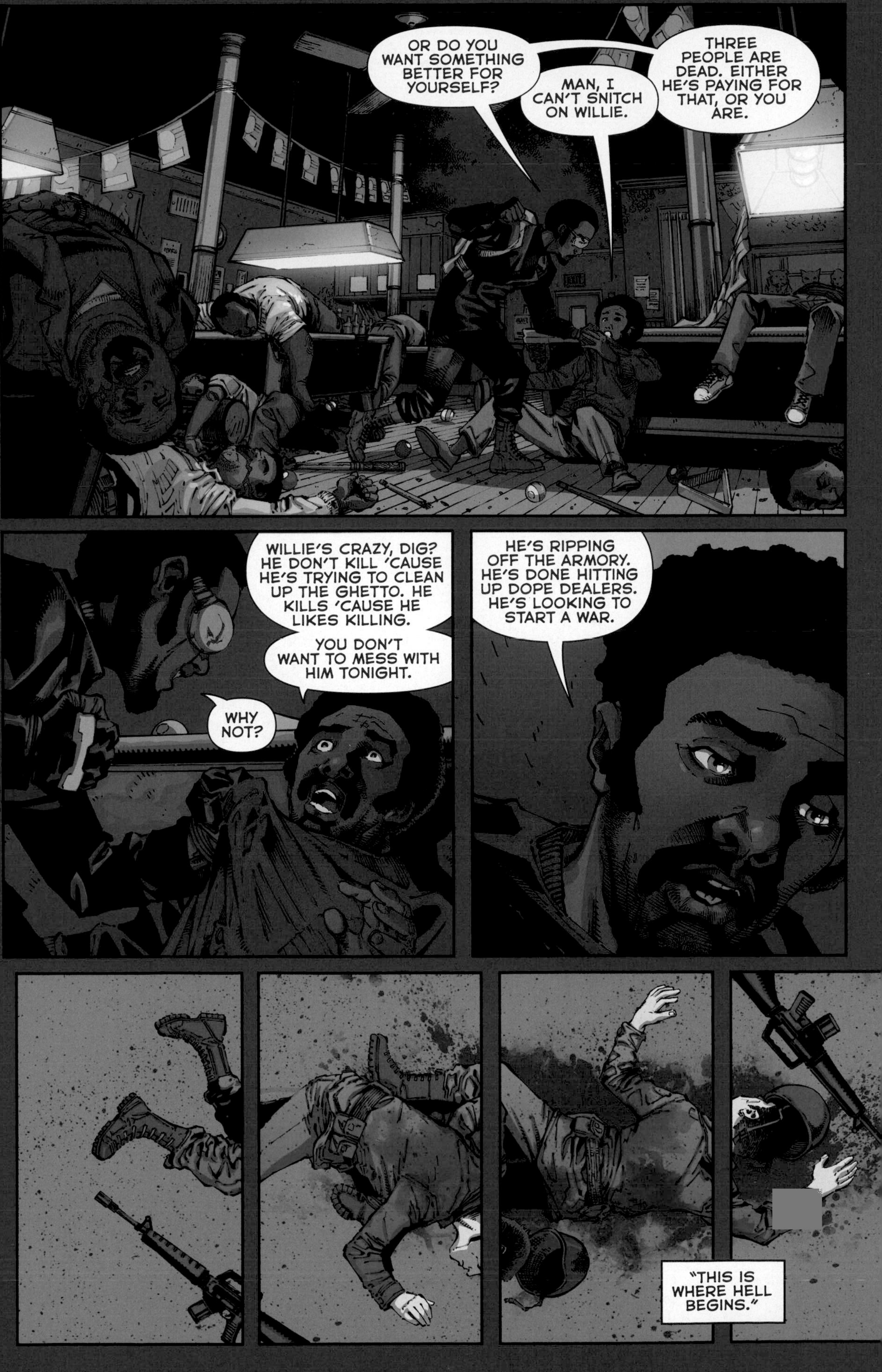

OR DO YOU WANT SOMETHING BETTER FOR YOURSELF?
MAN, I CAN'T SNITCH ON WILLIE.
THREE PEOPLE ARE DEAD. EITHER HE'S PAYING FOR THAT, OR YOU ARE.
WILLIE'S CRAZY, DIG? HE DON'T KILL 'CAUSE HE'S TRYING TO CLEAN UP THE GHETTO. HE KILLS 'CAUSE HE LIKES KILLING.
YOU DON'T WANT TO MESS WITH HIM TONIGHT.
WHY NOT?
HE'S RIPPING OFF THE ARMORY. HE'S DONE HITTING UP DOPE DEALERS. HE'S LOOKING TO START A WAR.
"THIS IS WHERE HELL BEGINS."

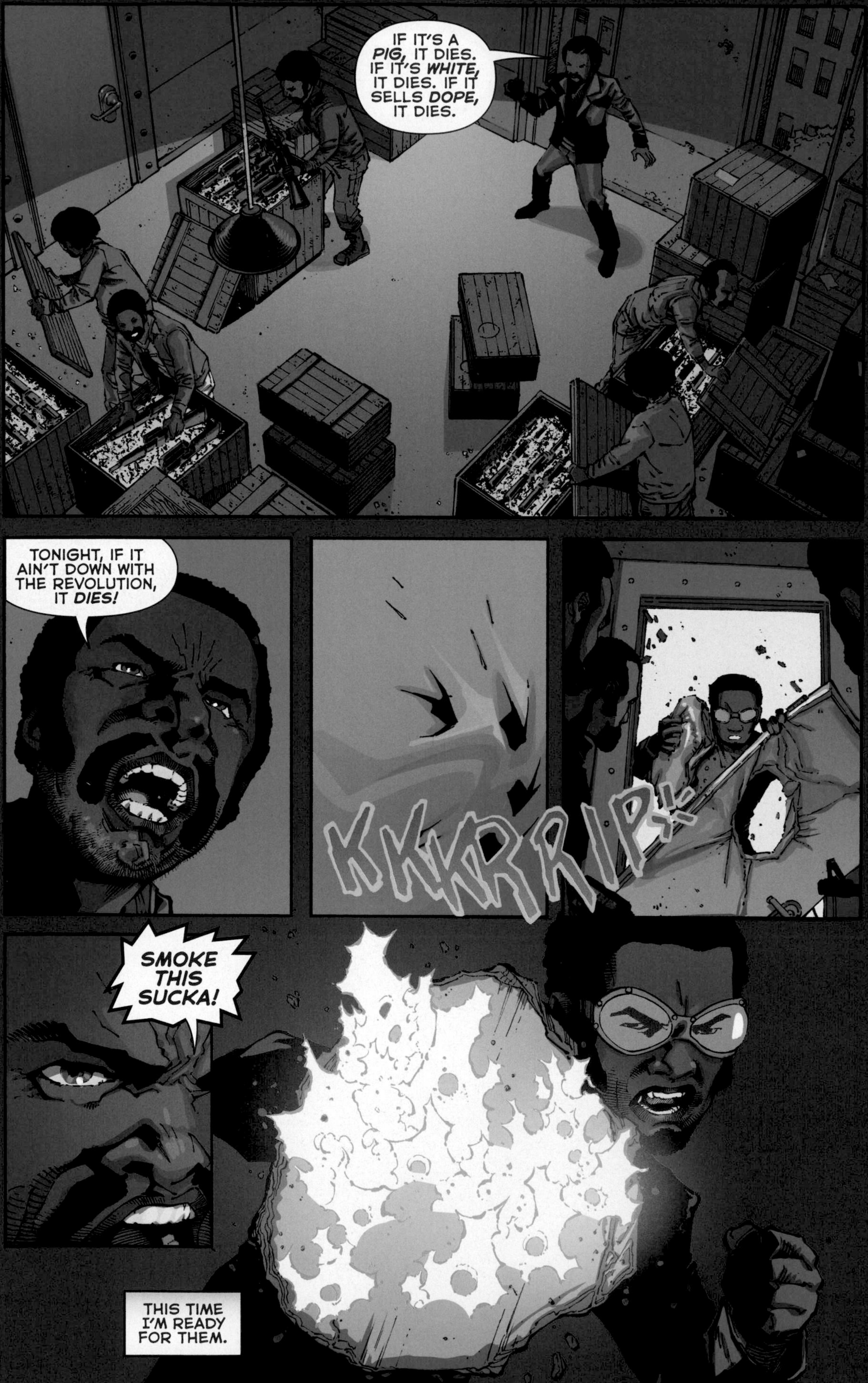
IF IT'S A PIG, IT DIES. IF IT'S WHITE, IT DIES. IF IT SELLS DOPE, IT DIES.
TONIGHT, IF IT AIN'T DOWN WITH THE REVOLUTION, IT DIES!
KKKRRIP!
SMOKE THIS SUCKA!
THIS TIME I'M READY FOR THEM.

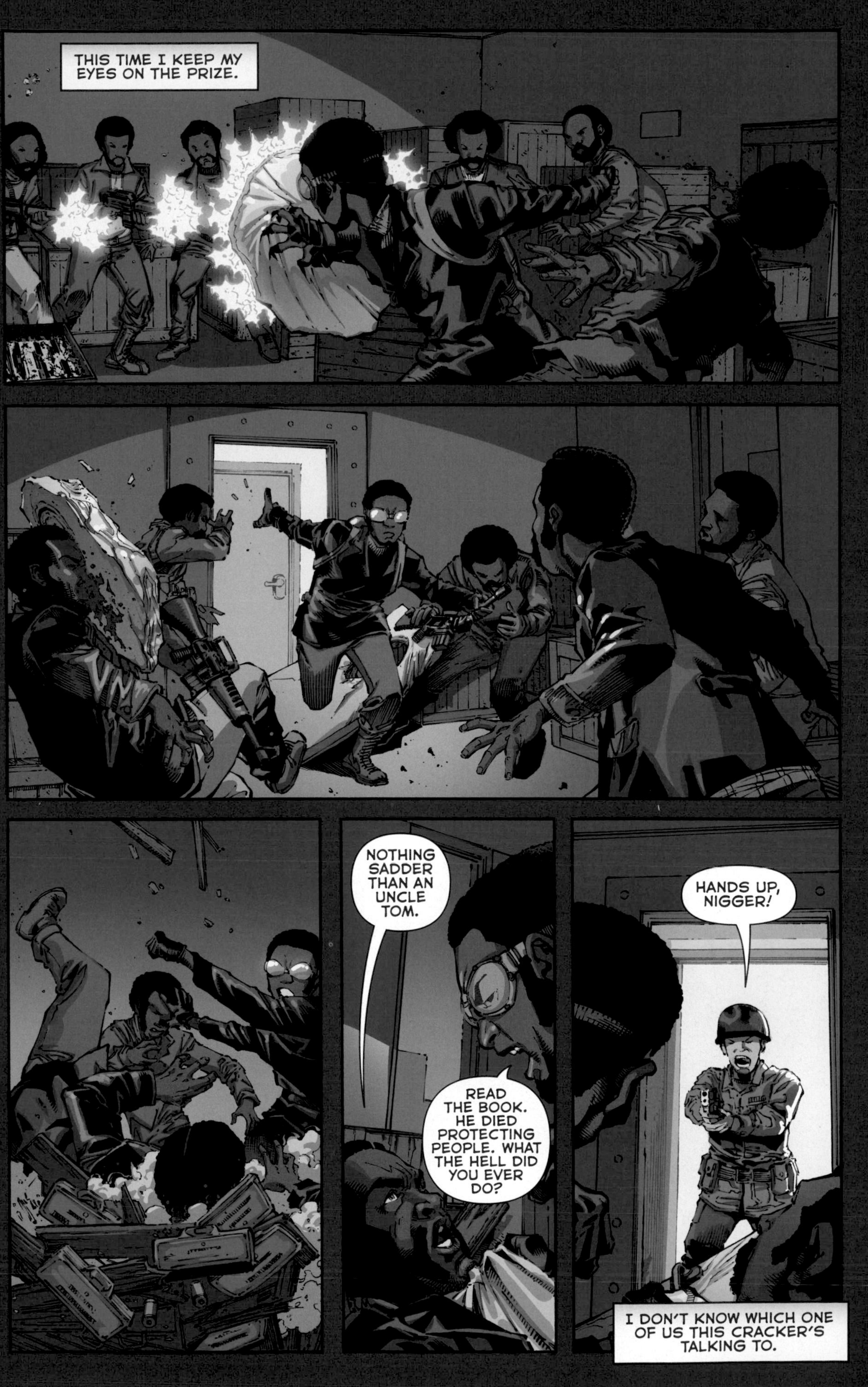
THIS TIME I KEEP MY EYES ON THE PRIZE.
NOTHING SADDER THAN AN UNCLE TOM.
READ THE BOOK. HE DIED PROTECTING PEOPLE. WHAT THE HELL DID YOU EVER DO?
HANDS UP, NIGGER!
I DON'T KNOW WHICH ONE OF US THIS CRACKER'S TALKING TO.

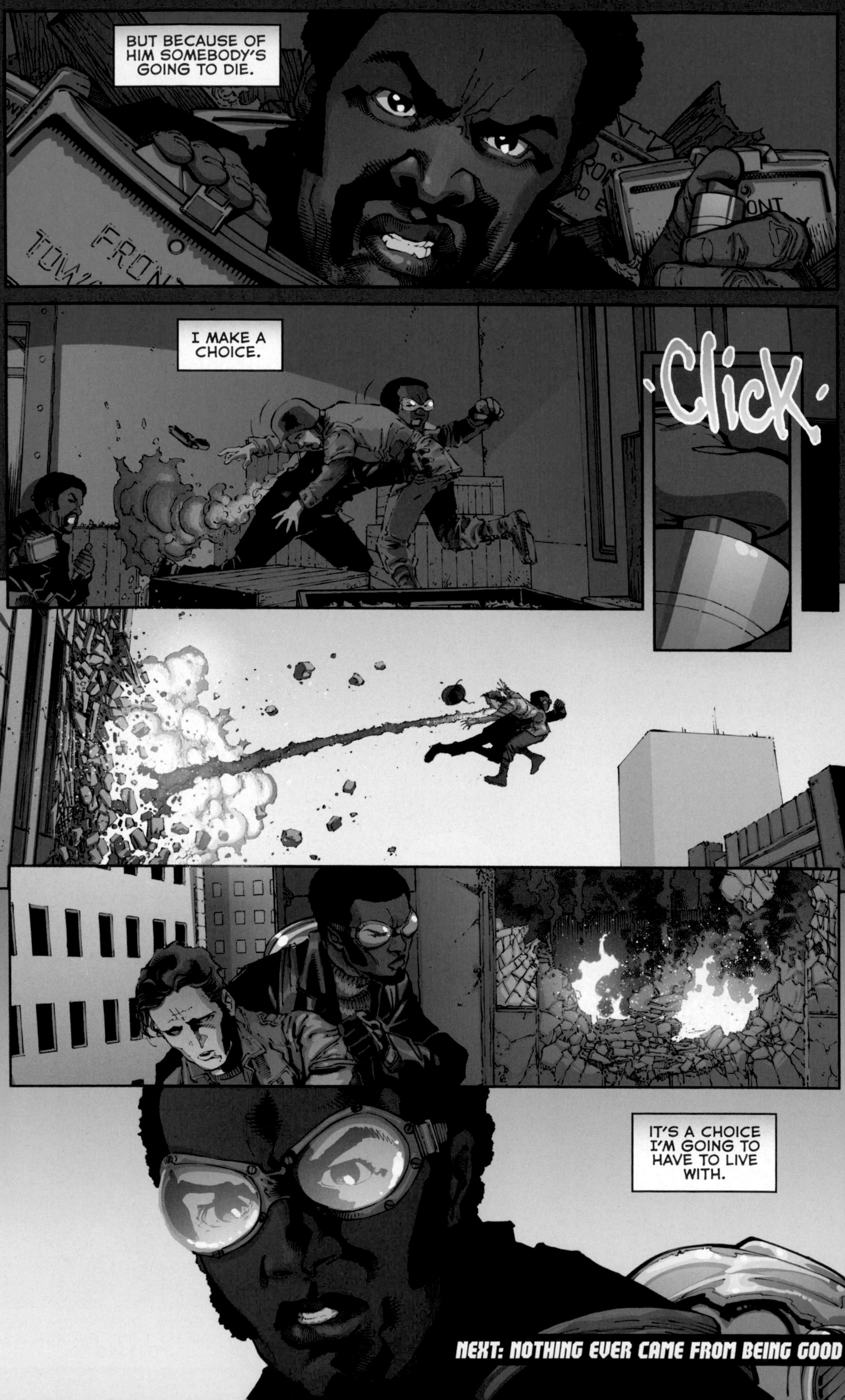
BUT BECAUSE OF HIM SOMEBODY'S GOING TO DIE.
FRONT
I MAKE A CHOICE.
CLICK
IT'S A CHOICE I'M GOING TO HAVE TO LIVE WITH.
NEXT: NOTHING EVER CAME FROM BEING GOOD

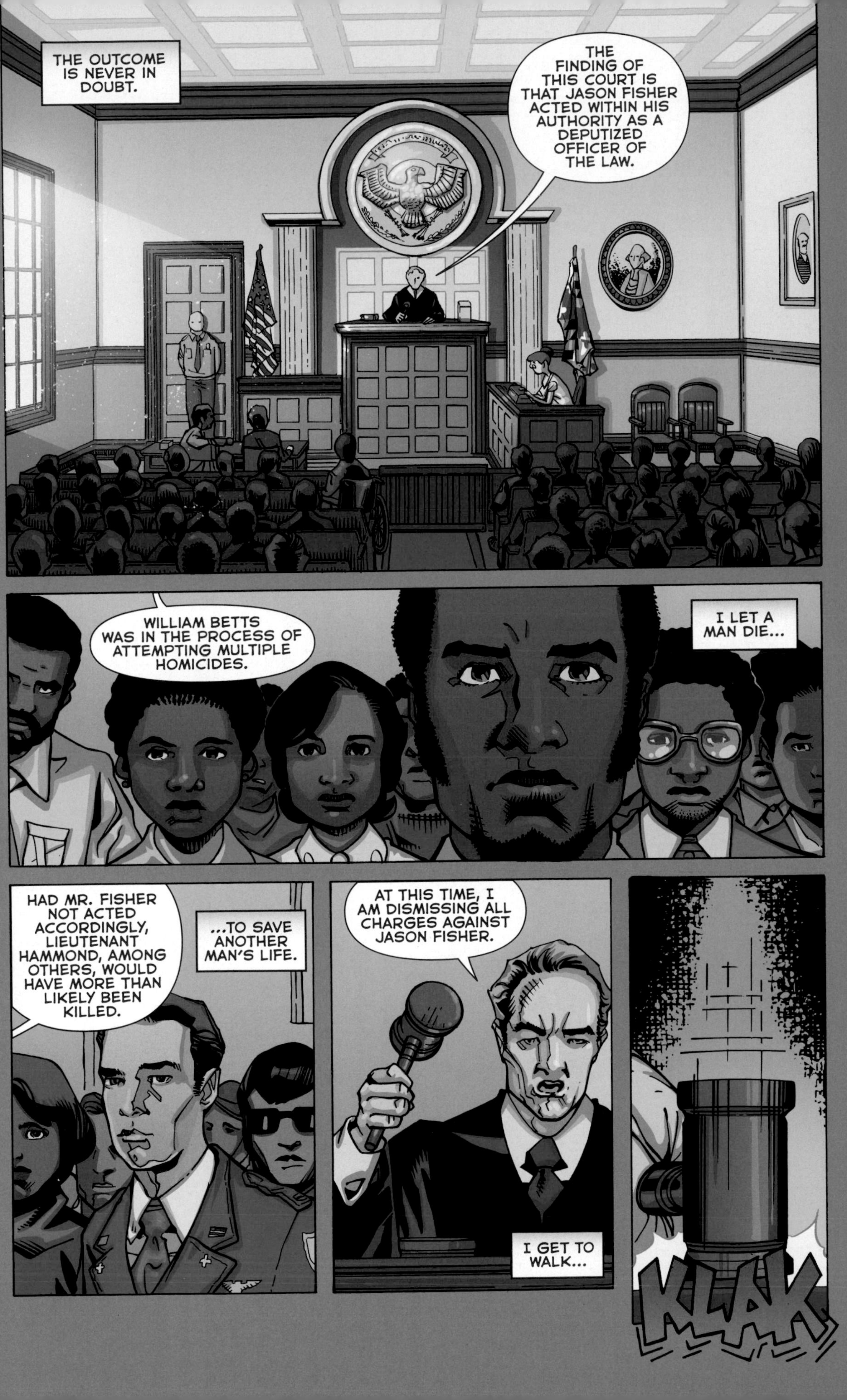
THE OUTCOME IS NEVER IN DOUBT.
THE FINDING OF THIS COURT IS THAT JASON FISHER ACTED WITHIN HIS AUTHORITY AS A DEPUTIZED OFFICER OF THE LAW.
WILLIAM BETTS WAS IN THE PROCESS OF ATTEMPTING MULTIPLE HOMICIDES.
I LET A MAN DIE...
HAD MR. FISHER NOT ACTED ACCORDINGLY, LIEUTENANT HAMMOND, AMONG OTHERS, WOULD HAVE MORE THAN LIKELY BEEN KILLED.
...TO SAVE ANOTHER MAN'S LIFE.
AT THIS TIME, I AM DISMISSING ALL CHARGES AGAINST JASON FISHER.
I GET TO WALK...
KLAK

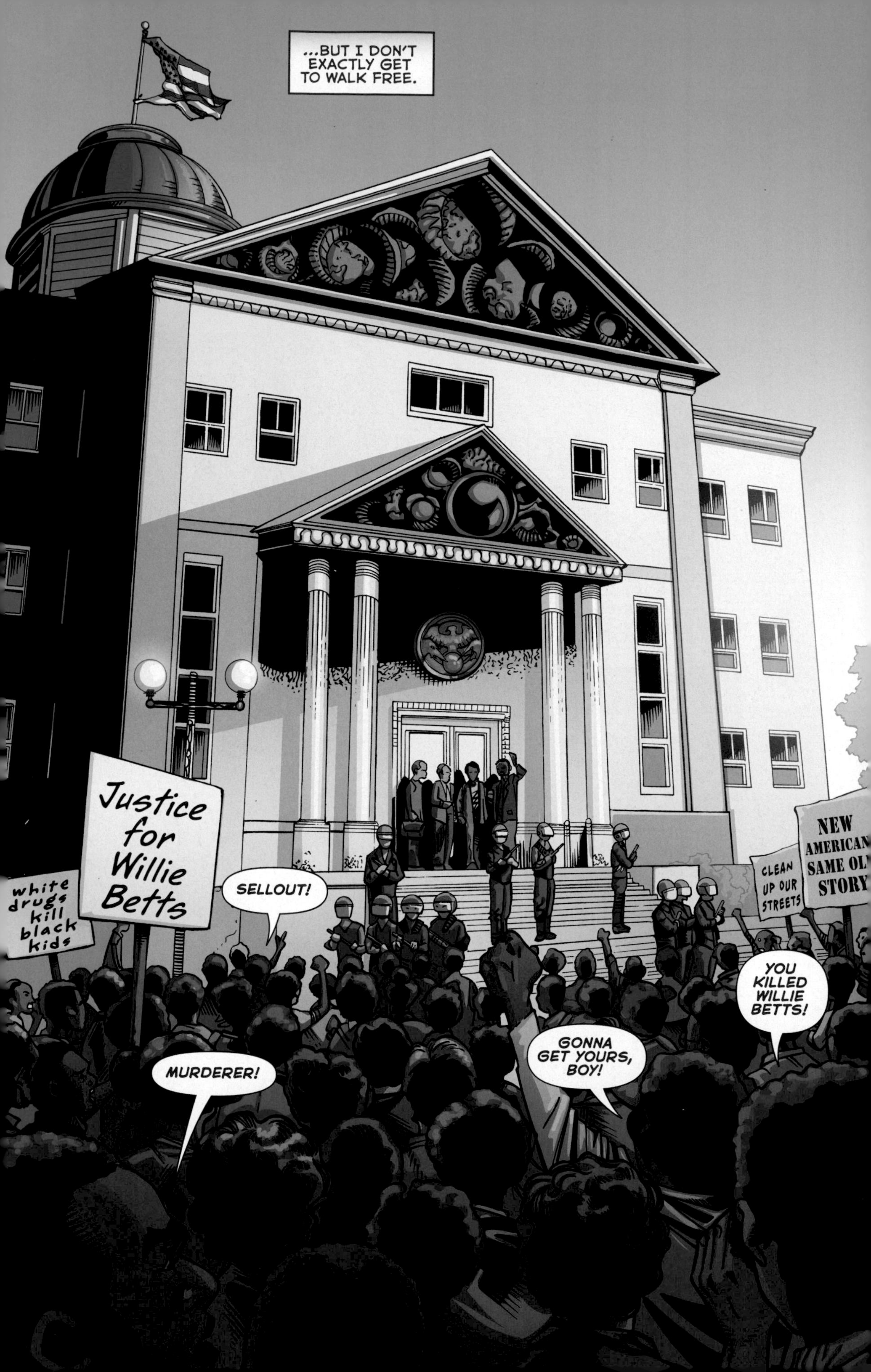
...BUT I DON'T EXACTLY GET TO WALK FREE.
Justice for Willie Betts
white drugs kill black kids
SELLOUT!
CLEAN UP OUR STREETS
NEW AMERICAN SAME OL STORY
YOU KILLED WILLIE BETTS!
GONNA GET YOURS, BOY!
MURDERER!

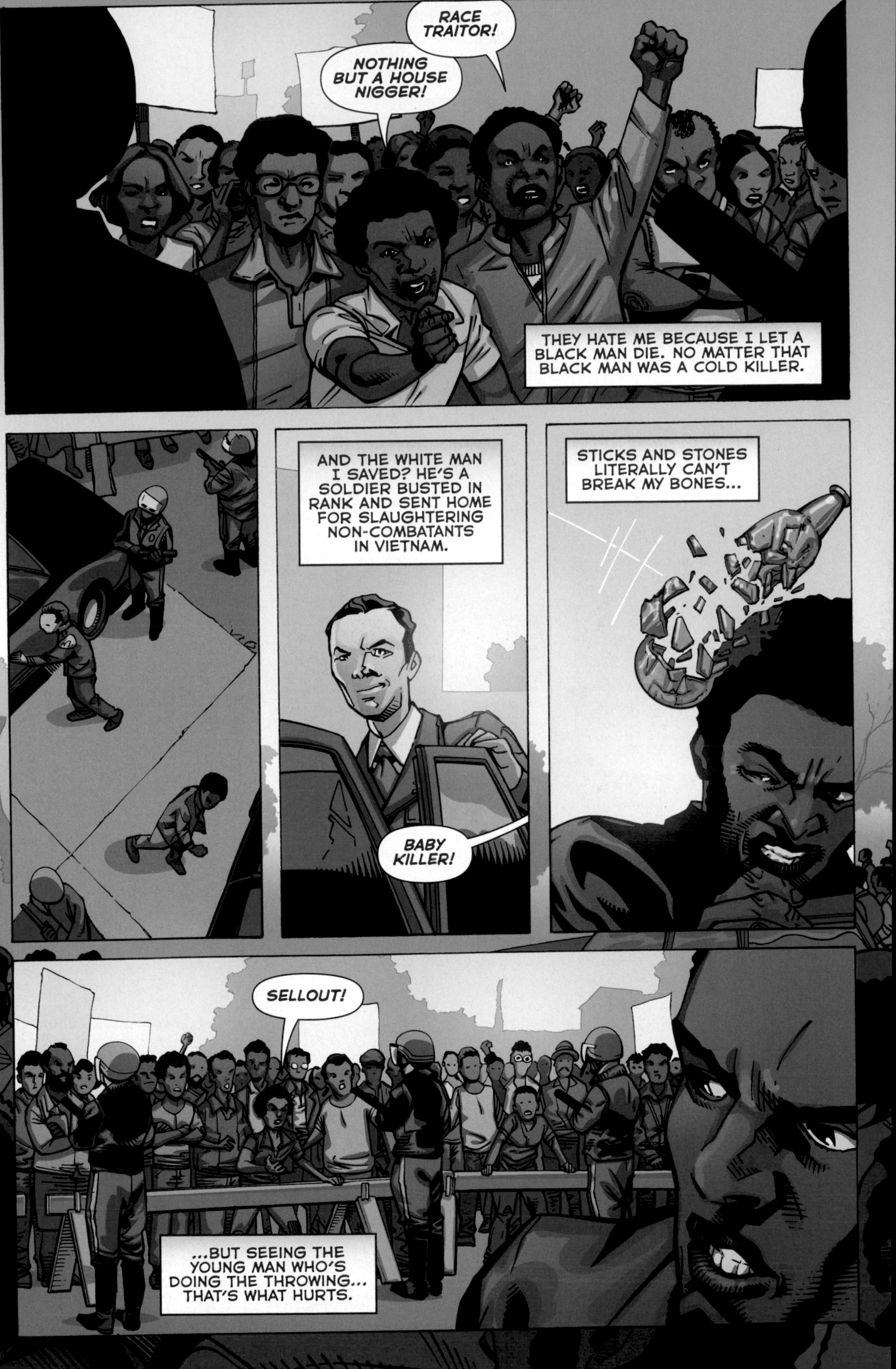
RACE TRAITOR!
NOTHING BUT A HOUSE NIGGER!
THEY HATE ME BECAUSE I LET A BLACK MAN DIE. NO MATTER THAT BLACK MAN WAS A COLD KILLER.
AND THE WHITE MAN I SAVED? HE'S A SOLDIER BUSTED IN RANK AND SENT HOME FOR SLAUGHTERING NON-COMBATANTS IN VIETNAM.
BABY KILLER!
STICKS AND STONES LITERALLY CAN'T BREAK MY BONES...
SELLOUT!
...BUT SEEING THE YOUNG MAN WHO'S DOING THE THROWING... THAT'S WHAT HURTS.

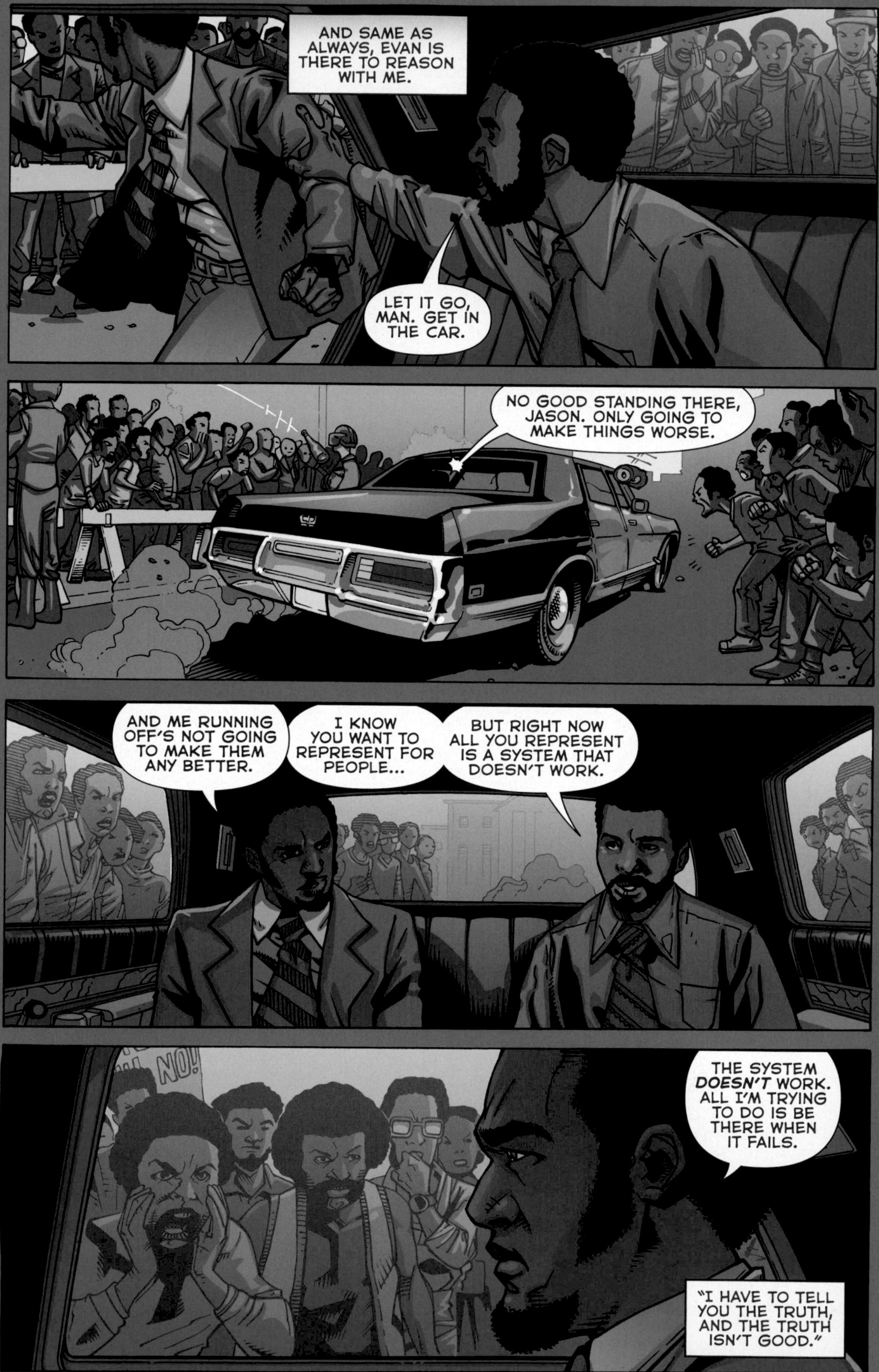
AND SAME AS ALWAYS, EVAN IS THERE TO REASON WITH ME.
LET IT GO, MAN. GET IN THE CAR.
NO GOOD STANDING THERE, JASON. ONLY GOING TO MAKE THINGS WORSE.
AND ME RUNNING OFF'S NOT GOING TO MAKE THEM ANY BETTER.
I KNOW YOU WANT TO REPRESENT FOR PEOPLE...
BUT RIGHT NOW ALL YOU REPRESENT IS A SYSTEM THAT DOESN'T WORK.
NO!
THE SYSTEM *DOESN'T* WORK. ALL I'M TRYING TO DO IS BE THERE WHEN IT FAILS.
"I HAVE TO TELL YOU THE TRUTH, AND THE TRUTH ISN'T GOOD."

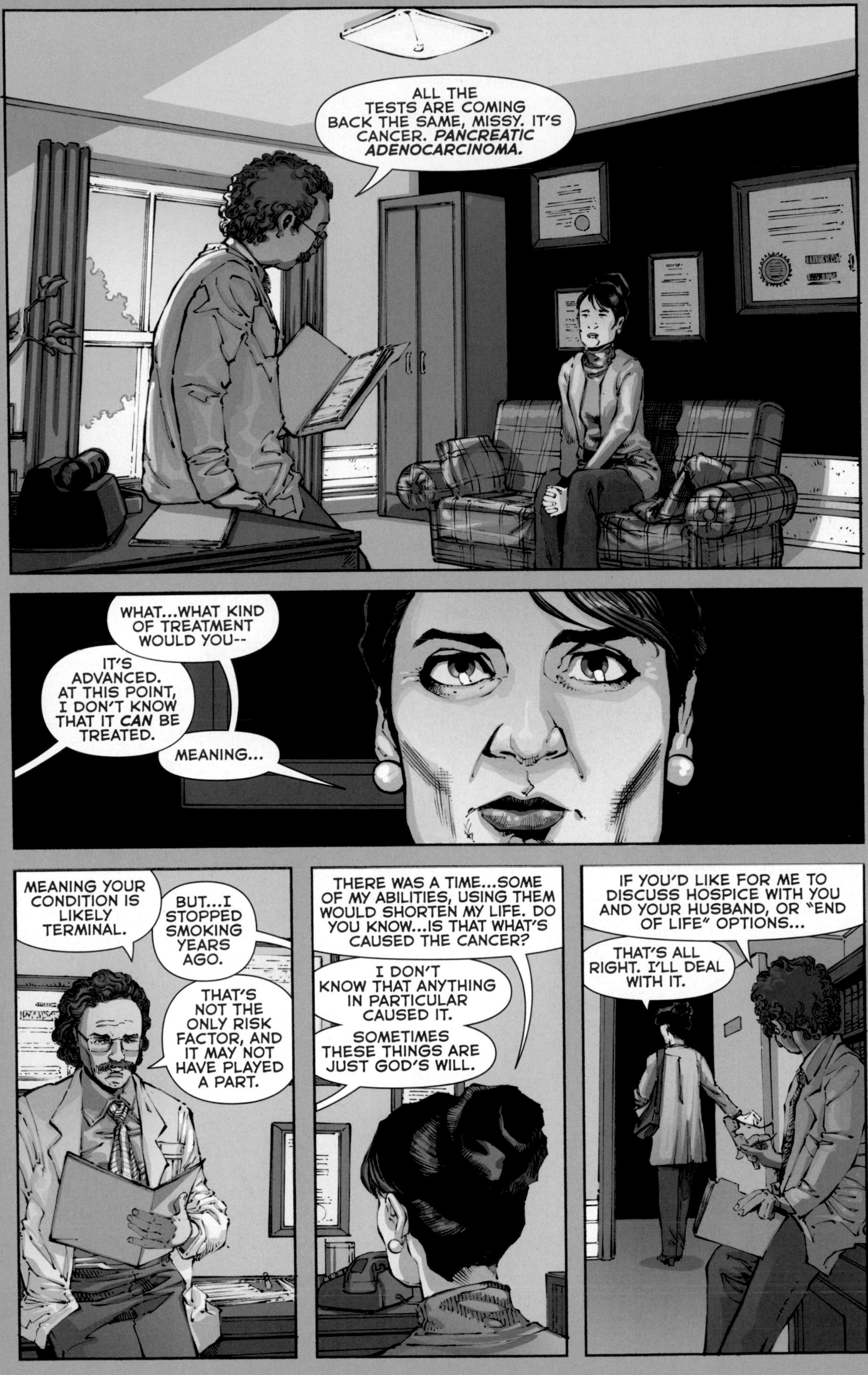
ALL THE TESTS ARE COMING BACK THE SAME, MISSY. IT'S CANCER. *PANCREATIC ADENOCARCINOMA.*
WHAT...WHAT KIND OF TREATMENT WOULD YOU--
IT'S ADVANCED. AT THIS POINT, I DON'T KNOW THAT IT *CAN* BE TREATED.
MEANING...
MEANING YOUR CONDITION IS LIKELY TERMINAL.
BUT...I STOPPED SMOKING YEARS AGO.
THAT'S NOT THE ONLY RISK FACTOR, AND IT MAY NOT HAVE PLAYED A PART.
THERE WAS A TIME...SOME OF MY ABILITIES, USING THEM WOULD SHORTEN MY LIFE. DO YOU KNOW...IS THAT WHAT'S CAUSED THE CANCER?
I DON'T KNOW THAT ANYTHING IN PARTICULAR CAUSED IT.
SOMETIMES THESE THINGS ARE JUST GOD'S WILL.
IF YOU'D LIKE FOR ME TO DISCUSS HOSPICE WITH YOU AND YOUR HUSBAND, OR "END OF LIFE" OPTIONS...
THAT'S ALL RIGHT. I'LL DEAL WITH IT.

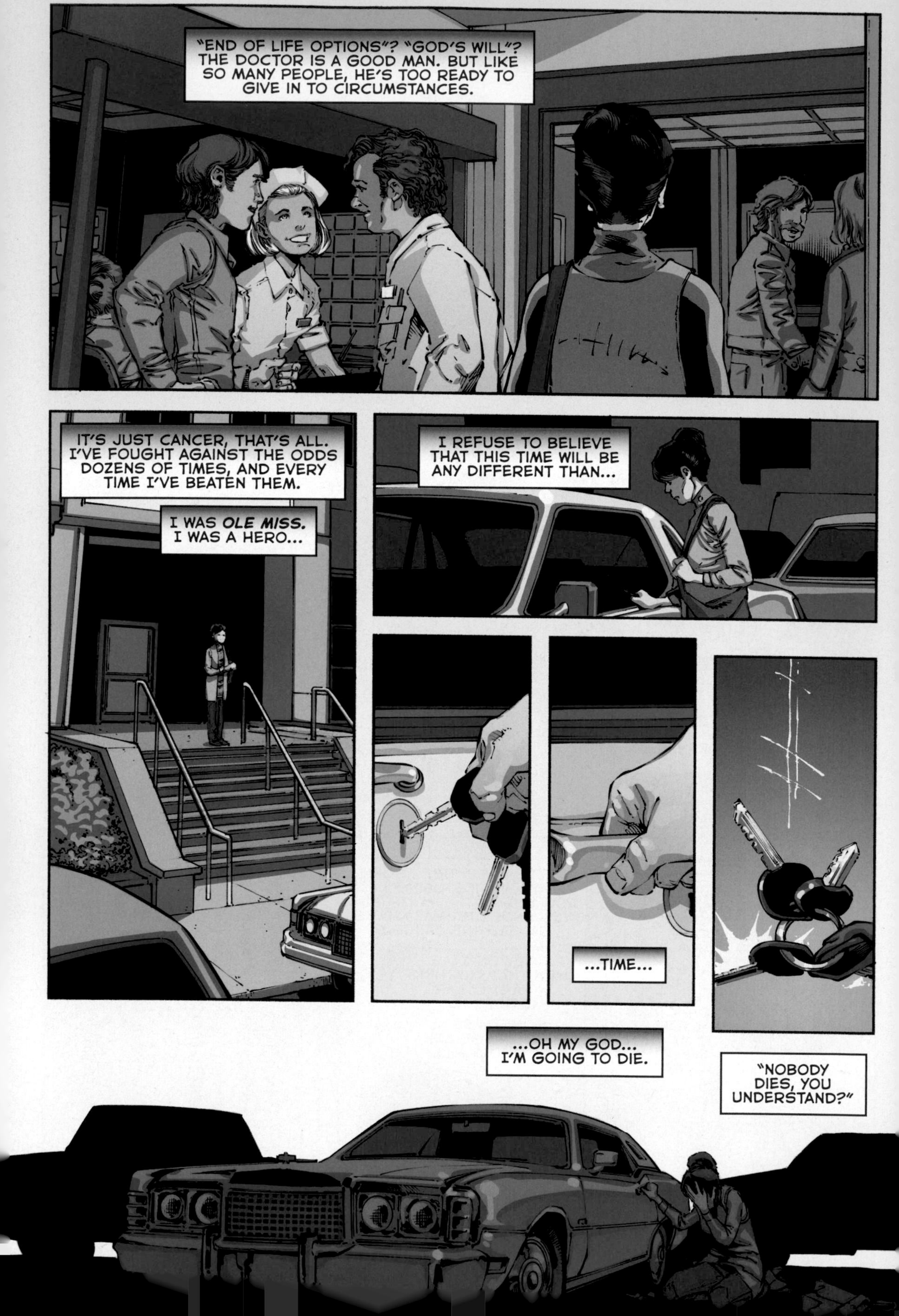
"END OF LIFE OPTIONS"? "GOD'S WILL"? THE DOCTOR IS A GOOD MAN. BUT LIKE SO MANY PEOPLE, HE'S TOO READY TO GIVE IN TO CIRCUMSTANCES.
IT'S JUST CANCER, THAT'S ALL. I'VE FOUGHT AGAINST THE ODDS DOZENS OF TIMES, AND EVERY TIME I'VE BEATEN THEM.
I WAS *OLE MISS.* I WAS A HERO...
I REFUSE TO BELIEVE THAT THIS TIME WILL BE ANY DIFFERENT THAN...
...TIME...
...OH MY GOD... I'M GOING TO DIE.
"NOBODY DIES, YOU UNDERSTAND?"

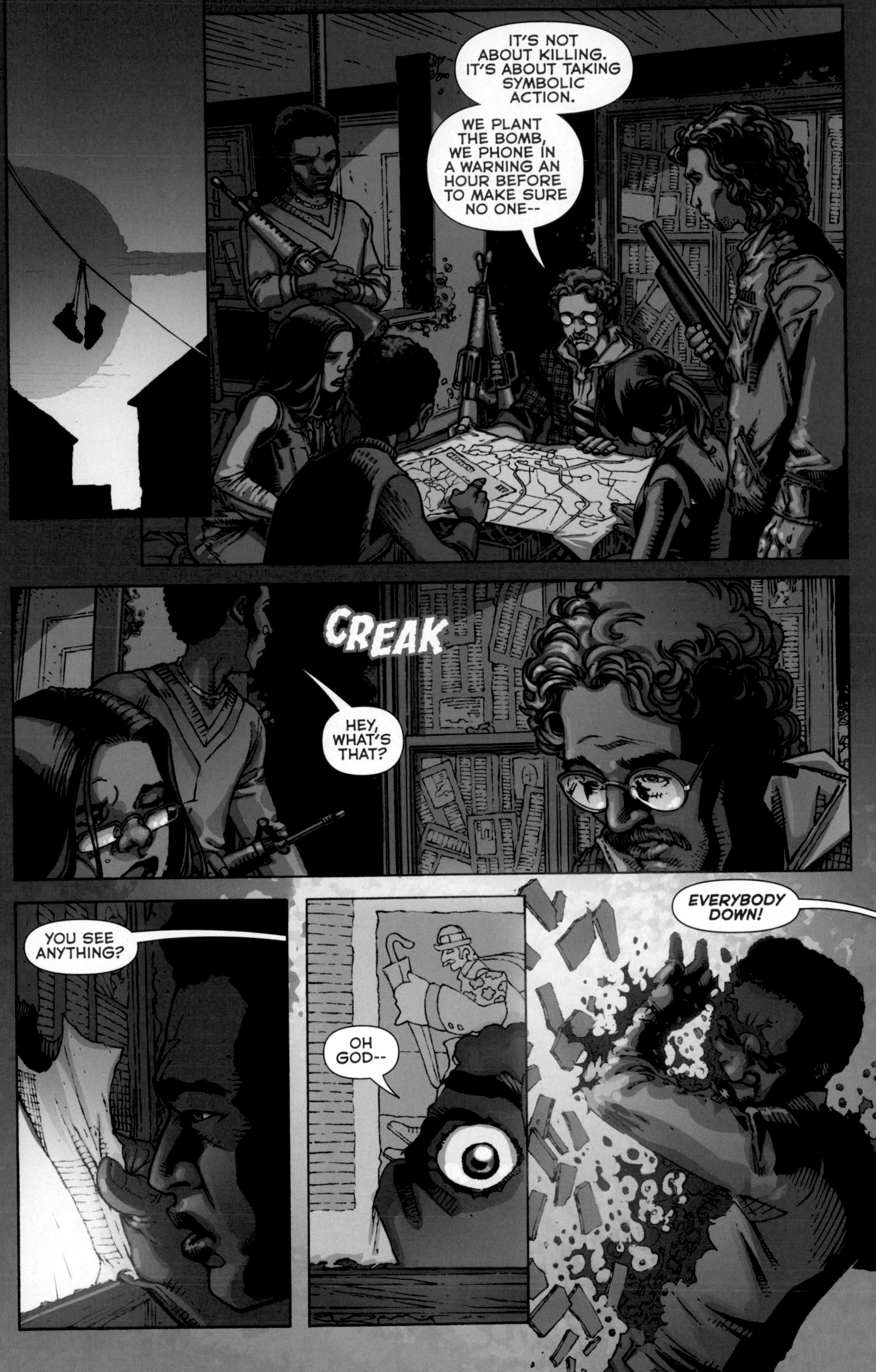
IT'S NOT ABOUT KILLING. IT'S ABOUT TAKING SYMBOLIC ACTION.
WE PLANT THE BOMB, WE PHONE IN A WARNING AN HOUR BEFORE TO MAKE SURE NO ONE--
CREAK
HEY, WHAT'S THAT?
YOU SEE ANYTHING?
OH GOD--
EVERYBODY DOWN!

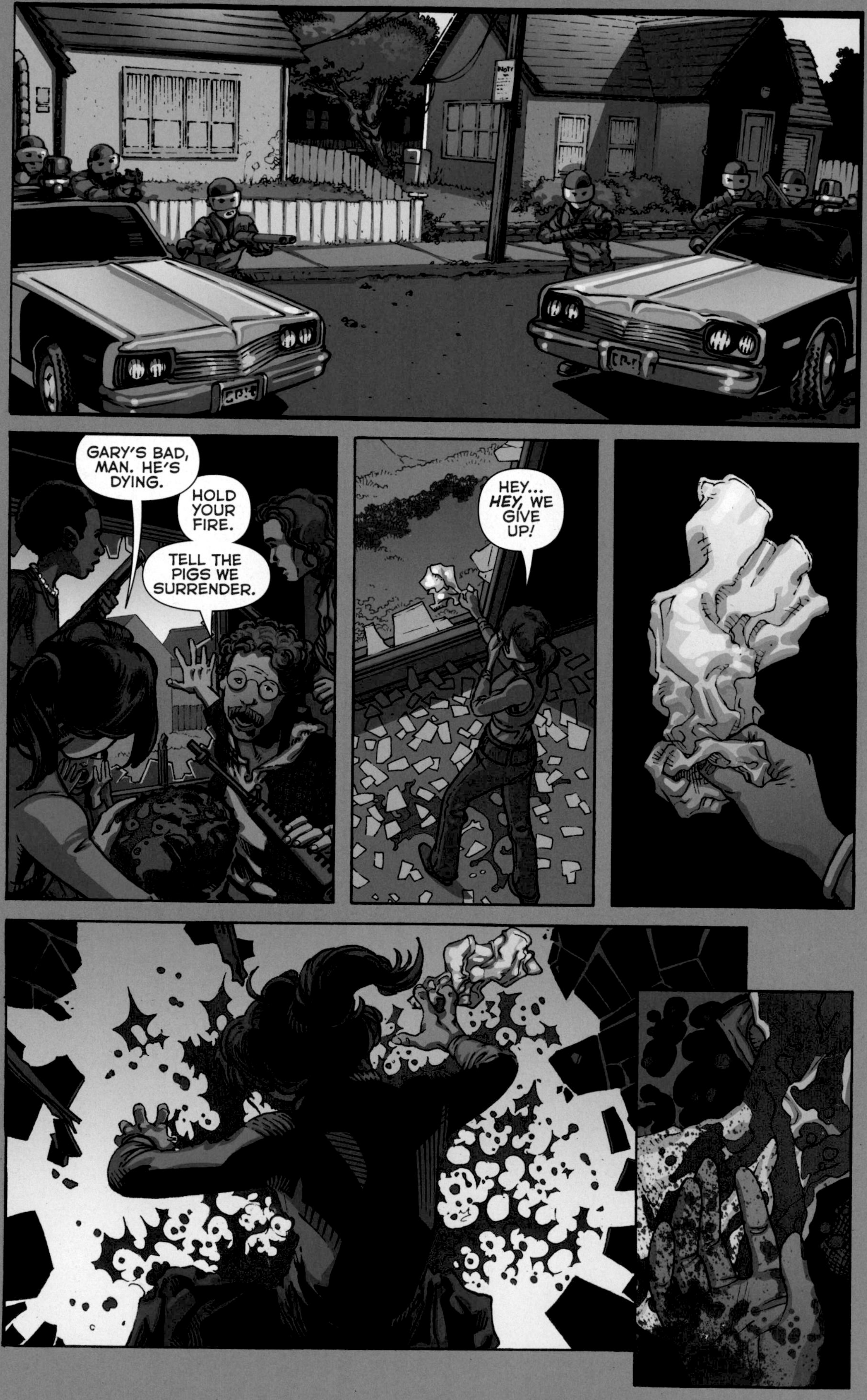
GARY'S BAD, MAN. HE'S DYING.
HOLD YOUR FIRE.
TELL THE PIGS WE SURRENDER.
HEY... HEY, WE GIVE UP!

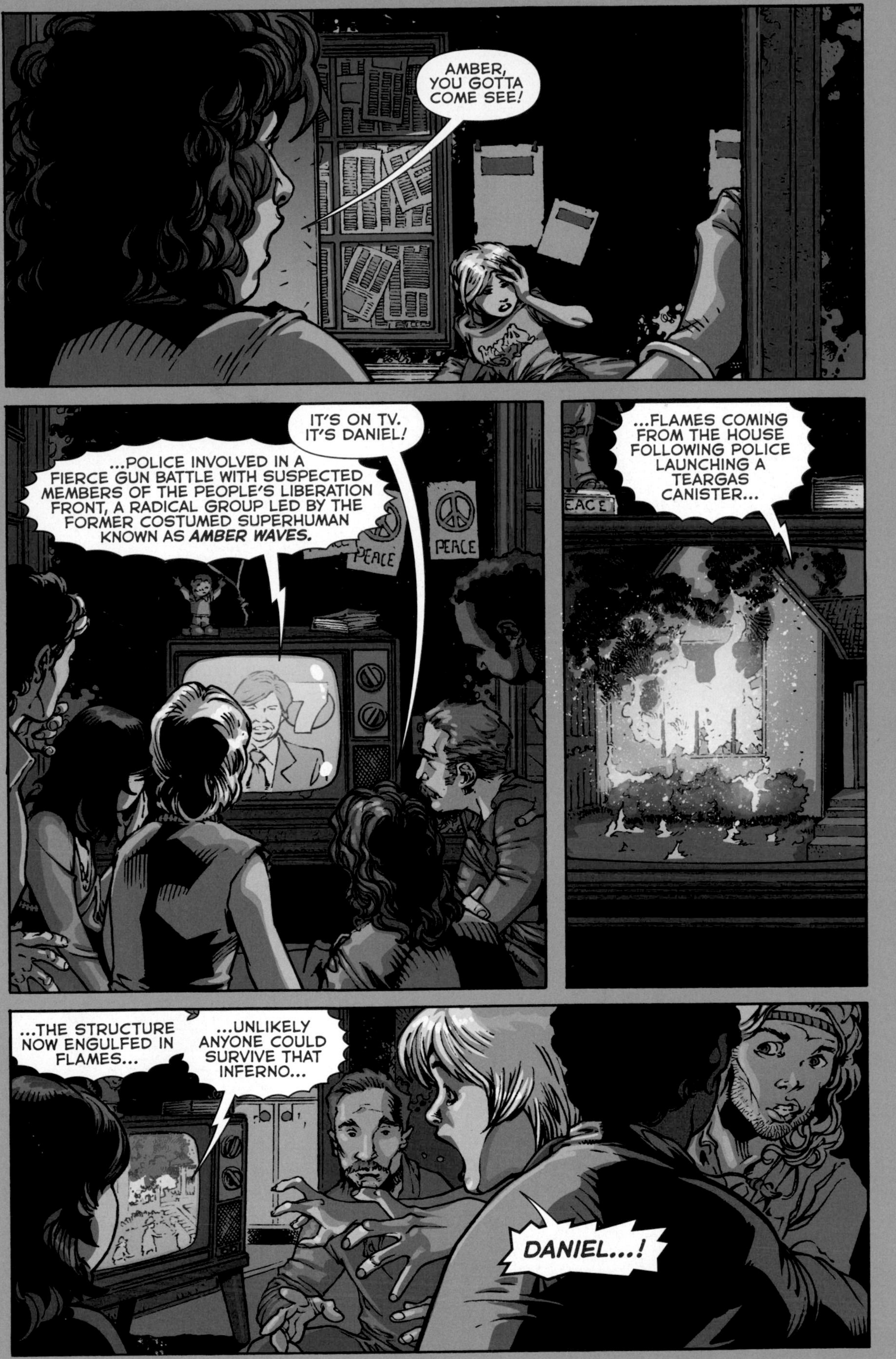
AMBER, YOU GOTTA COME SEE!
IT'S ON TV. IT'S DANIEL!
...POLICE INVOLVED IN A FIERCE GUN BATTLE WITH SUSPECTED MEMBERS OF THE PEOPLE'S LIBERATION FRONT, A RADICAL GROUP LED BY THE FORMER COSTUMED SUPERHUMAN KNOWN AS AMBER WAVES.
PEACE
PEACE
...FLAMES COMING FROM THE HOUSE FOLLOWING POLICE LAUNCHING A TEARGAS CANISTER...
...THE STRUCTURE NOW ENGULFED IN FLAMES...
...UNLIKELY ANYONE COULD SURVIVE THAT INFERNO...
DANIEL...!

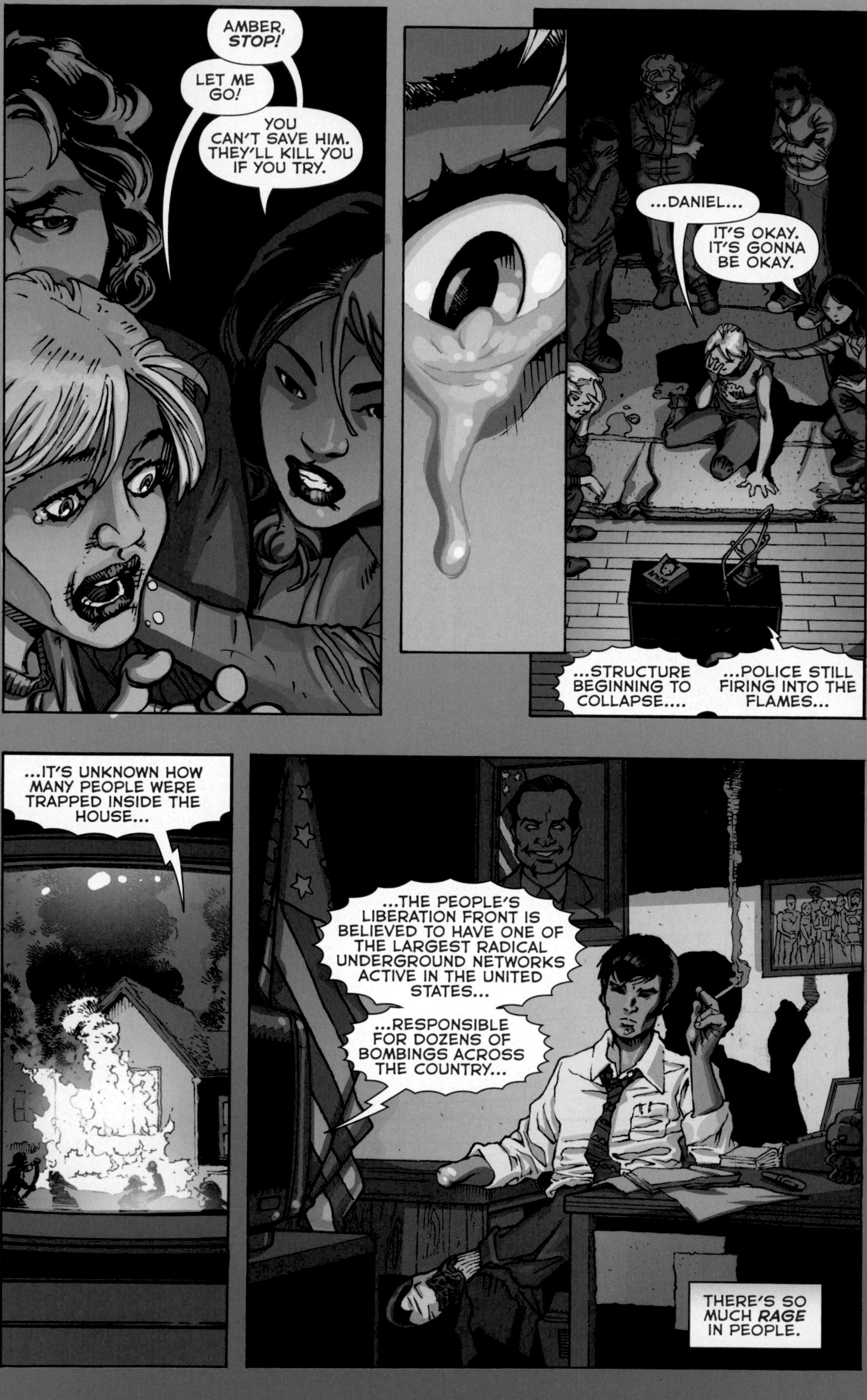
AMBER, STOP!
LET ME GO!
YOU CAN'T SAVE HIM. THEY'LL KILL YOU IF YOU TRY.
...DANIEL...
IT'S OKAY. IT'S GONNA BE OKAY.
...STRUCTURE BEGINNING TO COLLAPSE....
...POLICE STILL FIRING INTO THE FLAMES...
...IT'S UNKNOWN HOW MANY PEOPLE WERE TRAPPED INSIDE THE HOUSE...
...THE PEOPLE'S LIBERATION FRONT IS BELIEVED TO HAVE ONE OF THE LARGEST RADICAL UNDERGROUND NETWORKS ACTIVE IN THE UNITED STATES...
...RESPONSIBLE FOR DOZENS OF BOMBINGS ACROSS THE COUNTRY...
THERE'S SO MUCH RAGE IN PEOPLE.

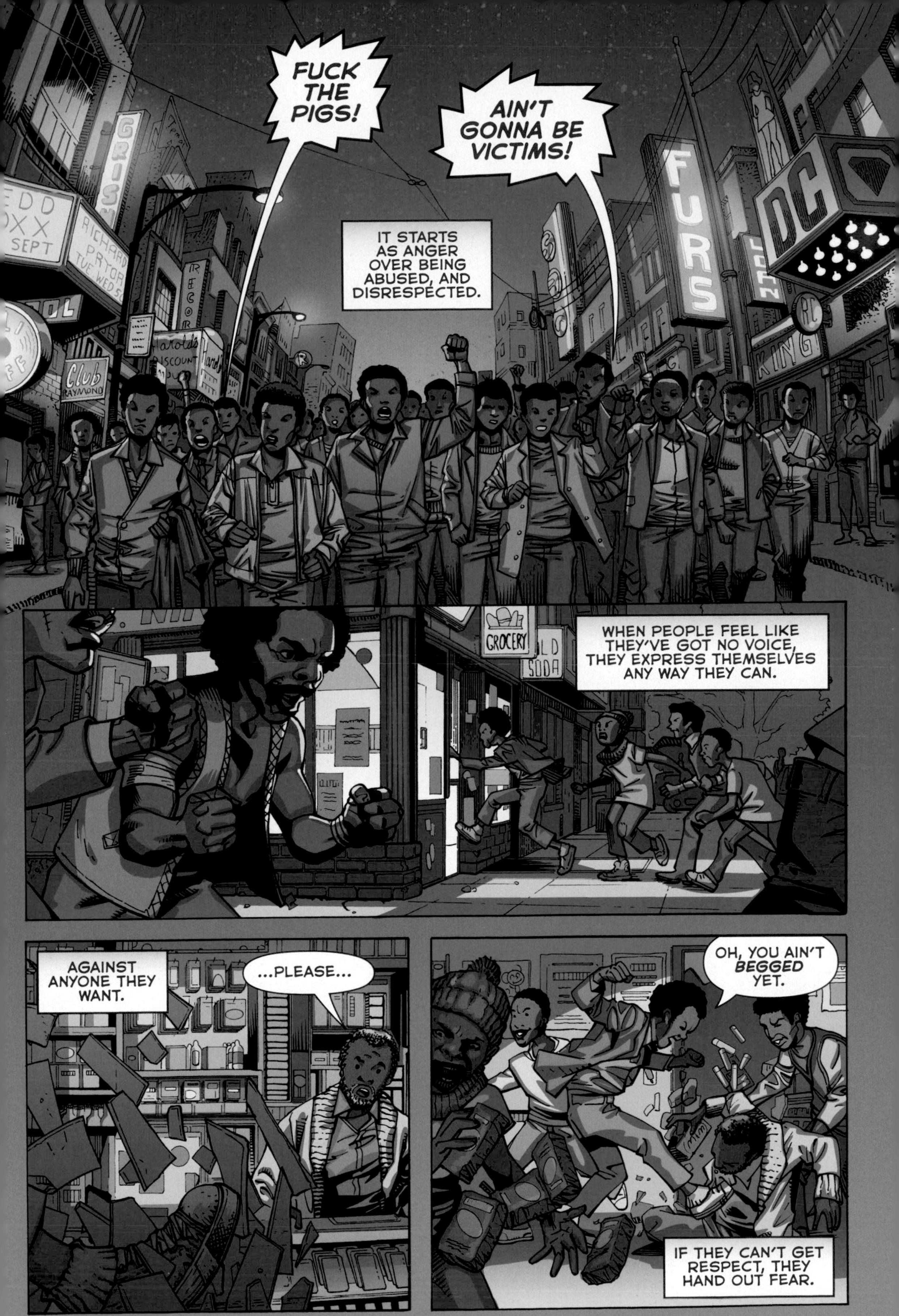
FUCK THE PIGS!
AIN'T GONNA BE VICTIMS!
IT STARTS AS ANGER OVER BEING ABUSED, AND DISRESPECTED.
WHEN PEOPLE FEEL LIKE THEY'VE GOT NO VOICE, THEY EXPRESS THEMSELVES ANY WAY THEY CAN.
GROCERY
SODA
AGAINST ANYONE THEY WANT.
...PLEASE...
OH, YOU AIN'T *BEGGED* YET.
IF THEY CAN'T GET RESPECT, THEY HAND OUT FEAR.

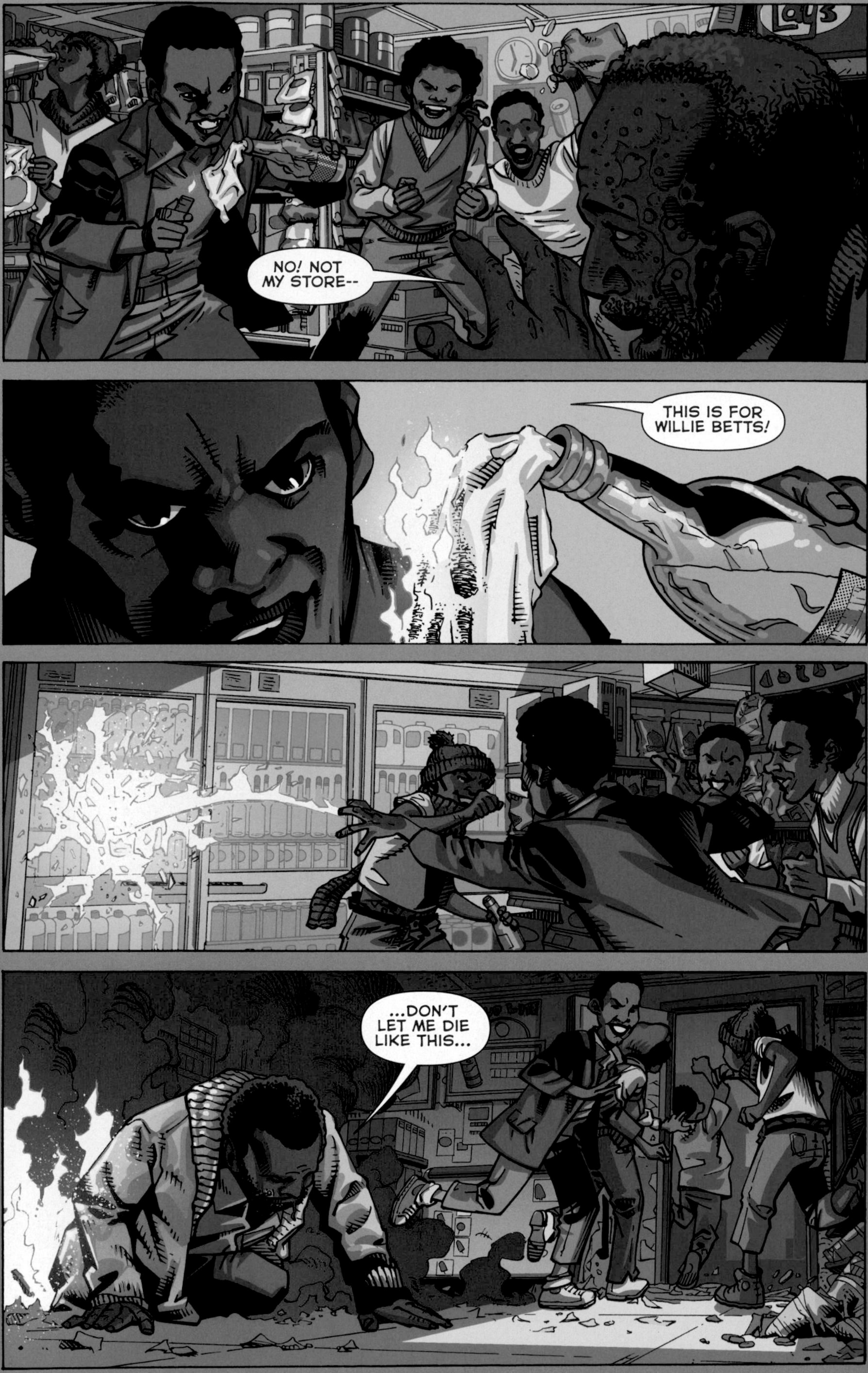
NO! NOT MY STORE--
THIS IS FOR WILLIE BETTS!
...DON'T LET ME DIE LIKE THIS...

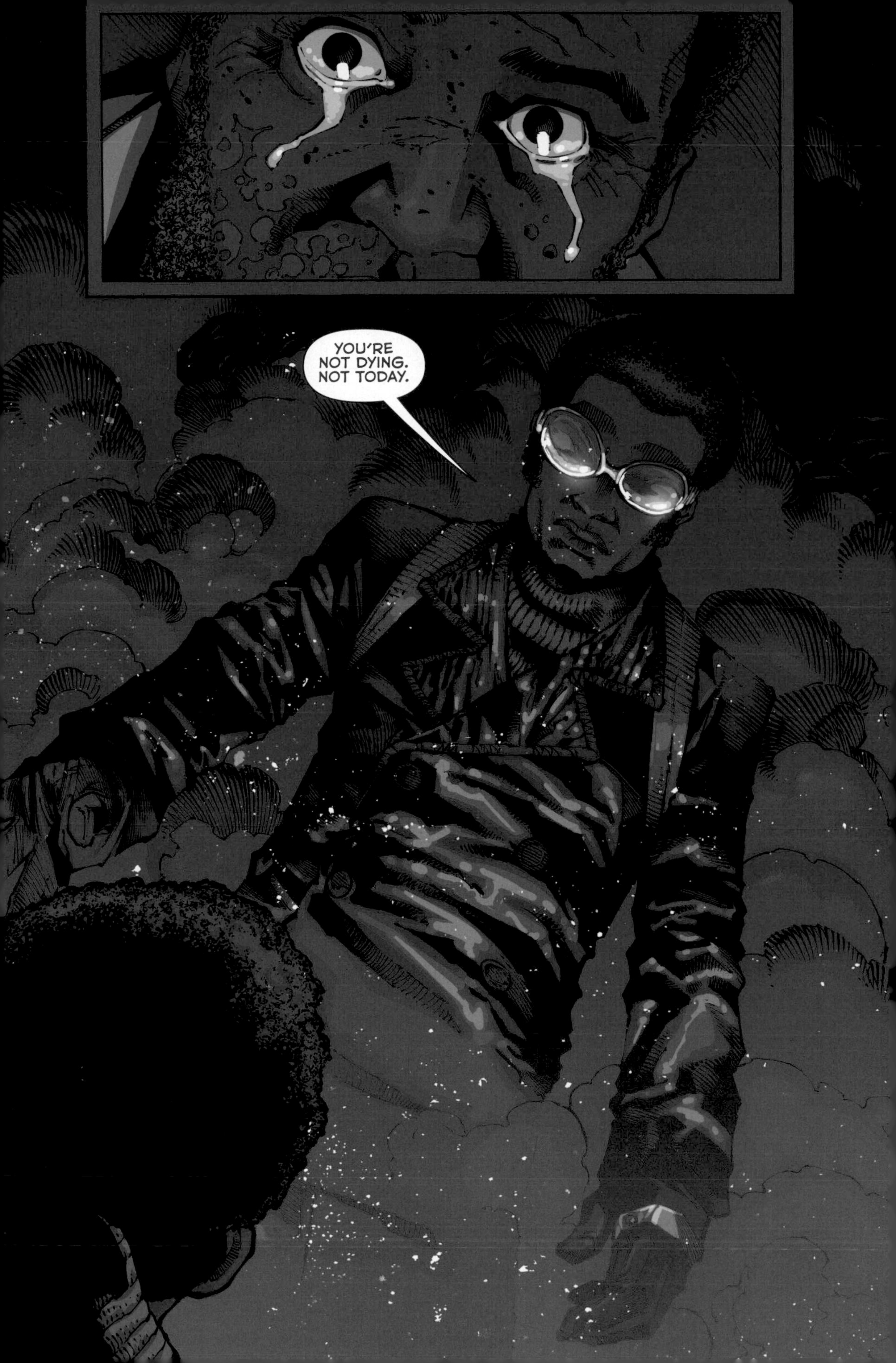
YOU'RE NOT DYING. NOT TODAY.

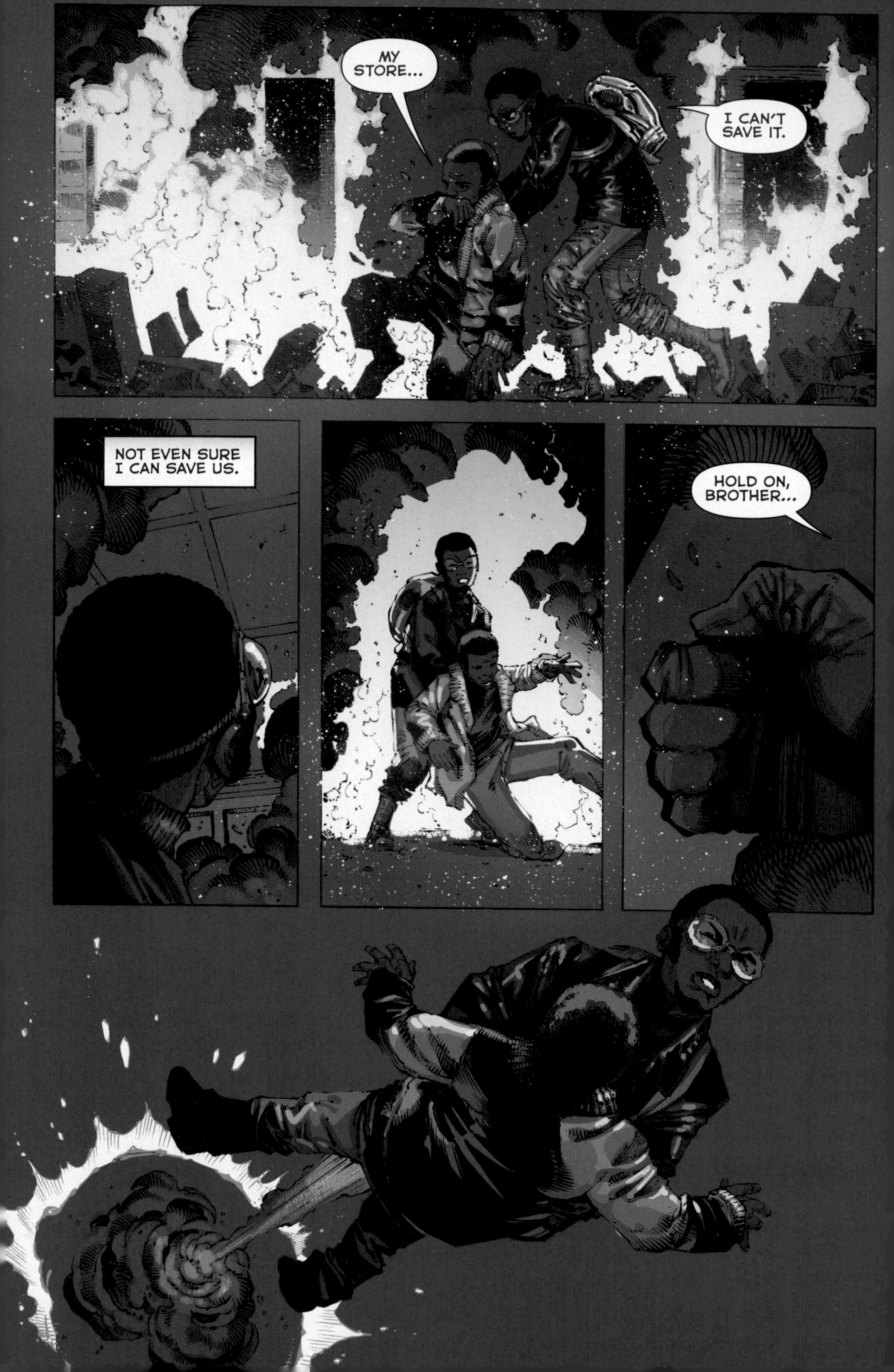

MY STORE...
I CAN'T SAVE IT.
NOT EVEN SURE I CAN SAVE US.
HOLD ON, BROTHER...

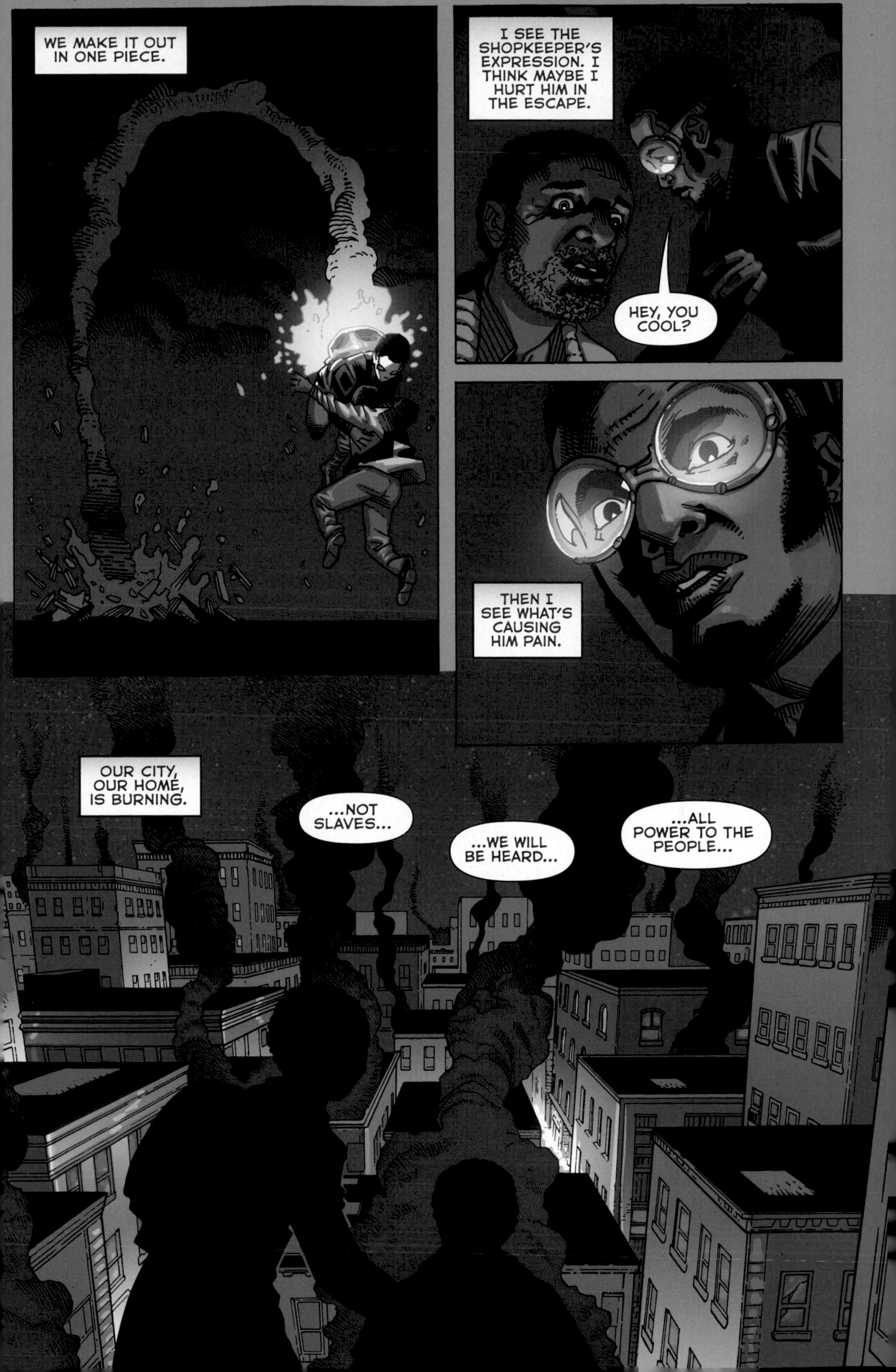
WE MAKE IT OUT IN ONE PIECE.
I SEE THE SHOPKEEPER'S EXPRESSION. I THINK MAYBE I HURT HIM IN THE ESCAPE.
HEY, YOU COOL?
THEN I SEE WHAT'S CAUSING HIM PAIN.
OUR CITY, OUR HOME, IS BURNING.
...NOT SLAVES...
...WE WILL BE HEARD...
...ALL POWER TO THE PEOPLE...

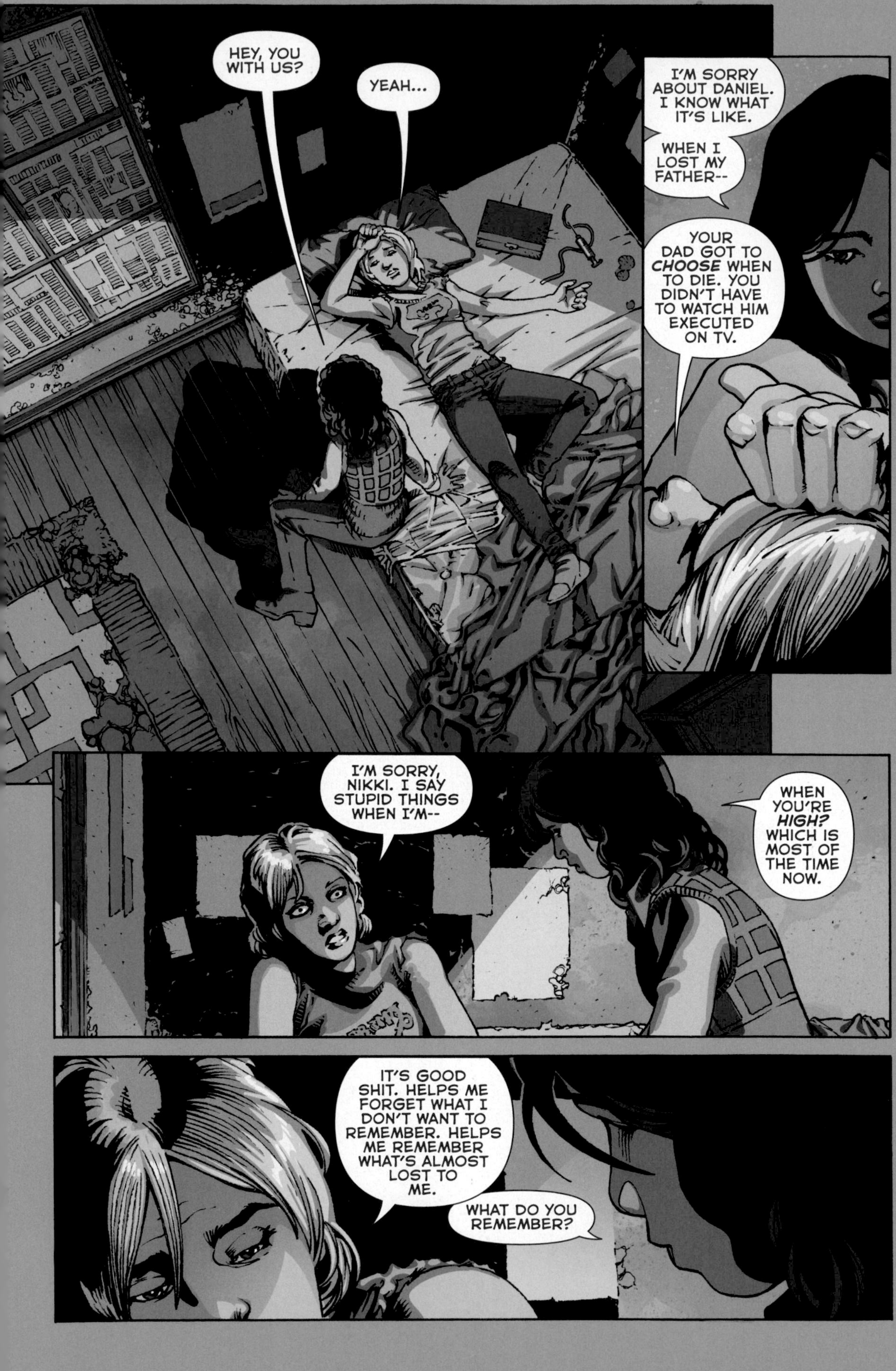
HEY, YOU WITH US?
YEAH...
I'M SORRY ABOUT DANIEL. I KNOW WHAT IT'S LIKE.
WHEN I LOST MY FATHER--
YOUR DAD GOT TO *CHOOSE* WHEN TO DIE. YOU DIDN'T HAVE TO WATCH HIM EXECUTED ON TV.
I'M SORRY, NIKKI. I SAY STUPID THINGS WHEN I'M--
WHEN YOU'RE *HIGH?* WHICH IS MOST OF THE TIME NOW.
IT'S GOOD SHIT. HELPS ME FORGET WHAT I DON'T WANT TO REMEMBER. HELPS ME REMEMBER WHAT'S ALMOST LOST TO ME.
WHAT DO YOU REMEMBER?

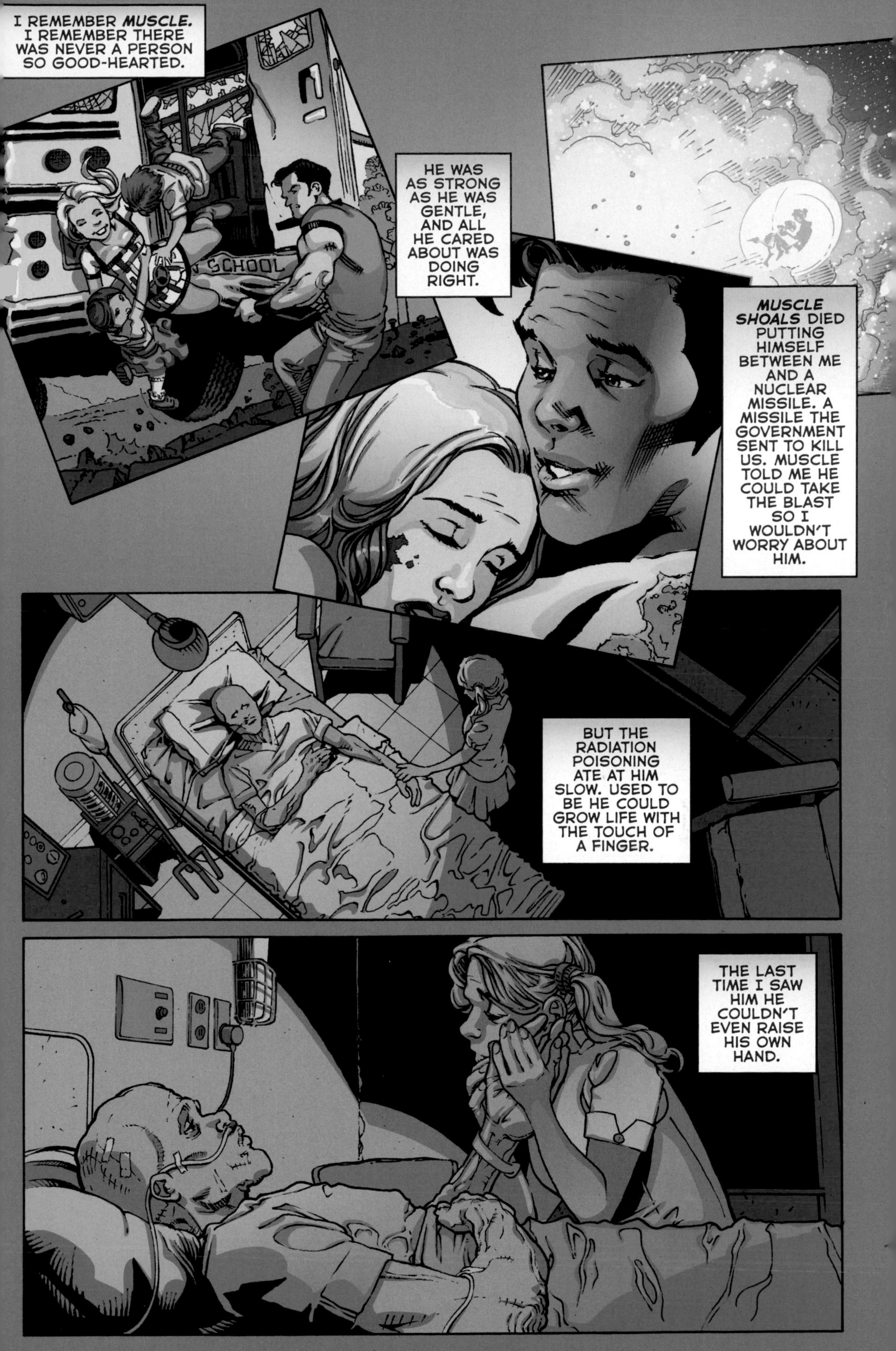
I REMEMBER *MUSCLE.* I REMEMBER THERE WAS NEVER A PERSON SO GOOD-HEARTED.
SCHOOL
HE WAS AS STRONG AS HE WAS GENTLE, AND ALL HE CARED ABOUT WAS DOING RIGHT.
MUSCLE SHOALS DIED PUTTING HIMSELF BETWEEN ME AND A NUCLEAR MISSILE. A MISSILE THE GOVERNMENT SENT TO KILL US. MUSCLE TOLD ME HE COULD TAKE THE BLAST SO I WOULDN'T WORRY ABOUT HIM.
BUT THE RADIATION POISONING ATE AT HIM SLOW. USED TO BE HE COULD GROW LIFE WITH THE TOUCH OF A FINGER.
THE LAST TIME I SAW HIM HE COULDN'T EVEN RAISE HIS OWN HAND.

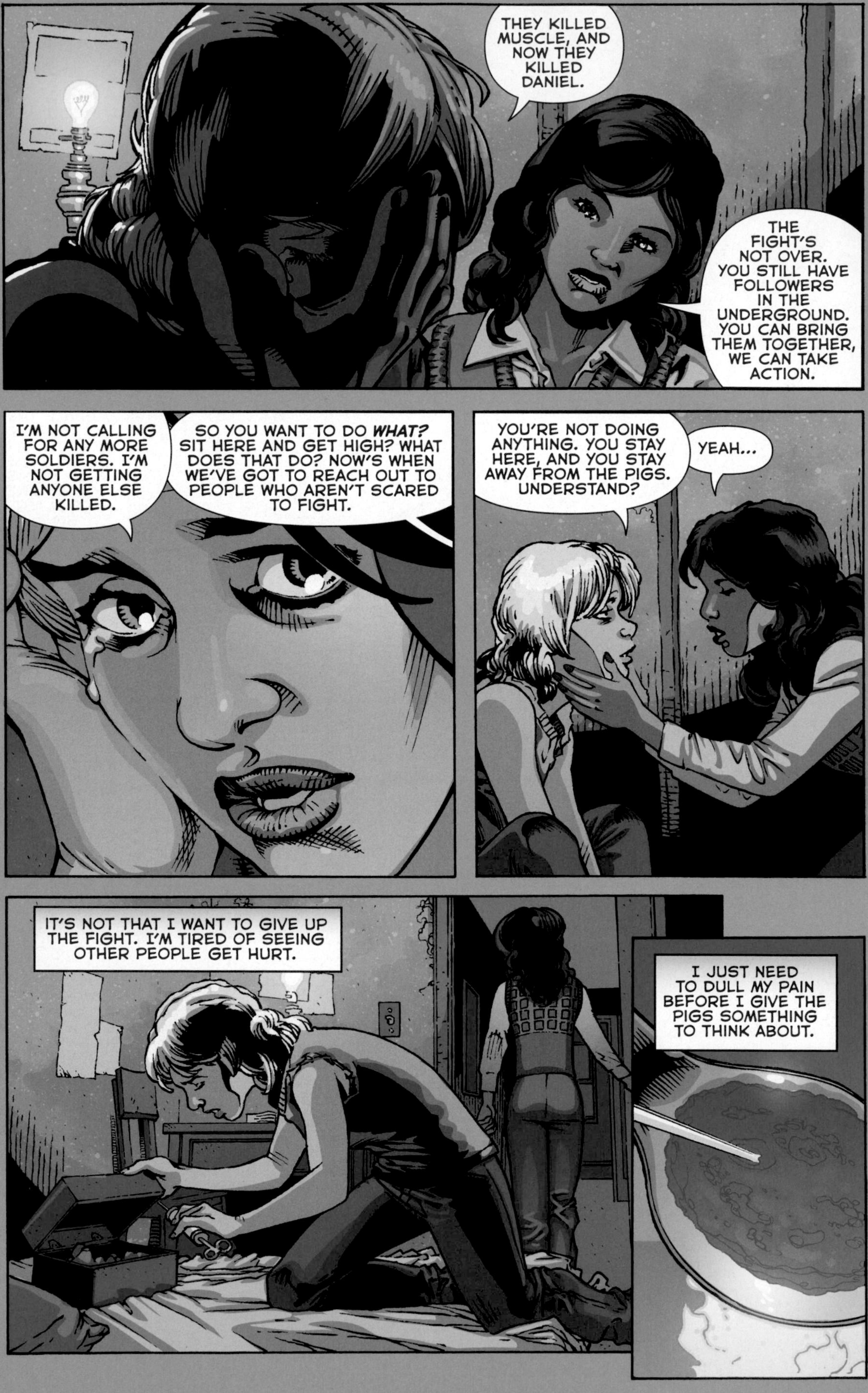
THEY KILLED MUSCLE, AND NOW THEY KILLED DANIEL.
THE FIGHT'S NOT OVER. YOU STILL HAVE FOLLOWERS IN THE UNDERGROUND. YOU CAN BRING THEM TOGETHER, WE CAN TAKE ACTION.
I'M NOT CALLING FOR ANY MORE SOLDIERS. I'M NOT GETTING ANYONE ELSE KILLED.
SO YOU WANT TO DO *WHAT?* SIT HERE AND GET HIGH? WHAT DOES THAT DO? NOW'S WHEN WE'VE GOT TO REACH OUT TO PEOPLE WHO AREN'T SCARED TO FIGHT.
YOU'RE NOT DOING ANYTHING. YOU STAY HERE, AND YOU STAY AWAY FROM THE PIGS. UNDERSTAND?
YEAH...
IT'S NOT THAT I WANT TO GIVE UP THE FIGHT. I'M TIRED OF SEEING OTHER PEOPLE GET HURT.
I JUST NEED TO DULL MY PAIN BEFORE I GIVE THE PIGS SOMETHING TO THINK ABOUT.

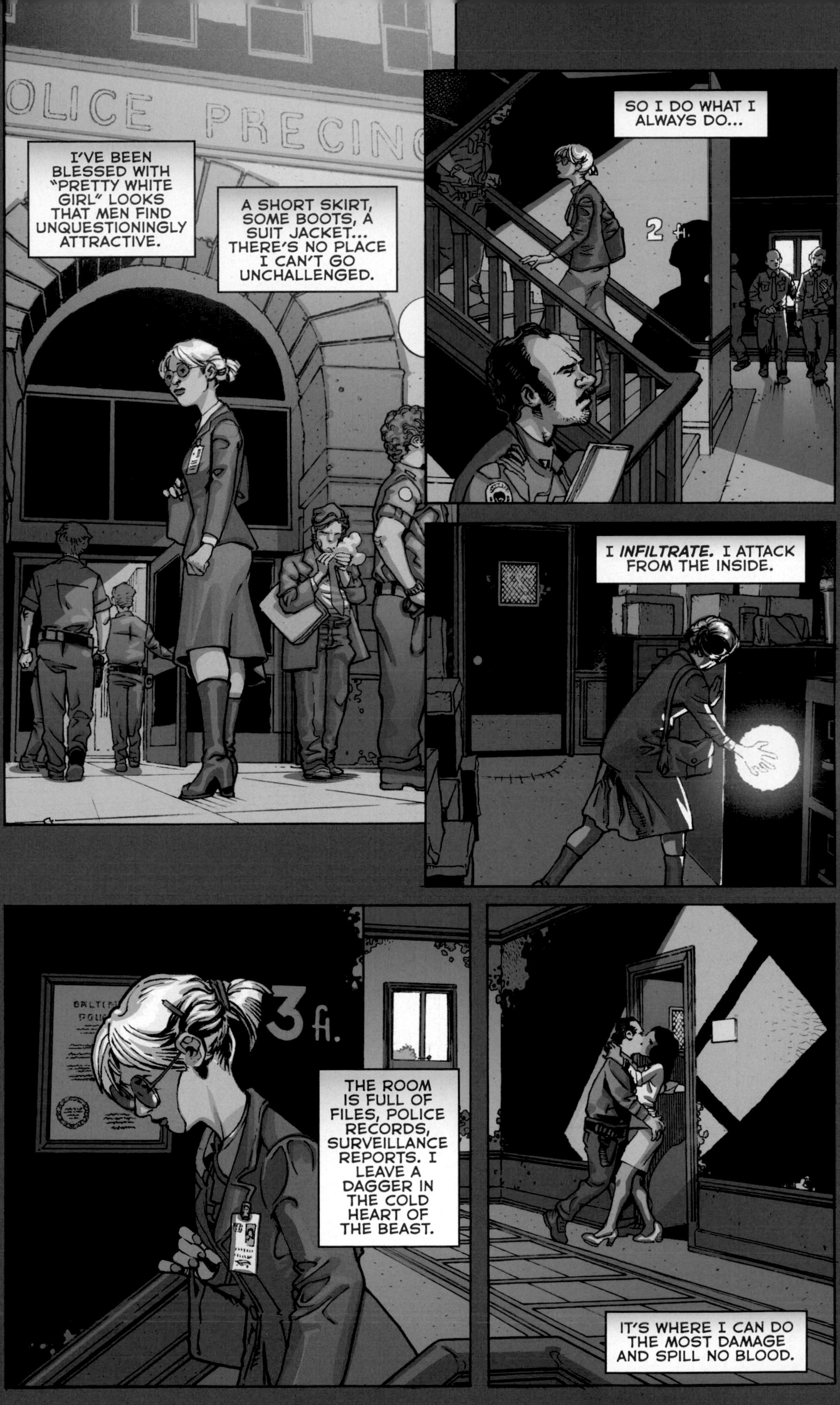

OLICE PRECINC
I'VE BEEN BLESSED WITH "PRETTY WHITE GIRL" LOOKS THAT MEN FIND UNQUESTIONINGLY ATTRACTIVE.
A SHORT SKIRT, SOME BOOTS, A SUIT JACKET... THERE'S NO PLACE I CAN'T GO UNCHALLENGED.
SO I DO WHAT I ALWAYS DO...
2 A.
I *INFILTRATE.* I ATTACK FROM THE INSIDE.
3 A.
THE ROOM IS FULL OF FILES, POLICE RECORDS, SURVEILLANCE REPORTS. I LEAVE A DAGGER IN THE COLD HEART OF THE BEAST.
IT'S WHERE I CAN DO THE MOST DAMAGE AND SPILL NO BLOOD.

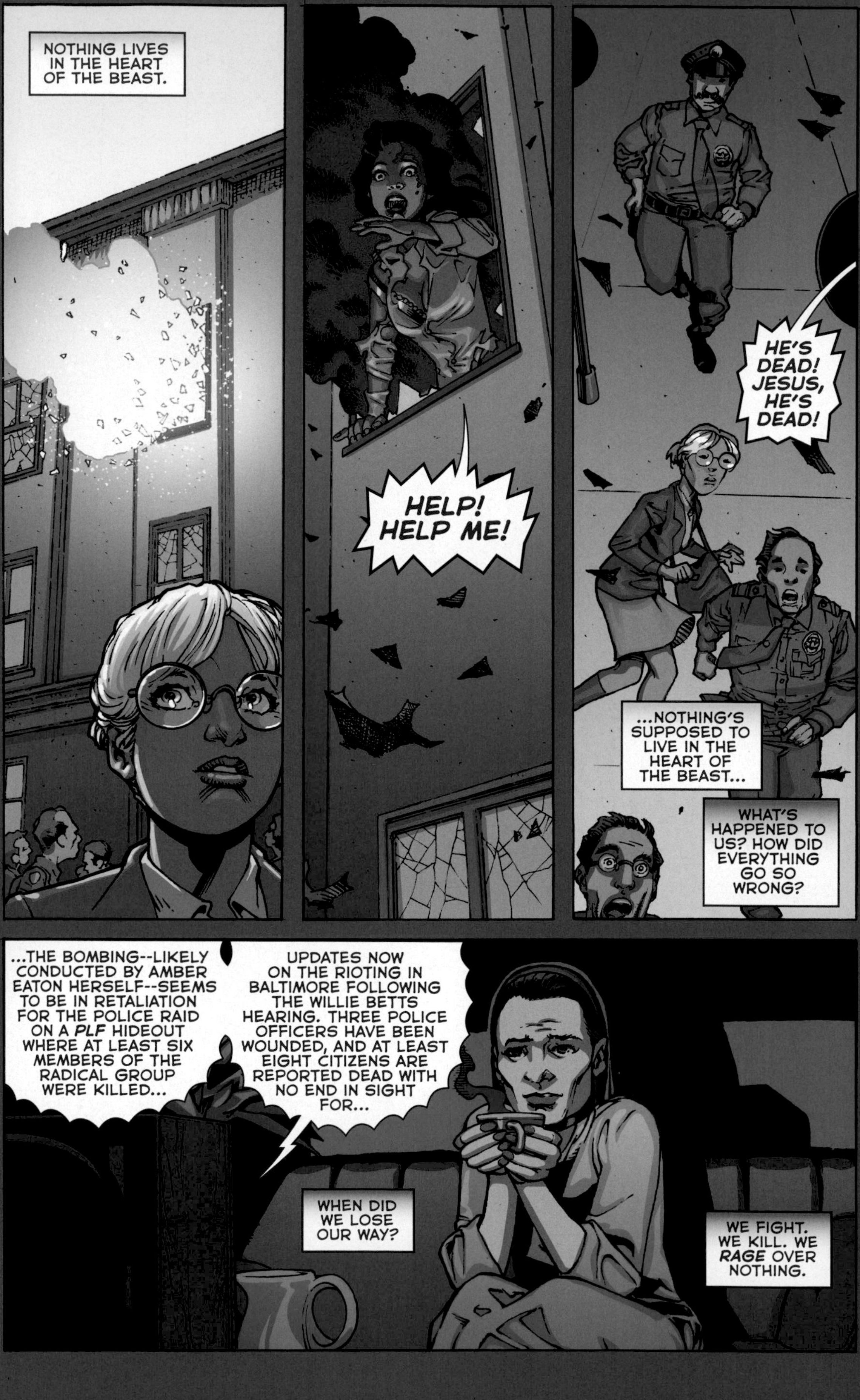
NOTHING LIVES IN THE HEART OF THE BEAST.
HELP! HELP ME!
HE'S DEAD! JESUS, HE'S DEAD!
...NOTHING'S SUPPOSED TO LIVE IN THE HEART OF THE BEAST...
WHAT'S HAPPENED TO US? HOW DID EVERYTHING GO SO WRONG?
...THE BOMBING--LIKELY CONDUCTED BY AMBER EATON HERSELF--SEEMS TO BE IN RETALIATION FOR THE POLICE RAID ON A *PLF* HIDEOUT WHERE AT LEAST SIX MEMBERS OF THE RADICAL GROUP WERE KILLED...
UPDATES NOW ON THE RIOTING IN BALTIMORE FOLLOWING THE WILLIE BETTS HEARING. THREE POLICE OFFICERS HAVE BEEN WOUNDED, AND AT LEAST EIGHT CITIZENS ARE REPORTED DEAD WITH NO END IN SIGHT FOR...
WHEN DID WE LOSE OUR WAY?
WE FIGHT. WE KILL. WE *RAGE* OVER NOTHING.

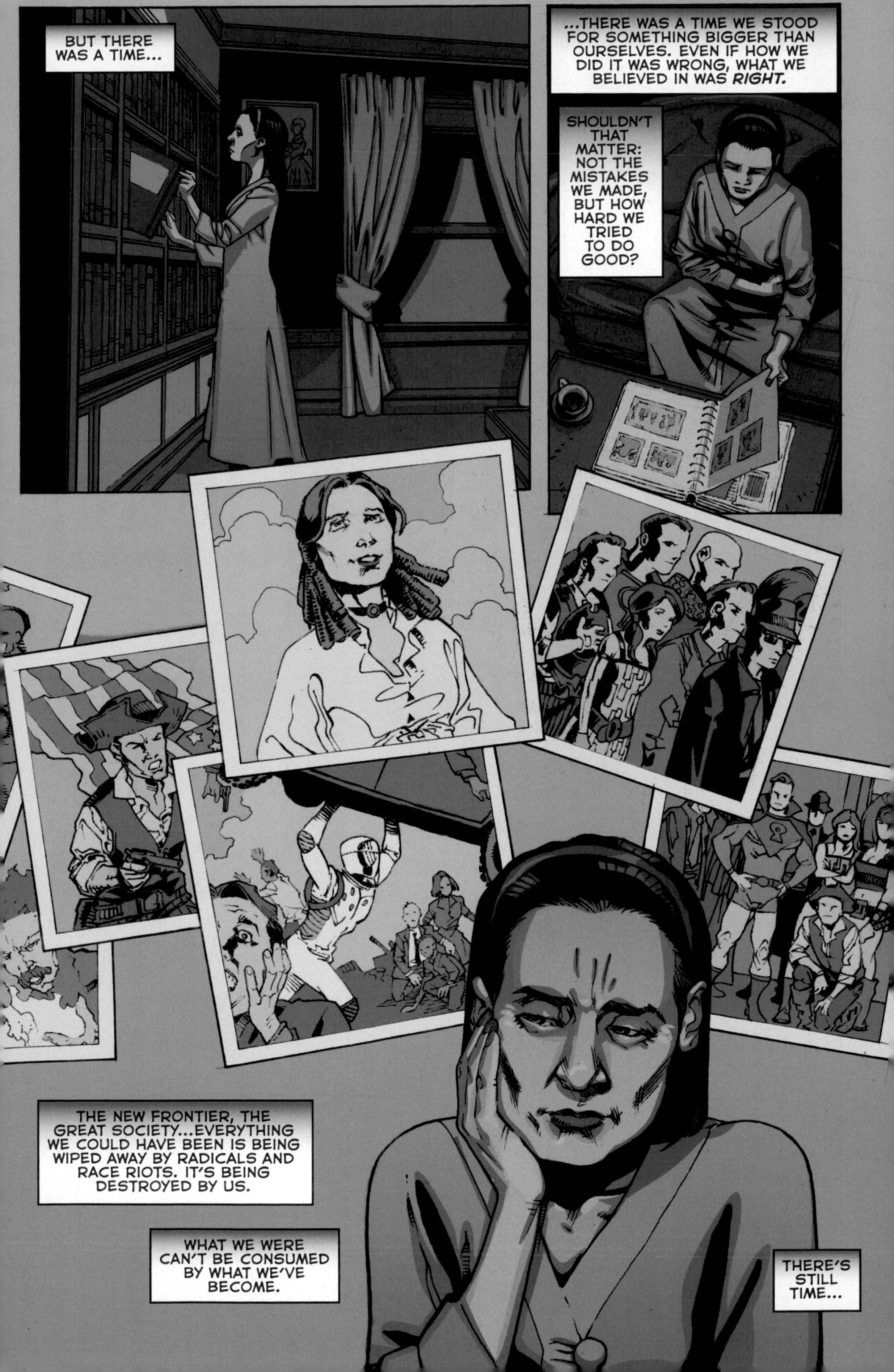
BUT THERE WAS A TIME...
...THERE WAS A TIME WE STOOD FOR SOMETHING BIGGER THAN OURSELVES. EVEN IF HOW WE DID IT WAS WRONG, WHAT WE BELIEVED IN WAS *RIGHT.*
SHOULDN'T THAT MATTER: NOT THE MISTAKES WE MADE, BUT HOW HARD WE TRIED TO DO GOOD?
THE NEW FRONTIER, THE GREAT SOCIETY...EVERYTHING WE COULD HAVE BEEN IS BEING WIPED AWAY BY RADICALS AND RACE RIOTS. IT'S BEING DESTROYED BY US.
WHAT WE WERE CAN'T BE CONSUMED BY WHAT WE'VE BECOME.
THERE'S STILL TIME...

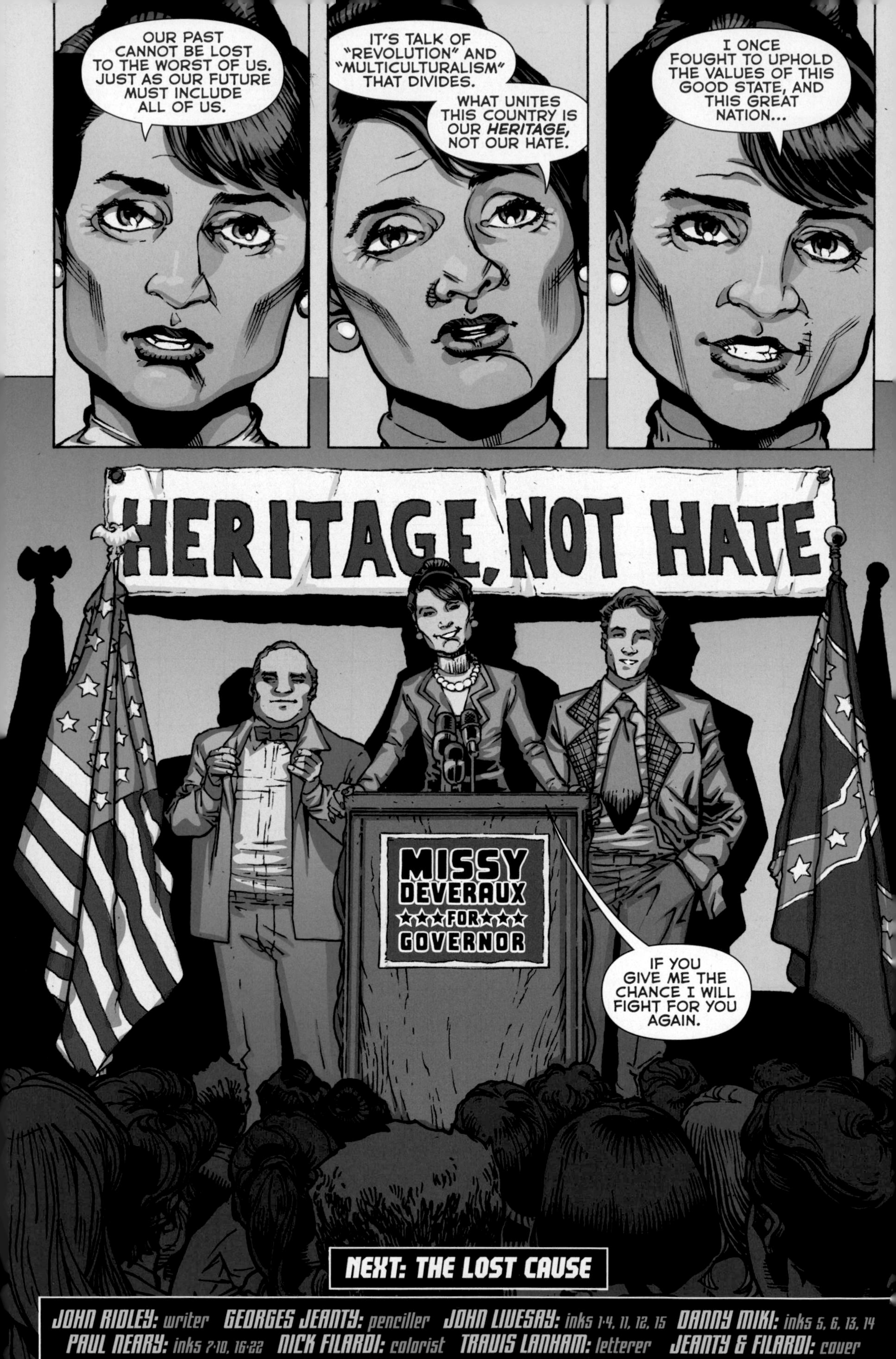

OUR PAST CANNOT BE LOST TO THE WORST OF US. JUST AS OUR FUTURE MUST INCLUDE ALL OF US.
IT'S TALK OF "REVOLUTION" AND "MULTICULTURALISM" THAT DIVIDES.
WHAT UNITES THIS COUNTRY IS OUR *HERITAGE*, NOT OUR HATE.
I ONCE FOUGHT TO UPHOLD THE VALUES OF THIS GOOD STATE, AND THIS GREAT NATION...
HERITAGE, NOT HATE
MISSY DEVERAUX FOR GOVERNOR
IF YOU GIVE ME THE CHANCE I WILL FIGHT FOR YOU AGAIN.
NEXT: THE LOST CAUSE

JOHN RIDLEY: writer **GEORGES JEANTY:** penciller **JOHN LIVESAY:** inks 1-4, 11, 12, 15 **DANNY MIKI:** inks 5, 6, 13, 14 **PAUL NEARY:** inks 7-10, 16-22 **NICK FILARDI:** colorist **TRAVIS LANHAM:** letterer **JEANTY & FILARDI:** cover **MAGGIE HOWELL:** asst. editor **JAMIE S. RICH:** editor

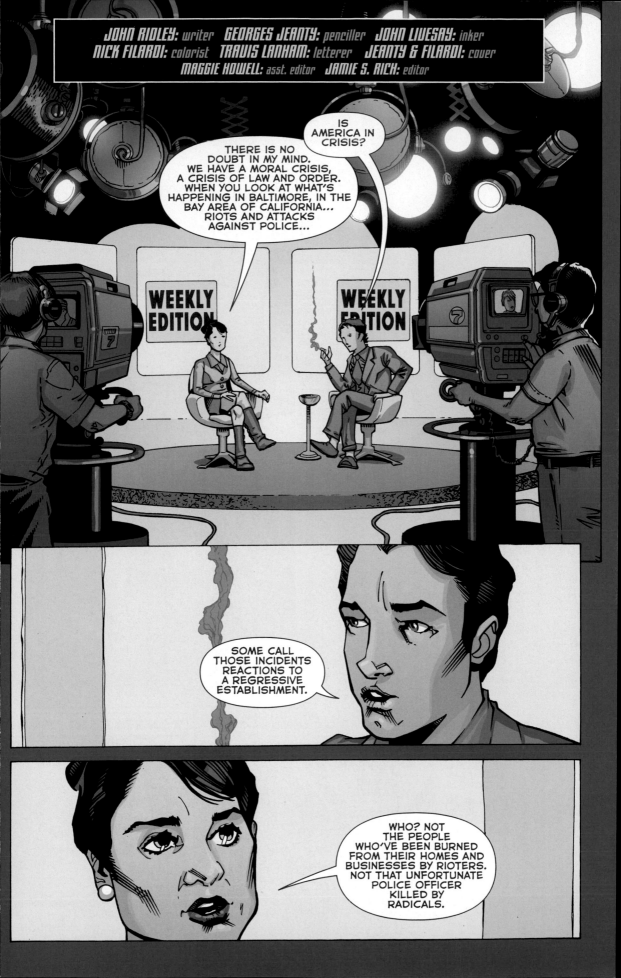

JOHN RIDLEY: writer **GEORGES JEANTY:** penciller **JOHN LIVESAY:** inker
NICK FILARDI: colorist **TRAVIS LANHAM:** letterer **JEANTY & FILARDI:** cover
MAGGIE HOWELL: asst. editor **JAMIE S. RICH:** editor

IS AMERICA IN CRISIS?

THERE IS NO DOUBT IN MY MIND. WE HAVE A MORAL CRISIS, A CRISIS OF LAW AND ORDER. WHEN YOU LOOK AT WHAT'S HAPPENING IN BALTIMORE, IN THE BAY AREA OF CALIFORNIA... RIOTS AND ATTACKS AGAINST POLICE...

WEEKLY EDITION

WEEKLY EDITION

SOME CALL THOSE INCIDENTS REACTIONS TO A REGRESSIVE ESTABLISHMENT.

WHO? NOT THE PEOPLE WHO'VE BEEN BURNED FROM THEIR HOMES AND BUSINESSES BY RIOTERS. NOT THAT UNFORTUNATE POLICE OFFICER KILLED BY RADICALS.

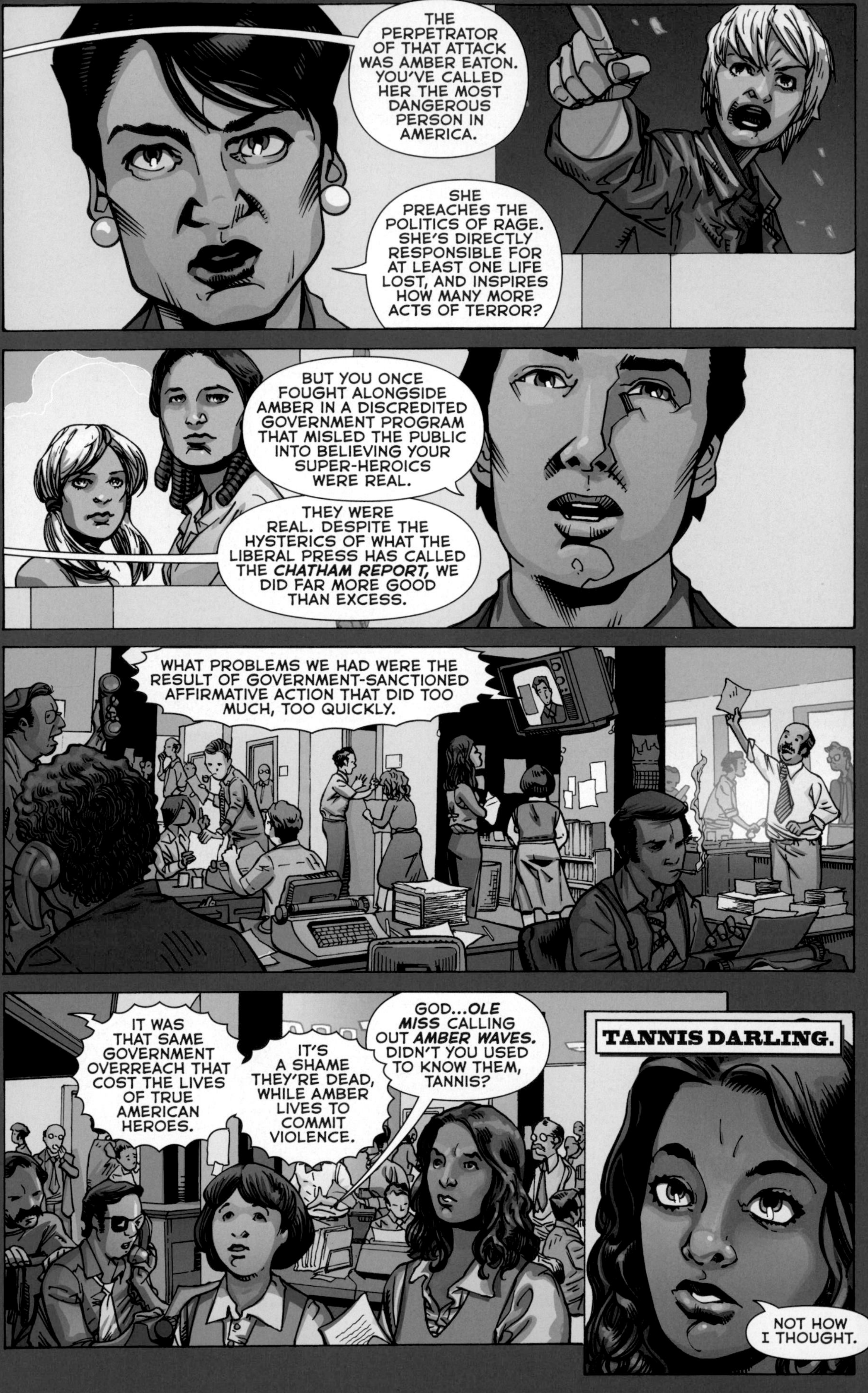
THE PERPETRATOR OF THAT ATTACK WAS AMBER EATON. YOU'VE CALLED HER THE MOST DANGEROUS PERSON IN AMERICA.
SHE PREACHES THE POLITICS OF RAGE. SHE'S DIRECTLY RESPONSIBLE FOR AT LEAST ONE LIFE LOST, AND INSPIRES HOW MANY MORE ACTS OF TERROR?
BUT YOU ONCE FOUGHT ALONGSIDE AMBER IN A DISCREDITED GOVERNMENT PROGRAM THAT MISLED THE PUBLIC INTO BELIEVING YOUR SUPER-HEROICS WERE REAL.
THEY WERE REAL. DESPITE THE HYSTERICS OF WHAT THE LIBERAL PRESS HAS CALLED THE *CHATHAM REPORT,* WE DID FAR MORE GOOD THAN EXCESS.
WHAT PROBLEMS WE HAD WERE THE RESULT OF GOVERNMENT-SANCTIONED AFFIRMATIVE ACTION THAT DID TOO MUCH, TOO QUICKLY.
IT WAS THAT SAME GOVERNMENT OVERREACH THAT COST THE LIVES OF TRUE AMERICAN HEROES.
IT'S A SHAME THEY'RE DEAD, WHILE AMBER LIVES TO COMMIT VIOLENCE.
GOD...*OLE MISS* CALLING OUT *AMBER WAVES.* DIDN'T YOU USED TO KNOW THEM, TANNIS?
TANNIS DARLING.
NOT HOW I THOUGHT.

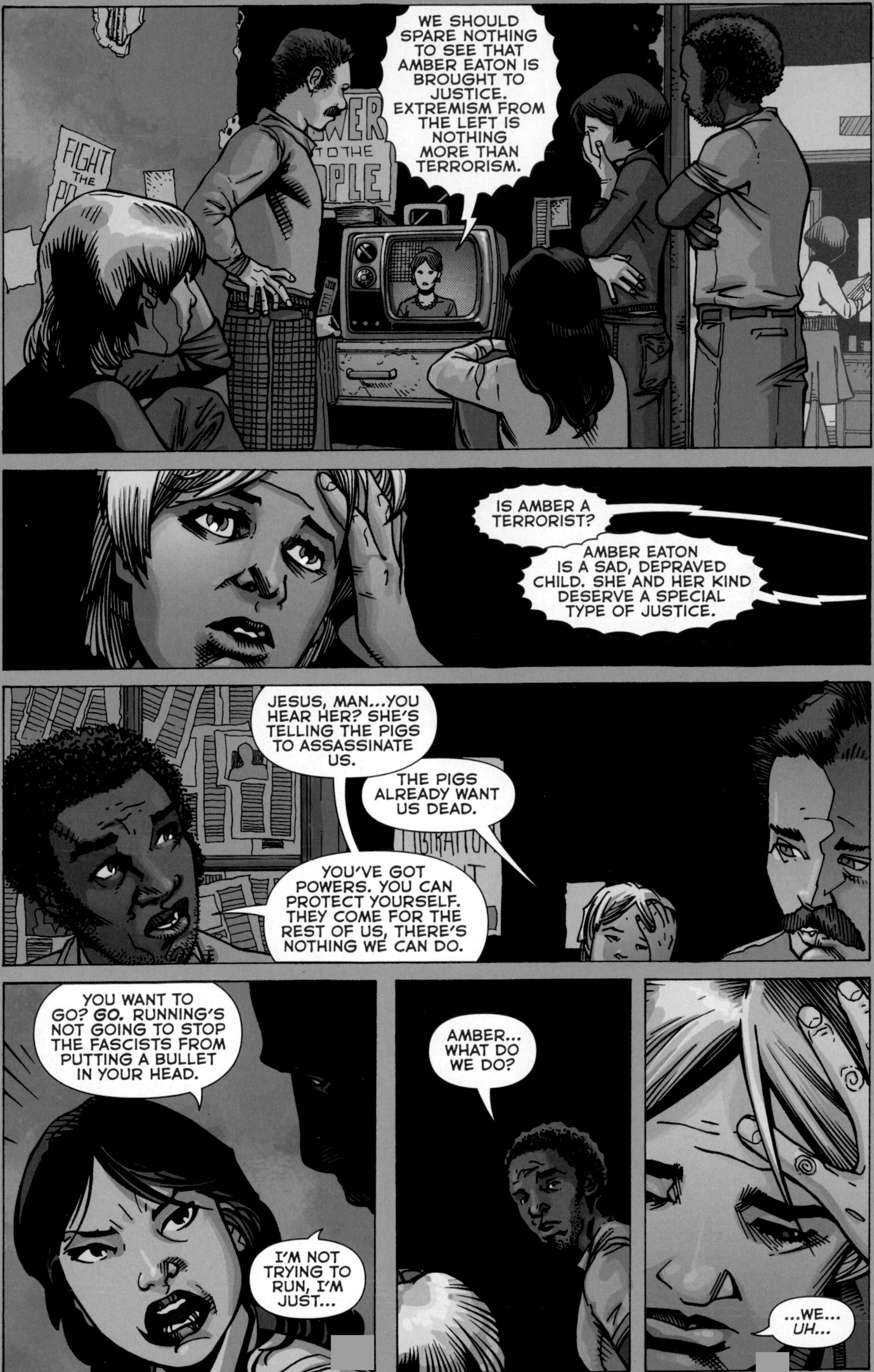

FIGHT THE PO
POWER TO THE PEOPLE
WE SHOULD SPARE NOTHING TO SEE THAT AMBER EATON IS BROUGHT TO JUSTICE. EXTREMISM FROM THE LEFT IS NOTHING MORE THAN TERRORISM.
IS AMBER A TERRORIST?
AMBER EATON IS A SAD, DEPRAVED CHILD. SHE AND HER KIND DESERVE A SPECIAL TYPE OF JUSTICE.
JESUS, MAN...YOU HEAR HER? SHE'S TELLING THE PIGS TO ASSASSINATE US.
THE PIGS ALREADY WANT US DEAD.
YOU'VE GOT POWERS. YOU CAN PROTECT YOURSELF. THEY COME FOR THE REST OF US, THERE'S NOTHING WE CAN DO.
YOU WANT TO GO? *GO.* RUNNING'S NOT GOING TO STOP THE FASCISTS FROM PUTTING A BULLET IN YOUR HEAD.
I'M NOT TRYING TO RUN, I'M JUST...
AMBER... WHAT DO WE DO?
...WE... UH...

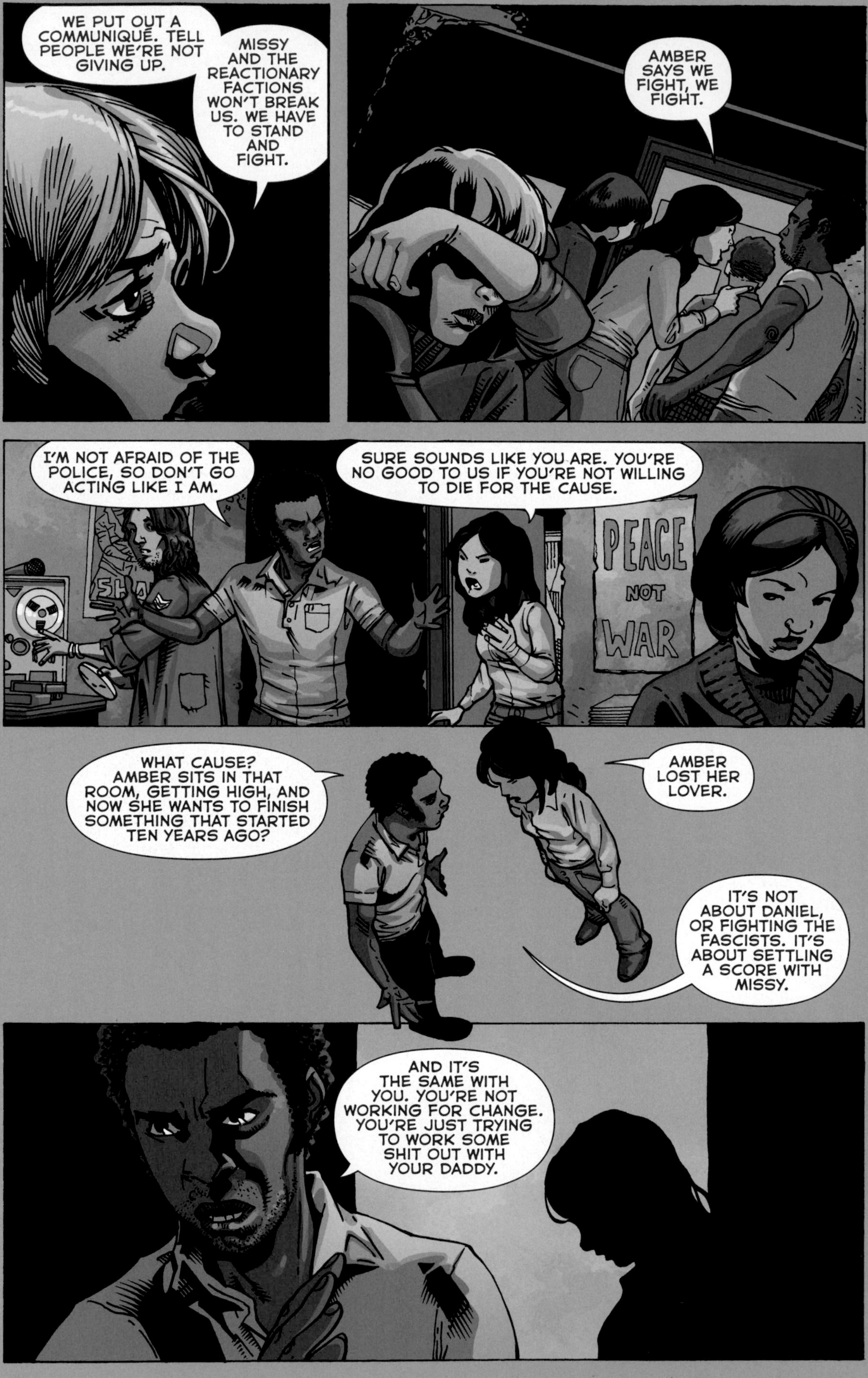
WE PUT OUT A COMMUNIQUÉ. TELL PEOPLE WE'RE NOT GIVING UP.
MISSY AND THE REACTIONARY FACTIONS WON'T BREAK US. WE HAVE TO STAND AND FIGHT.
AMBER SAYS WE FIGHT, WE FIGHT.
I'M NOT AFRAID OF THE POLICE, SO DON'T GO ACTING LIKE I AM.
SURE SOUNDS LIKE YOU ARE. YOU'RE NO GOOD TO US IF YOU'RE NOT WILLING TO DIE FOR THE CAUSE.
PEACE NOT WAR
WHAT CAUSE? AMBER SITS IN THAT ROOM, GETTING HIGH, AND NOW SHE WANTS TO FINISH SOMETHING THAT STARTED TEN YEARS AGO?
AMBER LOST HER LOVER.
IT'S NOT ABOUT DANIEL, OR FIGHTING THE FASCISTS. IT'S ABOUT SETTLING A SCORE WITH MISSY.
AND IT'S THE SAME WITH YOU. YOU'RE NOT WORKING FOR CHANGE. YOU'RE JUST TRYING TO WORK SOME SHIT OUT WITH YOUR DADDY.

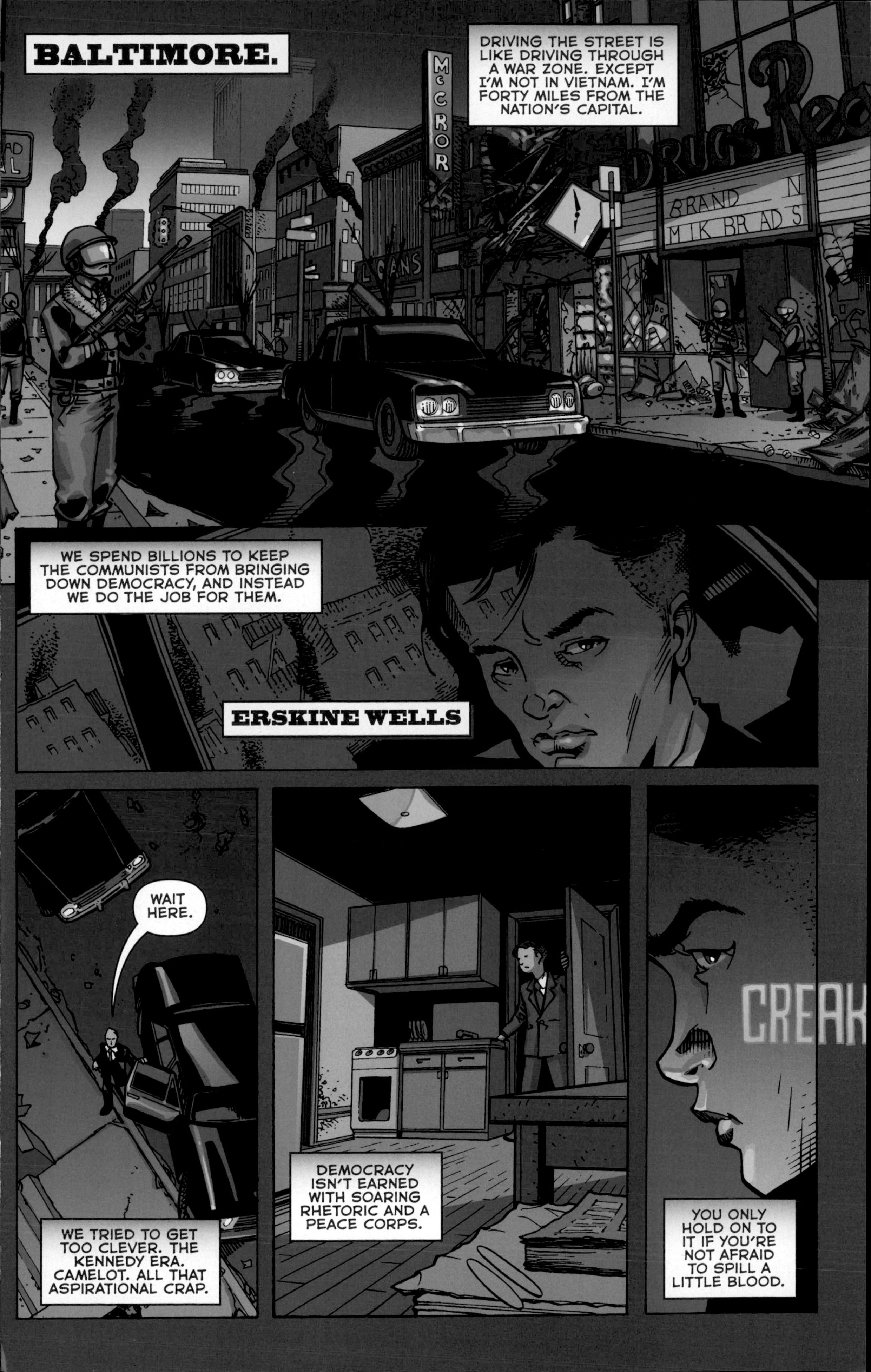
BALTIMORE.
DRIVING THE STREET IS LIKE DRIVING THROUGH A WAR ZONE. EXCEPT I'M NOT IN VIETNAM. I'M FORTY MILES FROM THE NATION'S CAPITAL.
McCROR
DRUGS
BRAND N
MIK BR AD S
LOANS
WE SPEND BILLIONS TO KEEP THE COMMUNISTS FROM BRINGING DOWN DEMOCRACY, AND INSTEAD WE DO THE JOB FOR THEM.
ERSKINE WELLS
WAIT HERE.
WE TRIED TO GET TOO CLEVER. THE KENNEDY ERA. CAMELOT. ALL THAT ASPIRATIONAL CRAP.
DEMOCRACY ISN'T EARNED WITH SOARING RHETORIC AND A PEACE CORPS.
CREAK
YOU ONLY HOLD ON TO IT IF YOU'RE NOT AFRAID TO SPILL A LITTLE BLOOD.

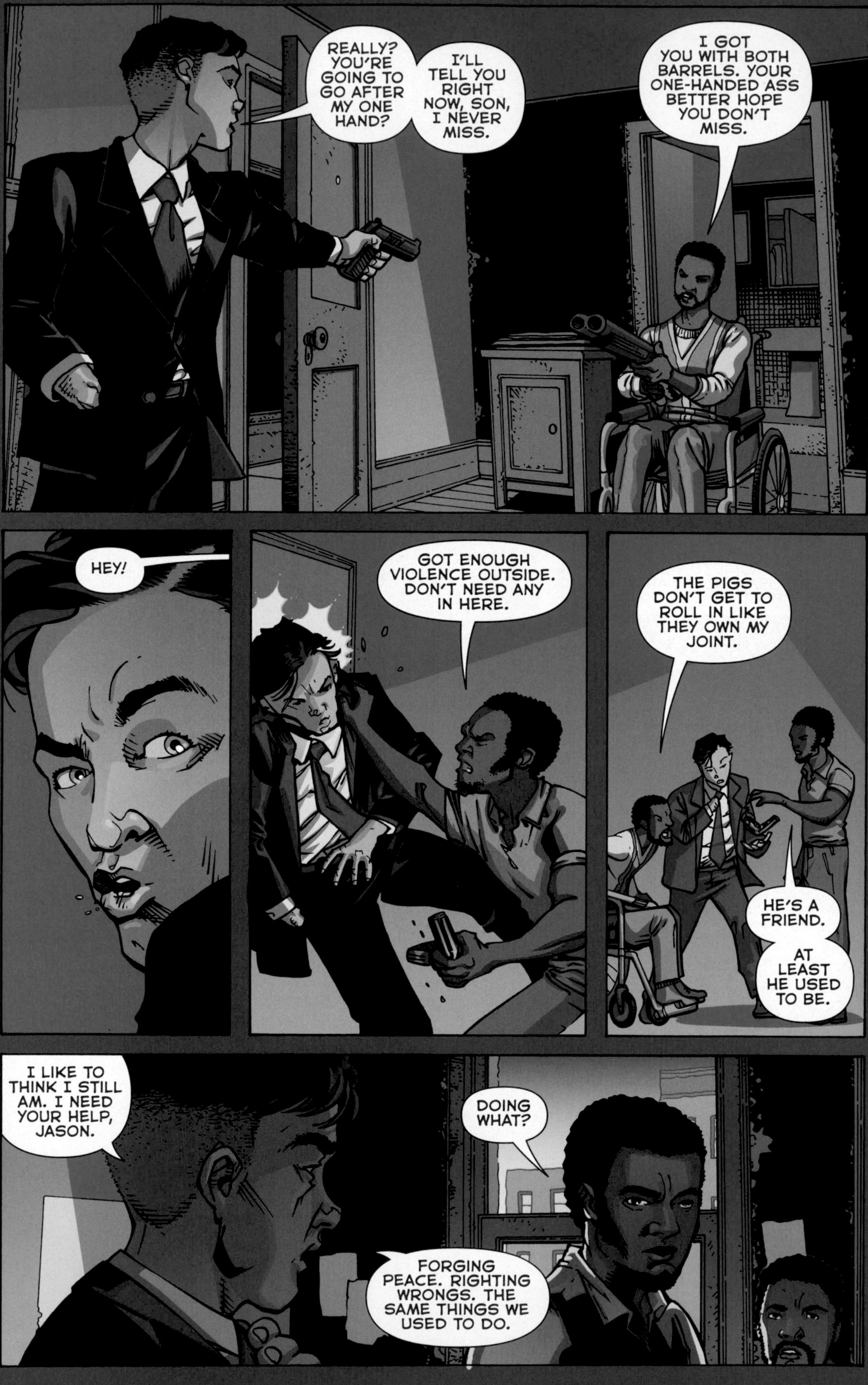

REALLY? YOU'RE GOING TO GO AFTER MY ONE HAND?
I'LL TELL YOU RIGHT NOW, SON, I NEVER MISS.
I GOT YOU WITH BOTH BARRELS. YOUR ONE-HANDED ASS BETTER HOPE YOU DON'T MISS.
HEY!
GOT ENOUGH VIOLENCE OUTSIDE. DON'T NEED ANY IN HERE.
THE PIGS DON'T GET TO ROLL IN LIKE THEY OWN MY JOINT.
HE'S A FRIEND.
AT LEAST HE USED TO BE.
I LIKE TO THINK I STILL AM. I NEED YOUR HELP, JASON.
DOING WHAT?
FORGING PEACE. RIGHTING WRONGS. THE SAME THINGS WE USED TO DO.

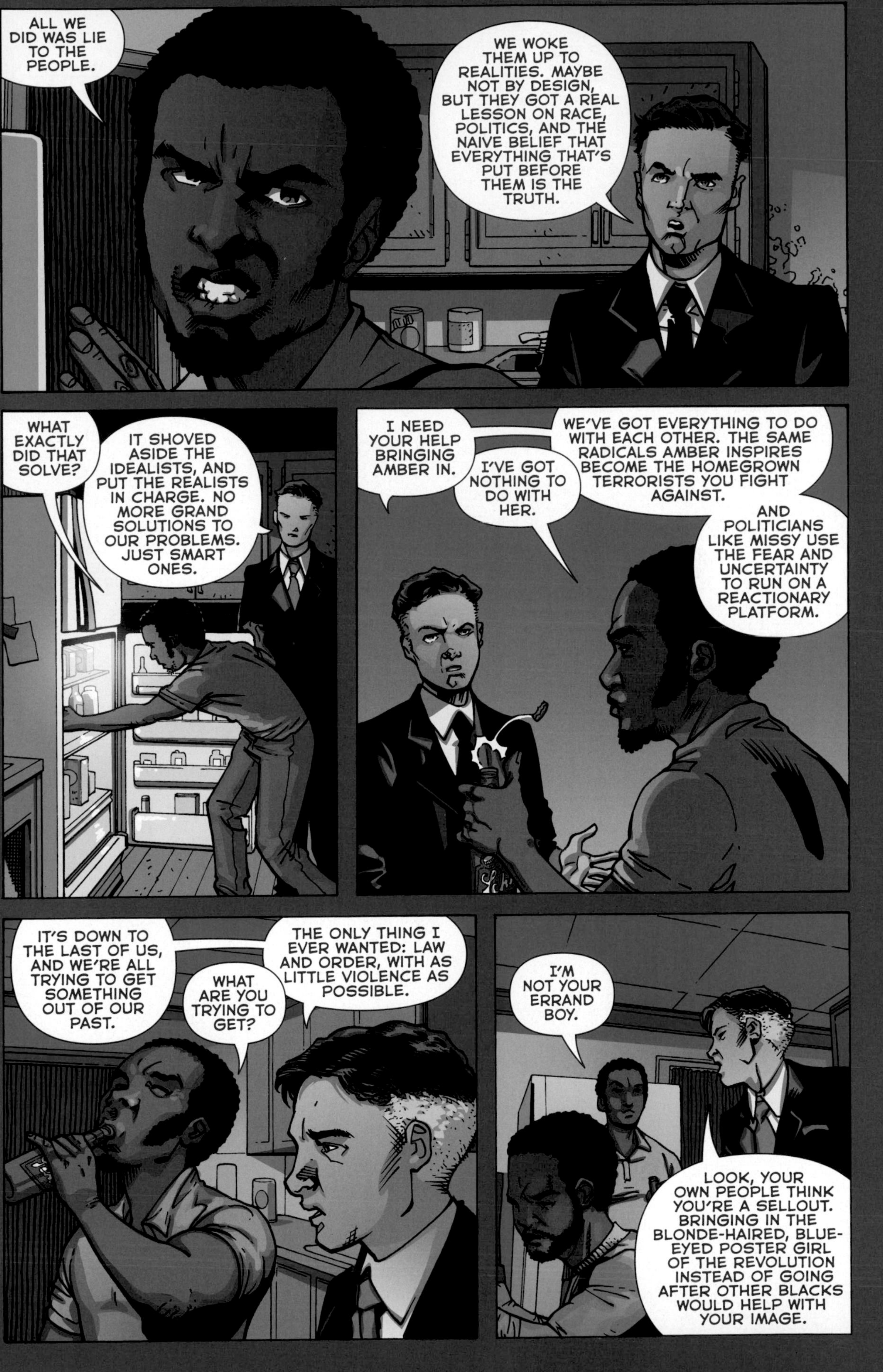

ALL WE DID WAS LIE TO THE PEOPLE.
WE WOKE THEM UP TO REALITIES. MAYBE NOT BY DESIGN, BUT THEY GOT A REAL LESSON ON RACE, POLITICS, AND THE NAIVE BELIEF THAT EVERYTHING THAT'S PUT BEFORE THEM IS THE TRUTH.
WHAT EXACTLY DID THAT SOLVE?
IT SHOVED ASIDE THE IDEALISTS, AND PUT THE REALISTS IN CHARGE. NO MORE GRAND SOLUTIONS TO OUR PROBLEMS. JUST SMART ONES.
I NEED YOUR HELP BRINGING AMBER IN.
I'VE GOT NOTHING TO DO WITH HER.
WE'VE GOT EVERYTHING TO DO WITH EACH OTHER. THE SAME RADICALS AMBER INSPIRES BECOME THE HOMEGROWN TERRORISTS YOU FIGHT AGAINST.
AND POLITICIANS LIKE MISSY USE THE FEAR AND UNCERTAINTY TO RUN ON A REACTIONARY PLATFORM.
IT'S DOWN TO THE LAST OF US, AND WE'RE ALL TRYING TO GET SOMETHING OUT OF OUR PAST.
WHAT ARE YOU TRYING TO GET?
THE ONLY THING I EVER WANTED: LAW AND ORDER, WITH AS LITTLE VIOLENCE AS POSSIBLE.
I'M NOT YOUR ERRAND BOY.
LOOK, YOUR OWN PEOPLE THINK YOU'RE A SELLOUT. BRINGING IN THE BLONDE-HAIRED, BLUE-EYED POSTER GIRL OF THE REVOLUTION INSTEAD OF GOING AFTER OTHER BLACKS WOULD HELP WITH YOUR IMAGE.

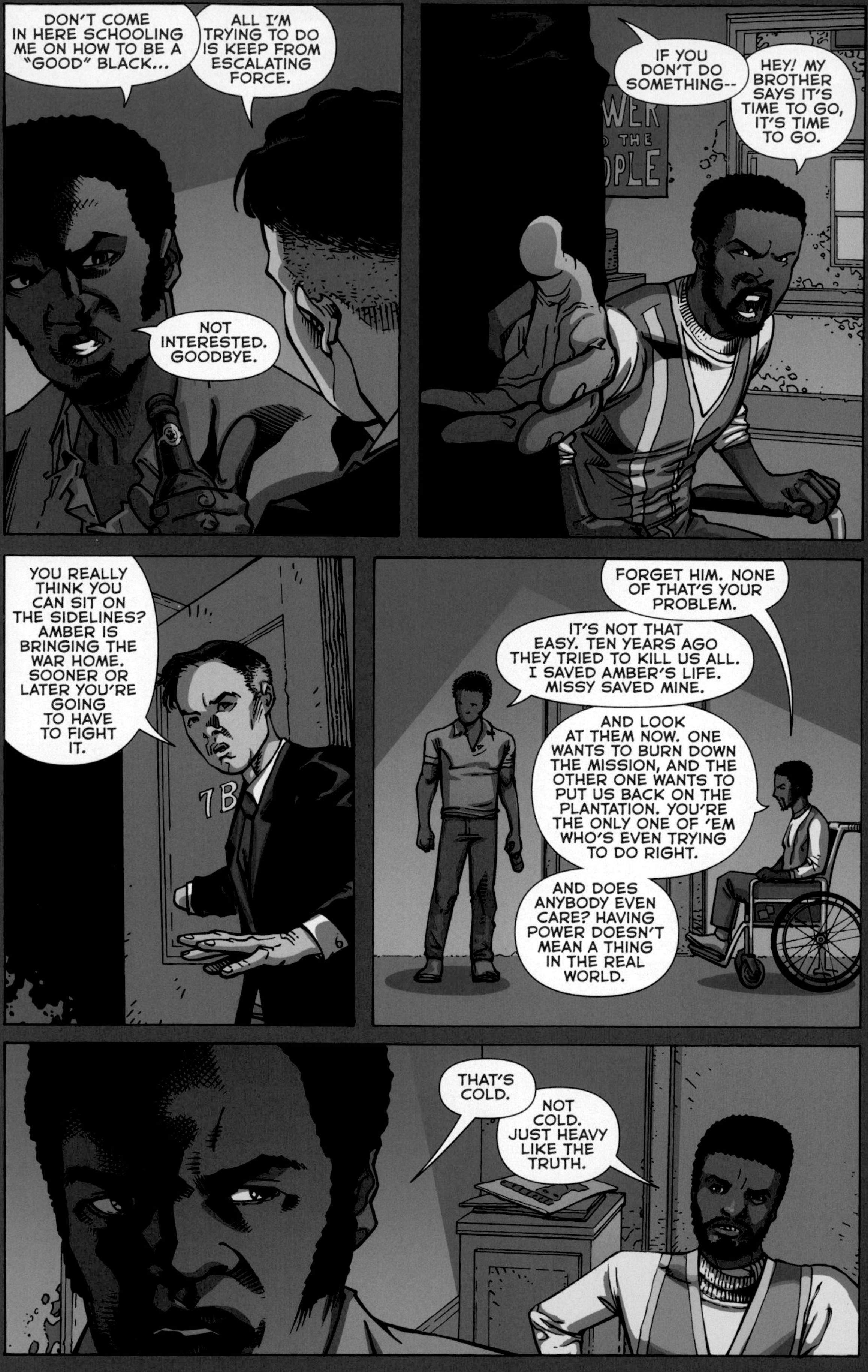
DON'T COME IN HERE SCHOOLING ME ON HOW TO BE A "GOOD" BLACK...
ALL I'M TRYING TO DO IS KEEP FROM ESCALATING FORCE.
NOT INTERESTED. GOODBYE.
IF YOU DON'T DO SOMETHING--
HEY! MY BROTHER SAYS IT'S TIME TO GO, IT'S TIME TO GO.
YOU REALLY THINK YOU CAN SIT ON THE SIDELINES? AMBER IS BRINGING THE WAR HOME. SOONER OR LATER YOU'RE GOING TO HAVE TO FIGHT IT.
7B
FORGET HIM. NONE OF THAT'S YOUR PROBLEM.
IT'S NOT THAT EASY. TEN YEARS AGO THEY TRIED TO KILL US ALL. I SAVED AMBER'S LIFE. MISSY SAVED MINE.
AND LOOK AT THEM NOW. ONE WANTS TO BURN DOWN THE MISSION, AND THE OTHER ONE WANTS TO PUT US BACK ON THE PLANTATION. YOU'RE THE ONLY ONE OF 'EM WHO'S EVEN TRYING TO DO RIGHT.
AND DOES ANYBODY EVEN CARE? HAVING POWER DOESN'T MEAN A THING IN THE REAL WORLD.
THAT'S COLD.
NOT COLD. JUST HEAVY LIKE THE TRUTH.

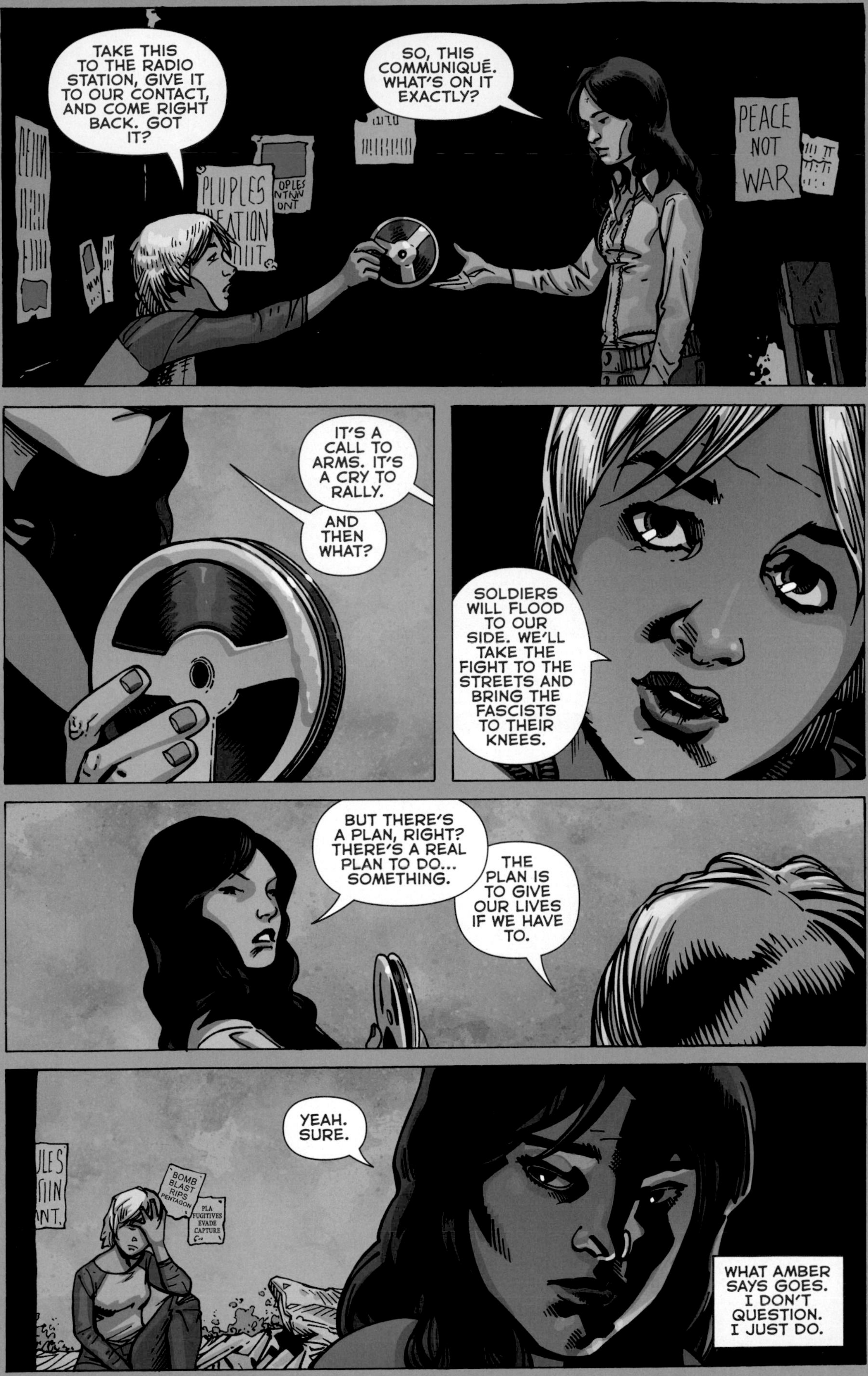
TAKE THIS TO THE RADIO STATION, GIVE IT TO OUR CONTACT, AND COME RIGHT BACK. GOT IT?
SO, THIS COMMUNIQUÉ. WHAT'S ON IT EXACTLY?
PEACE NOT WAR
PLUPLES
IT'S A CALL TO ARMS. IT'S A CRY TO RALLY.
AND THEN WHAT?
SOLDIERS WILL FLOOD TO OUR SIDE. WE'LL TAKE THE FIGHT TO THE STREETS AND BRING THE FASCISTS TO THEIR KNEES.
BUT THERE'S A PLAN, RIGHT? THERE'S A REAL PLAN TO DO... SOMETHING.
THE PLAN IS TO GIVE OUR LIVES IF WE HAVE TO.
YEAH. SURE.
BOMB BLAST RIPS PENTAGON
FUGITIVES EVADE CAPTURE
WHAT AMBER SAYS GOES. I DON'T QUESTION. I JUST DO.

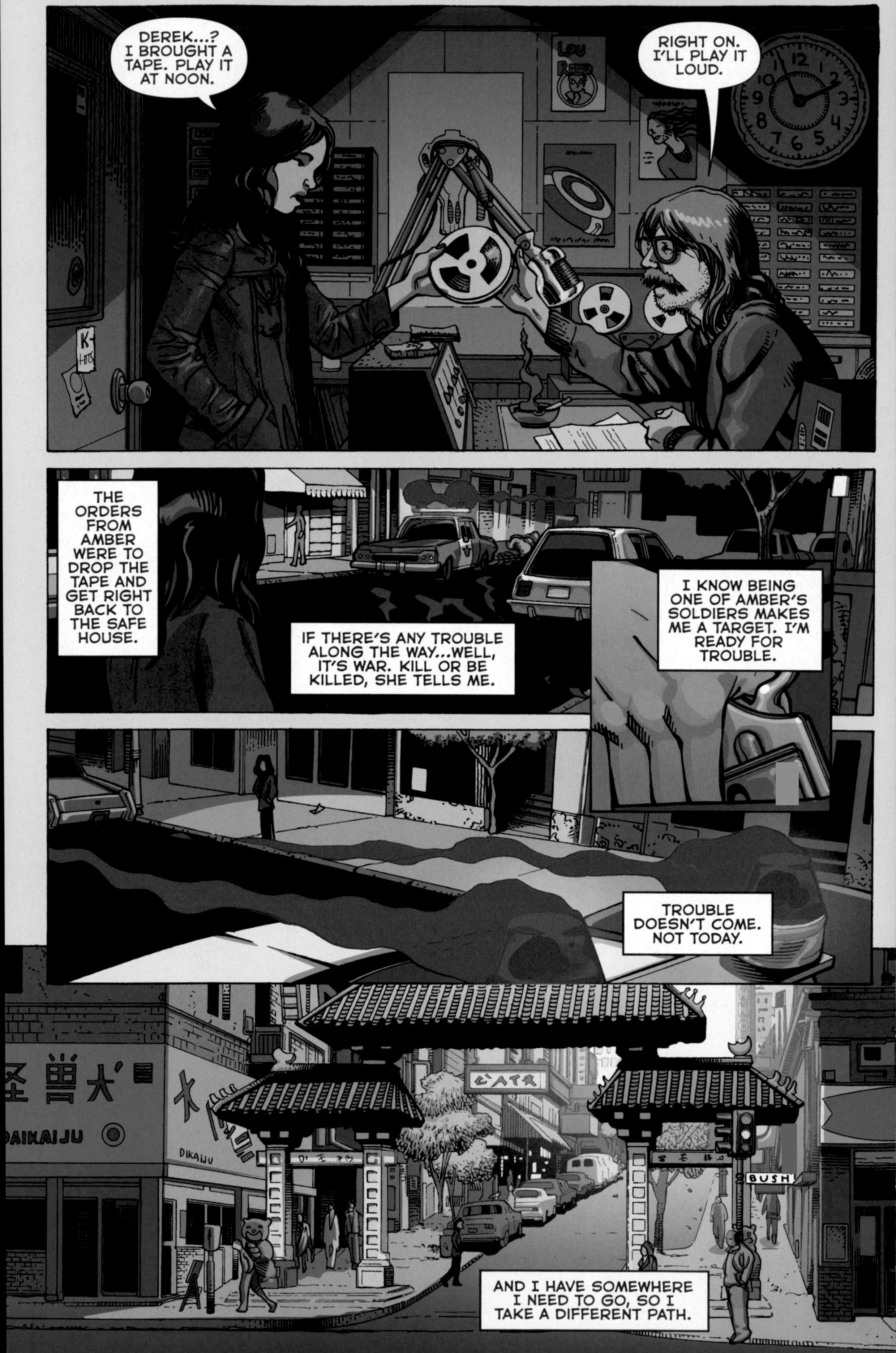
DEREK...? I BROUGHT A TAPE. PLAY IT AT NOON.
RIGHT ON. I'LL PLAY IT LOUD.
THE ORDERS FROM AMBER WERE TO DROP THE TAPE AND GET RIGHT BACK TO THE SAFE HOUSE.
IF THERE'S ANY TROUBLE ALONG THE WAY...WELL, IT'S WAR. KILL OR BE KILLED, SHE TELLS ME.
I KNOW BEING ONE OF AMBER'S SOLDIERS MAKES ME A TARGET. I'M READY FOR TROUBLE.
TROUBLE DOESN'T COME. NOT TODAY.
DAIKAIJU
DIKAIJU
BUSH
AND I HAVE SOMEWHERE I NEED TO GO, SO I TAKE A DIFFERENT PATH.

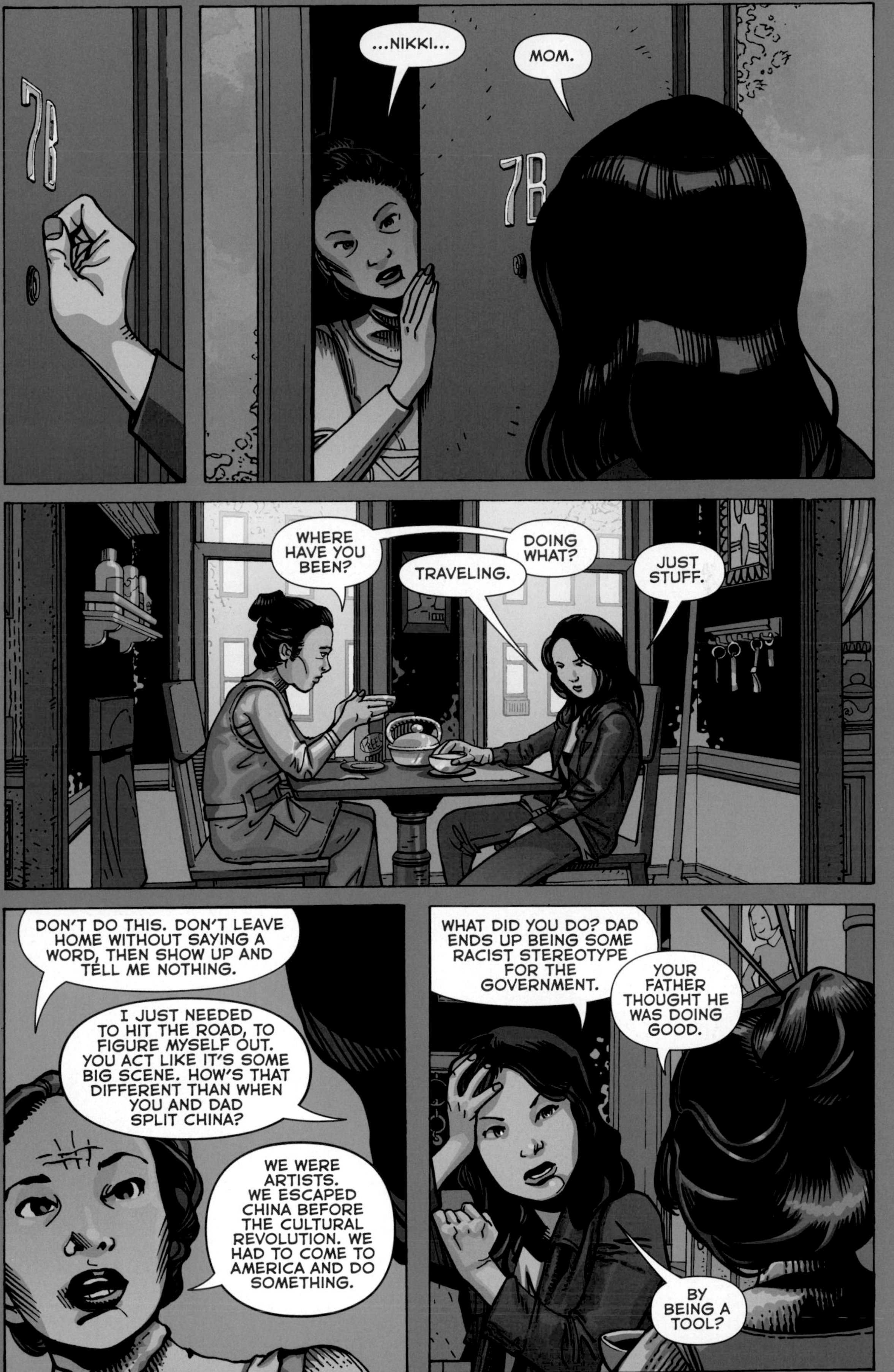
...NIKKI...
MOM.
WHERE HAVE YOU BEEN?
TRAVELING.
DOING WHAT?
JUST STUFF.
DON'T DO THIS. DON'T LEAVE HOME WITHOUT SAYING A WORD, THEN SHOW UP AND TELL ME NOTHING.
I JUST NEEDED TO HIT THE ROAD, TO FIGURE MYSELF OUT. YOU ACT LIKE IT'S SOME BIG SCENE. HOW'S THAT DIFFERENT THAN WHEN YOU AND DAD SPLIT CHINA?
WE WERE ARTISTS. WE ESCAPED CHINA BEFORE THE CULTURAL REVOLUTION. WE HAD TO COME TO AMERICA AND DO SOMETHING.
WHAT DID YOU DO? DAD ENDS UP BEING SOME RACIST STEREOTYPE FOR THE GOVERNMENT.
YOUR FATHER THOUGHT HE WAS DOING GOOD.
BY BEING A TOOL?

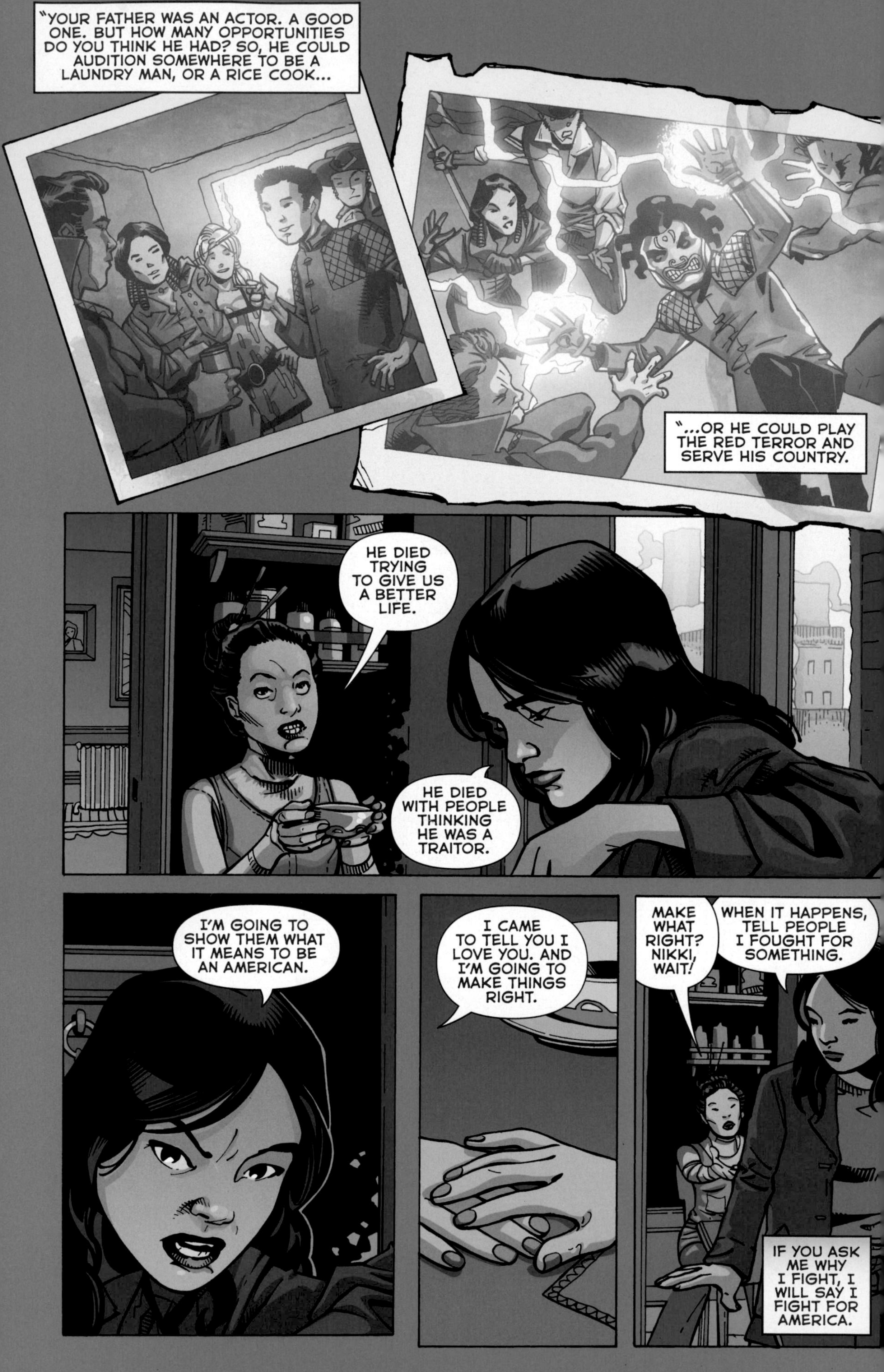
"YOUR FATHER WAS AN ACTOR. A GOOD ONE. BUT HOW MANY OPPORTUNITIES DO YOU THINK HE HAD? SO, HE COULD AUDITION SOMEWHERE TO BE A LAUNDRY MAN, OR A RICE COOK...
"...OR HE COULD PLAY THE RED TERROR AND SERVE HIS COUNTRY.
HE DIED TRYING TO GIVE US A BETTER LIFE.
HE DIED WITH PEOPLE THINKING HE WAS A TRAITOR.
I'M GOING TO SHOW THEM WHAT IT MEANS TO BE AN AMERICAN.
I CAME TO TELL YOU I LOVE YOU. AND I'M GOING TO MAKE THINGS RIGHT.
MAKE WHAT RIGHT? NIKKI, WAIT!
WHEN IT HAPPENS, TELL PEOPLE I FOUGHT FOR SOMETHING.
IF YOU ASK ME WHY I FIGHT, I WILL SAY I FIGHT FOR AMERICA.

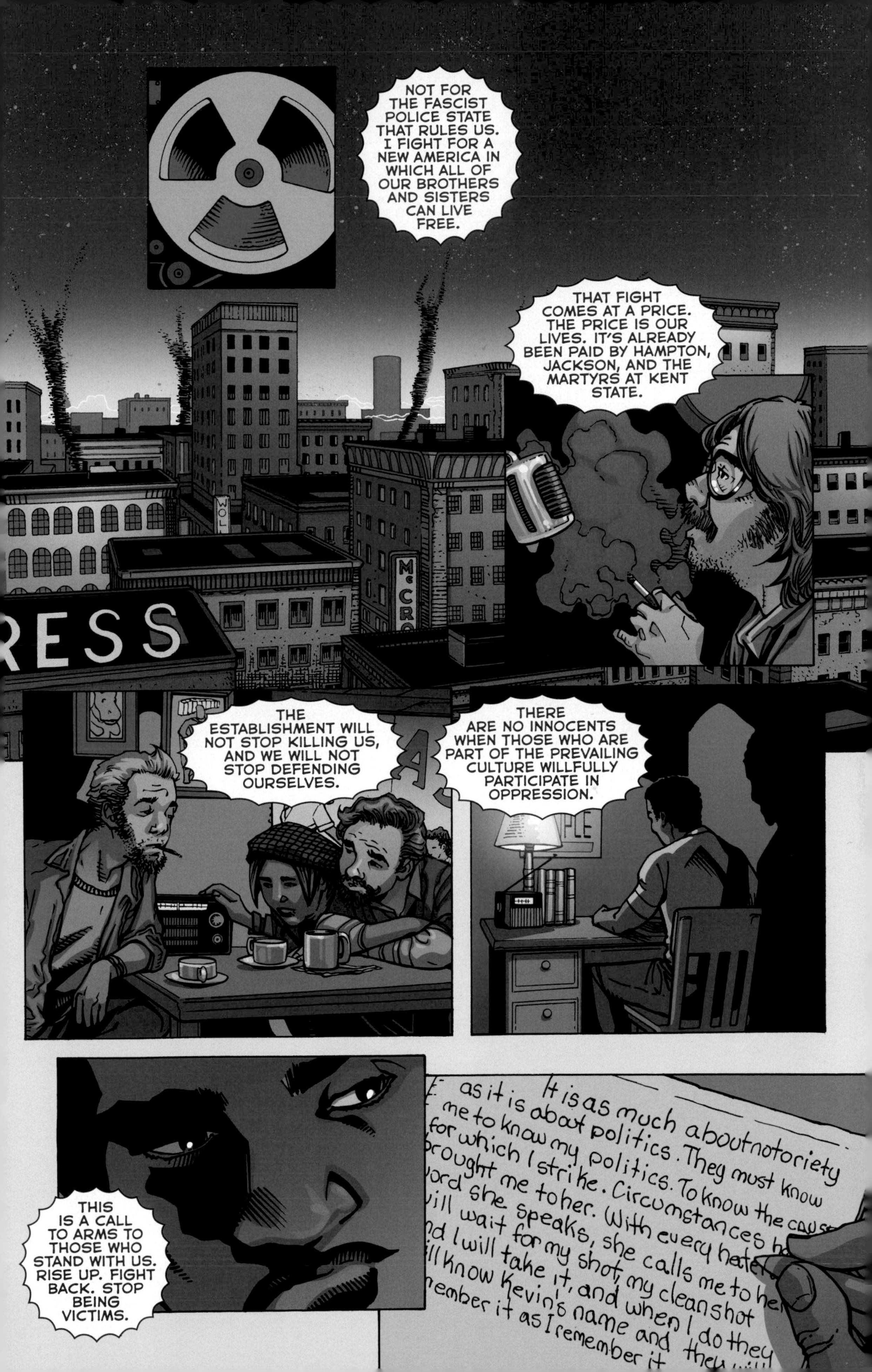
NOT FOR THE FASCIST POLICE STATE THAT RULES US. I FIGHT FOR A NEW AMERICA IN WHICH ALL OF OUR BROTHERS AND SISTERS CAN LIVE FREE.
THAT FIGHT COMES AT A PRICE. THE PRICE IS OUR LIVES. IT'S ALREADY BEEN PAID BY HAMPTON, JACKSON, AND THE MARTYRS AT KENT STATE.
WOL
McCRO
RESS
THE ESTABLISHMENT WILL NOT STOP KILLING US, AND WE WILL NOT STOP DEFENDING OURSELVES.
THERE ARE NO INNOCENTS WHEN THOSE WHO ARE PART OF THE PREVAILING CULTURE WILLFULLY PARTICIPATE IN OPPRESSION.
THIS IS A CALL TO ARMS TO THOSE WHO STAND WITH US. RISE UP. FIGHT BACK. STOP BEING VICTIMS.
It is as much aboutnotoriety
as it is about politics. They must know
me to know my politics. To know the caus
for which I strike. Circumstances ha
rought me to her. With every hate
ord she speaks, she calls me to her
ill wait for my shot, my cleanshot
nd I will take it, and when I do they
ill know Kevin's name and they
emember it as I remember it

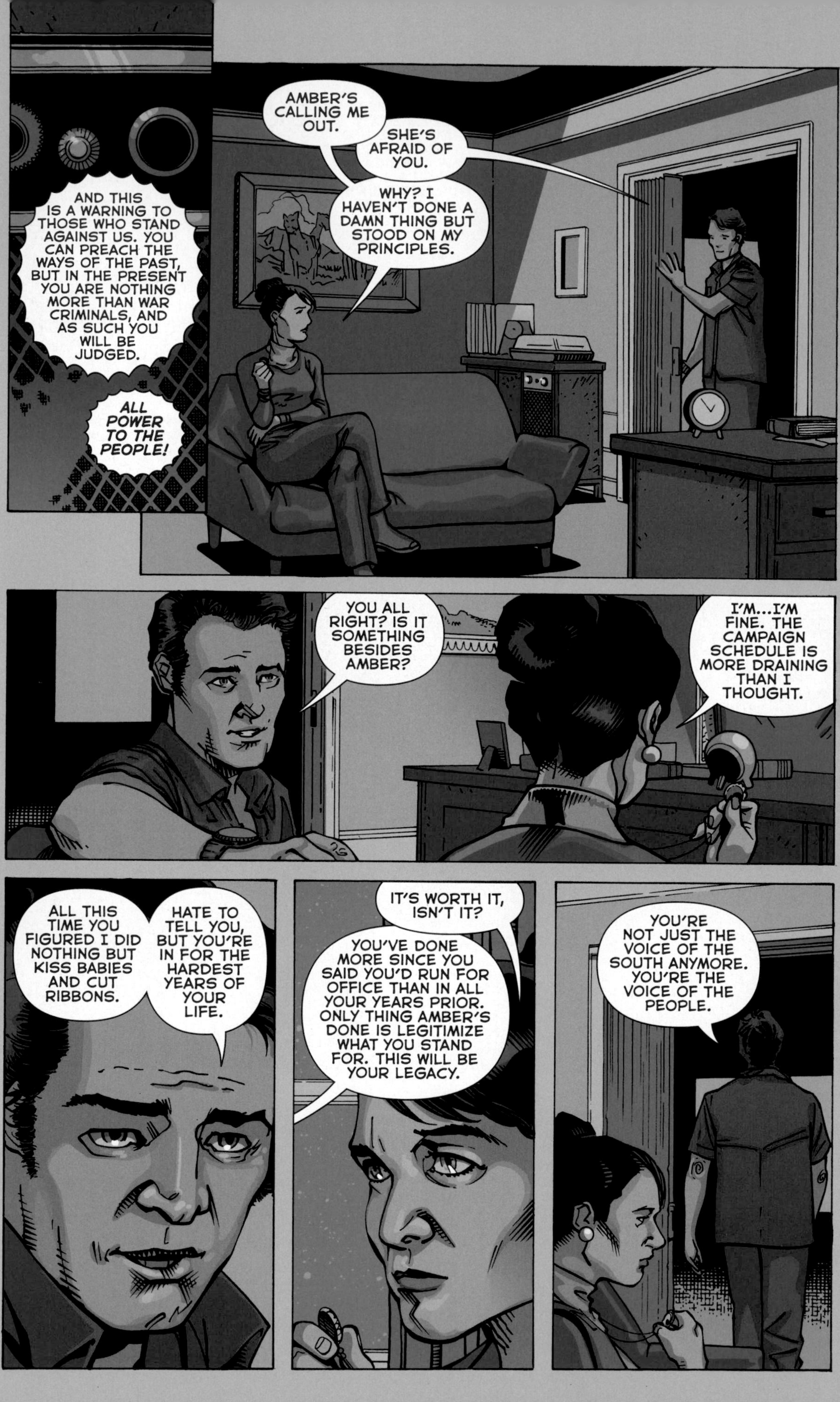
AND THIS IS A WARNING TO THOSE WHO STAND AGAINST US. YOU CAN PREACH THE WAYS OF THE PAST, BUT IN THE PRESENT YOU ARE NOTHING MORE THAN WAR CRIMINALS, AND AS SUCH YOU WILL BE JUDGED.
ALL POWER TO THE PEOPLE!
AMBER'S CALLING ME OUT.
SHE'S AFRAID OF YOU.
WHY? I HAVEN'T DONE A DAMN THING BUT STOOD ON MY PRINCIPLES.
YOU ALL RIGHT? IS IT SOMETHING BESIDES AMBER?
I'M...I'M FINE. THE CAMPAIGN SCHEDULE IS MORE DRAINING THAN I THOUGHT.
ALL THIS TIME YOU FIGURED I DID NOTHING BUT KISS BABIES AND CUT RIBBONS.
HATE TO TELL YOU, BUT YOU'RE IN FOR THE HARDEST YEARS OF YOUR LIFE.
IT'S WORTH IT, ISN'T IT?
YOU'VE DONE MORE SINCE YOU SAID YOU'D RUN FOR OFFICE THAN IN ALL YOUR YEARS PRIOR. ONLY THING AMBER'S DONE IS LEGITIMIZE WHAT YOU STAND FOR. THIS WILL BE YOUR LEGACY.
YOU'RE NOT JUST THE VOICE OF THE SOUTH ANYMORE. YOU'RE THE VOICE OF THE PEOPLE.

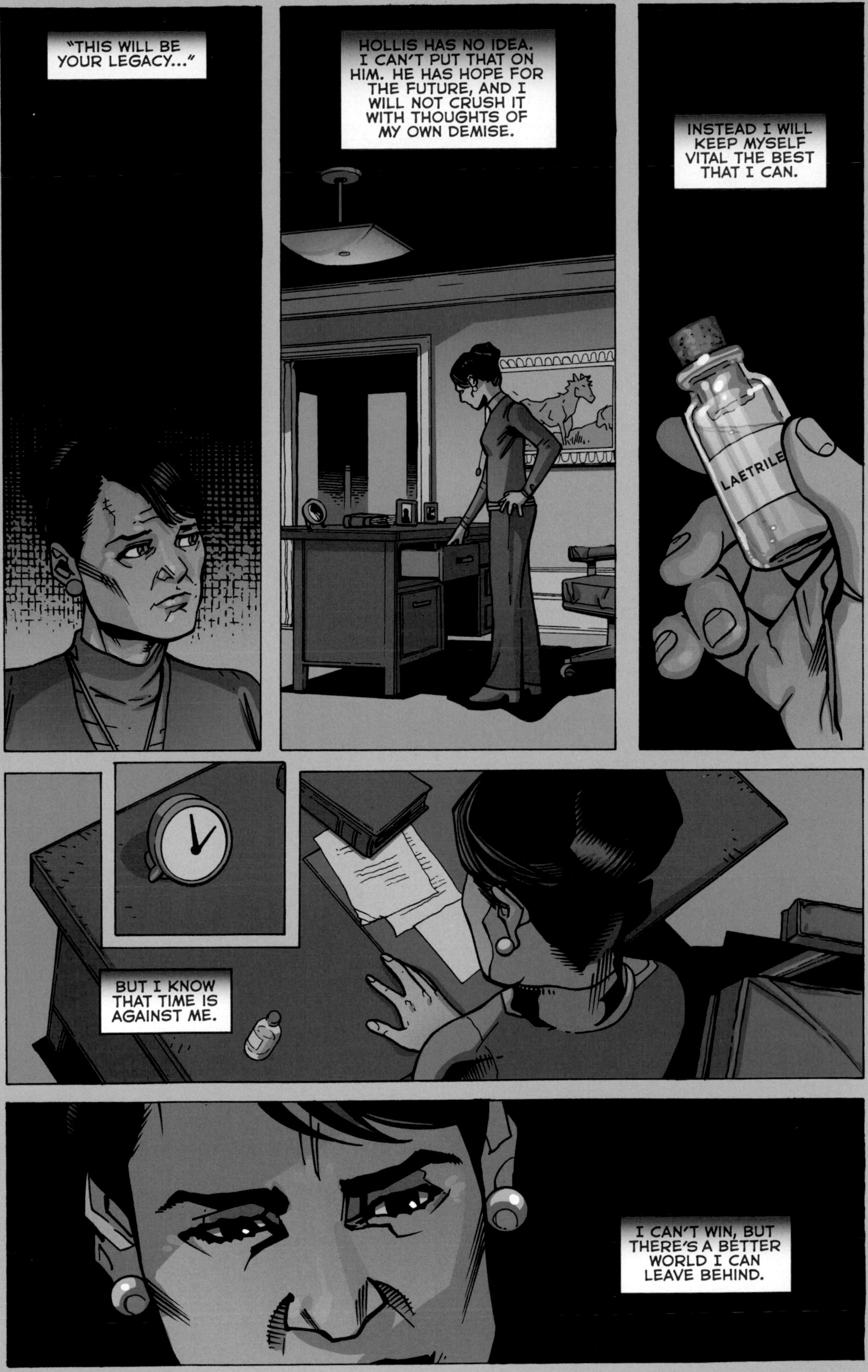
"THIS WILL BE YOUR LEGACY..."
HOLLIS HAS NO IDEA. I CAN'T PUT THAT ON HIM. HE HAS HOPE FOR THE FUTURE, AND I WILL NOT CRUSH IT WITH THOUGHTS OF MY OWN DEMISE.
INSTEAD I WILL KEEP MYSELF VITAL THE BEST THAT I CAN.
LAETRILE
BUT I KNOW THAT TIME IS AGAINST ME.
I CAN'T WIN, BUT THERE'S A BETTER WORLD I CAN LEAVE BEHIND.

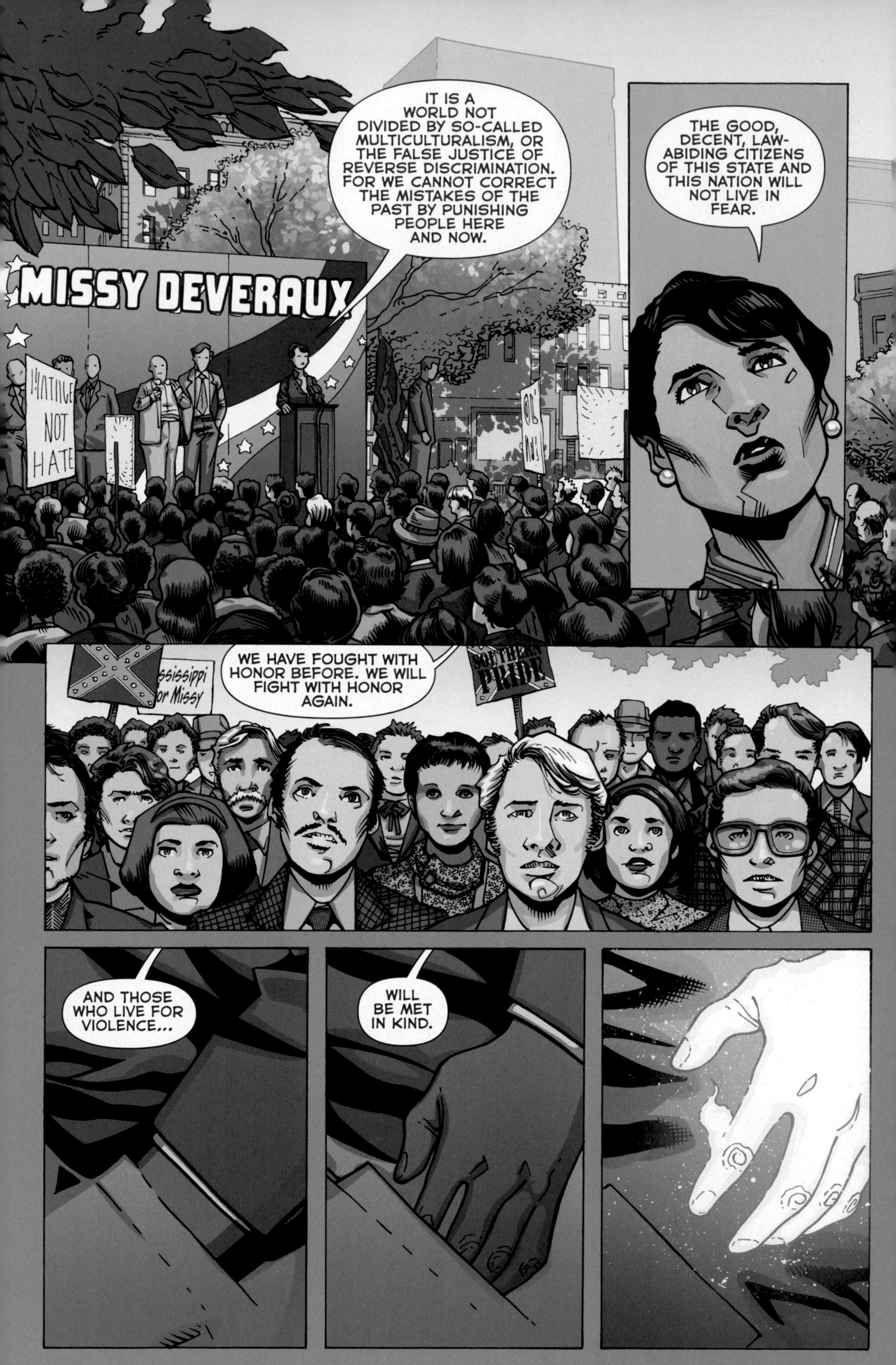
MISSY DEVERAUX
IT IS A WORLD NOT DIVIDED BY SO-CALLED MULTICULTURALISM, OR THE FALSE JUSTICE OF REVERSE DISCRIMINATION. FOR WE CANNOT CORRECT THE MISTAKES OF THE PAST BY PUNISHING PEOPLE HERE AND NOW.
HATING NOT HATE
THE GOOD, DECENT, LAW-ABIDING CITIZENS OF THIS STATE AND THIS NATION WILL NOT LIVE IN FEAR.
WE HAVE FOUGHT WITH HONOR BEFORE. WE WILL FIGHT WITH HONOR AGAIN.
SOUTHERN PRIDE
AND THOSE WHO LIVE FOR VIOLENCE...
WILL BE MET IN KIND.

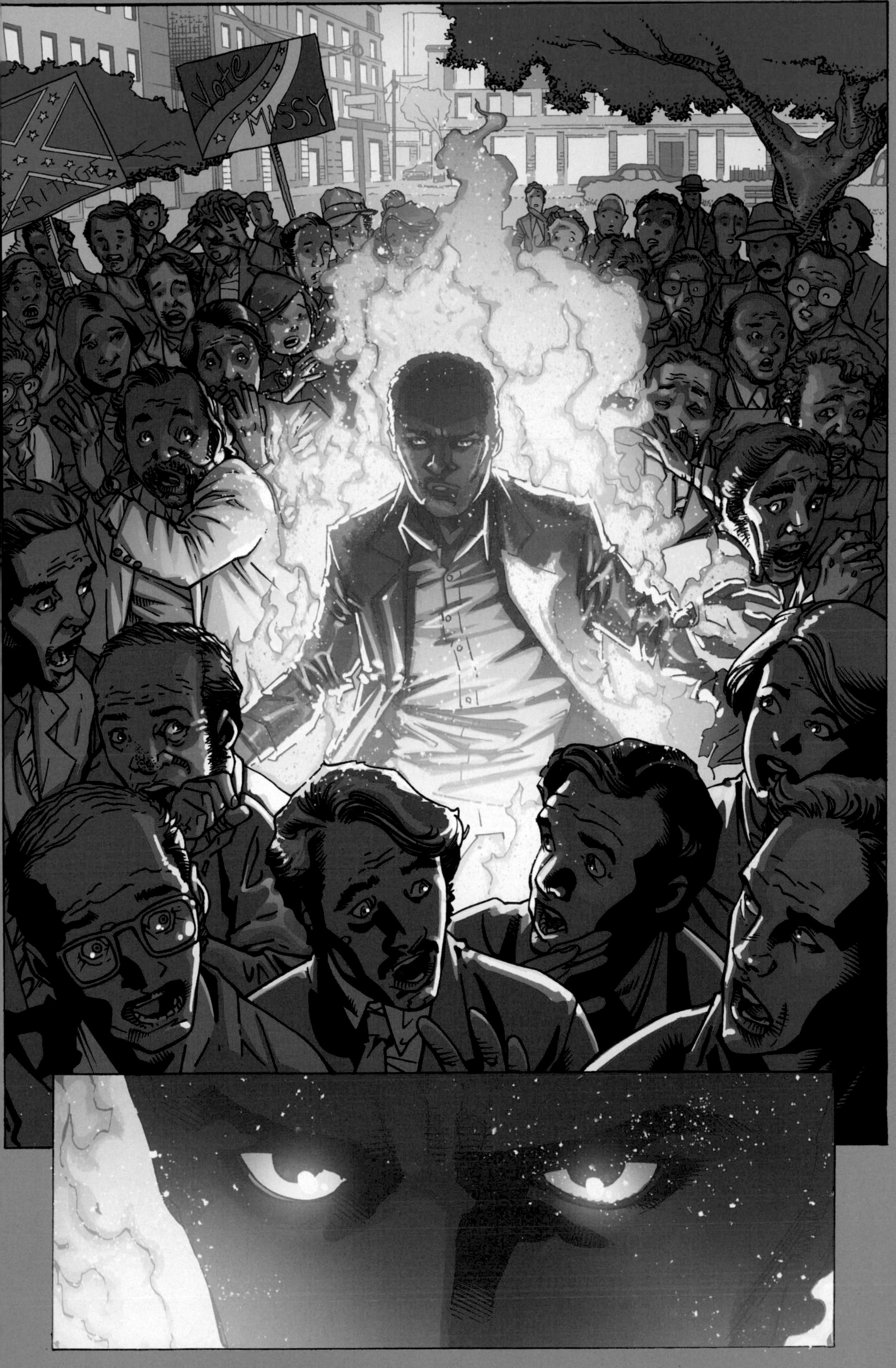
Vote MISSY

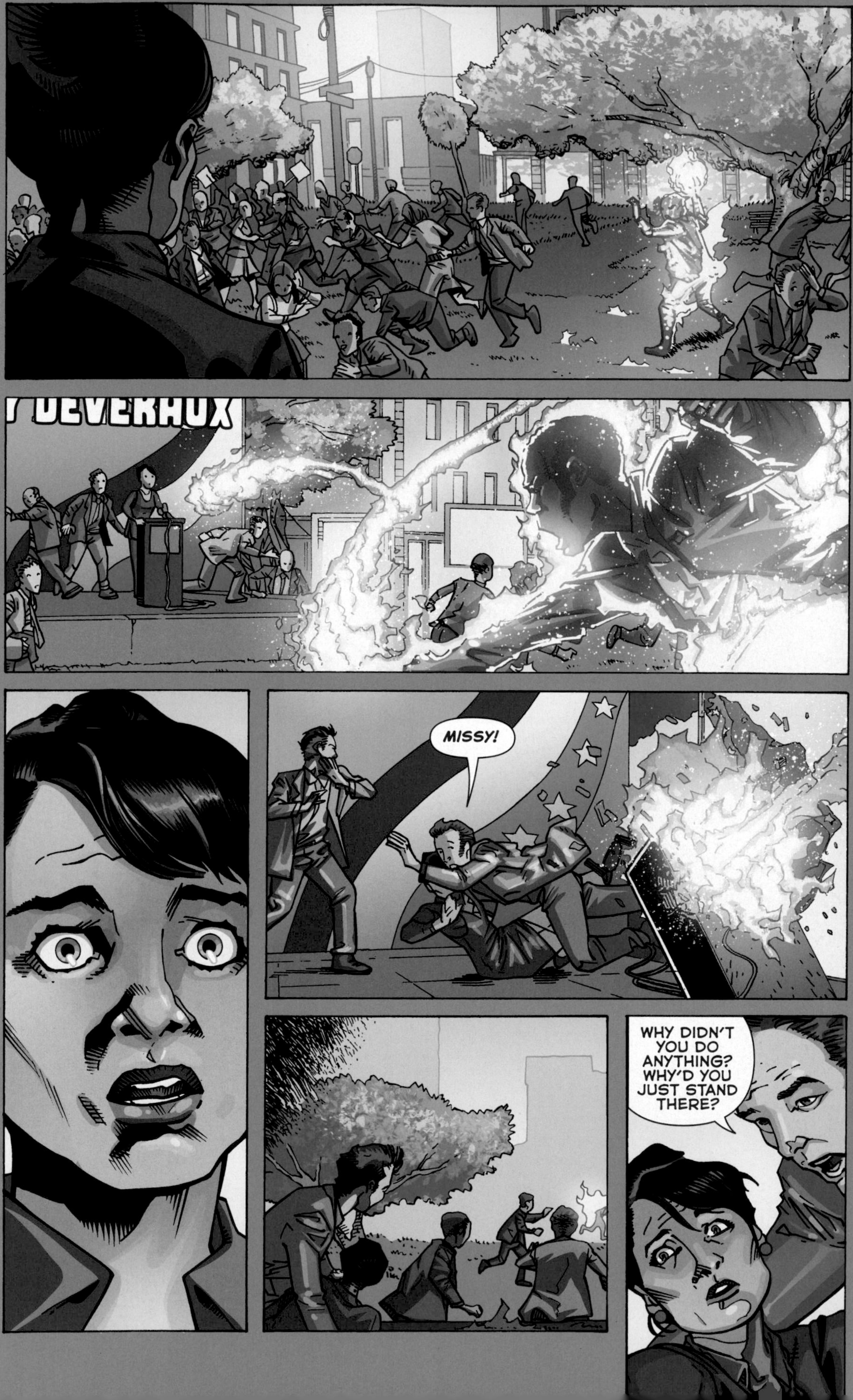
DEVERAUX
MISSY!
WHY DIDN'T YOU DO ANYTHING? WHY'D YOU JUST STAND THERE?

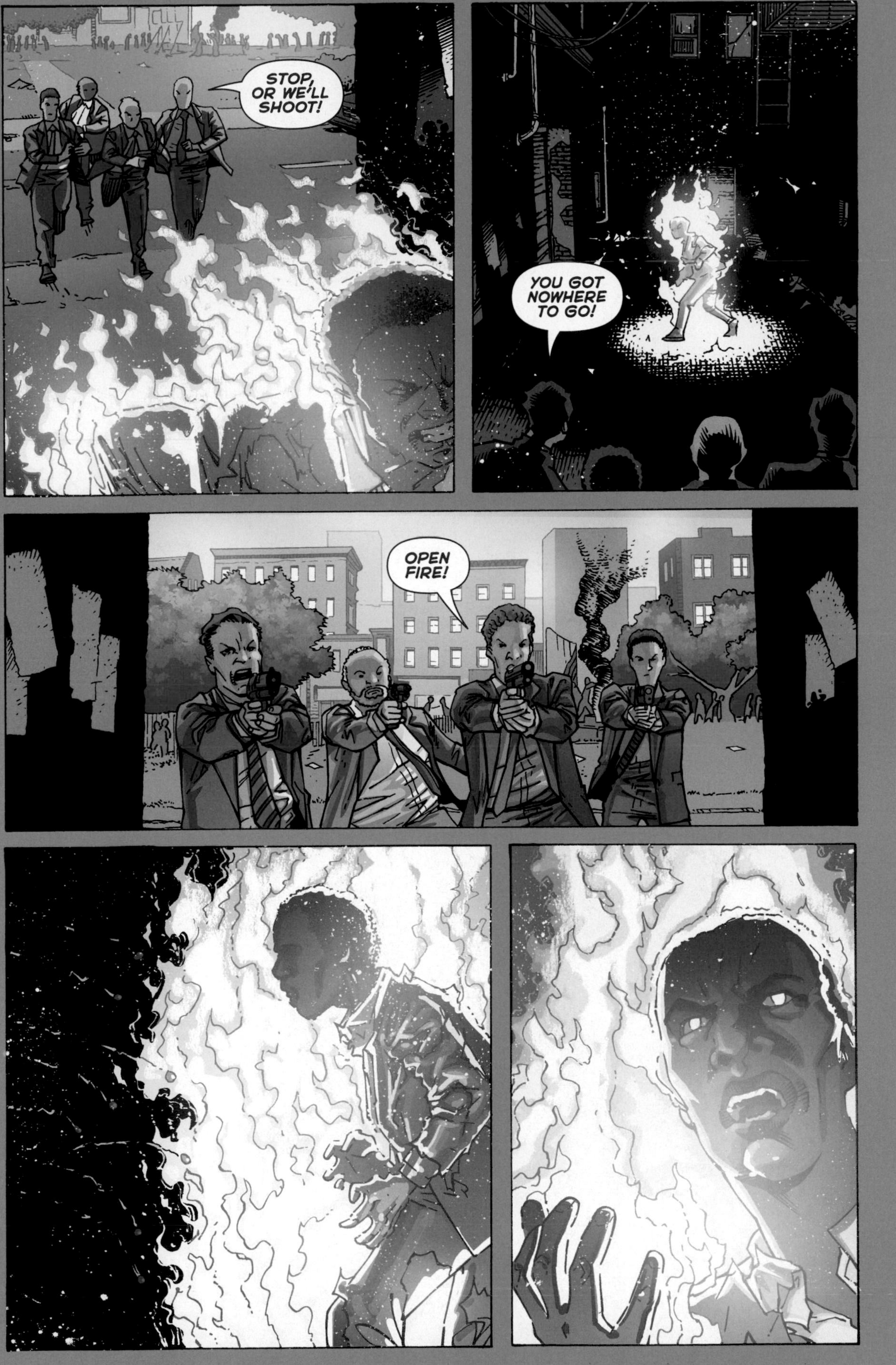
STOP, OR WE'LL SHOOT!
YOU GOT NOWHERE TO GO!
OPEN FIRE!

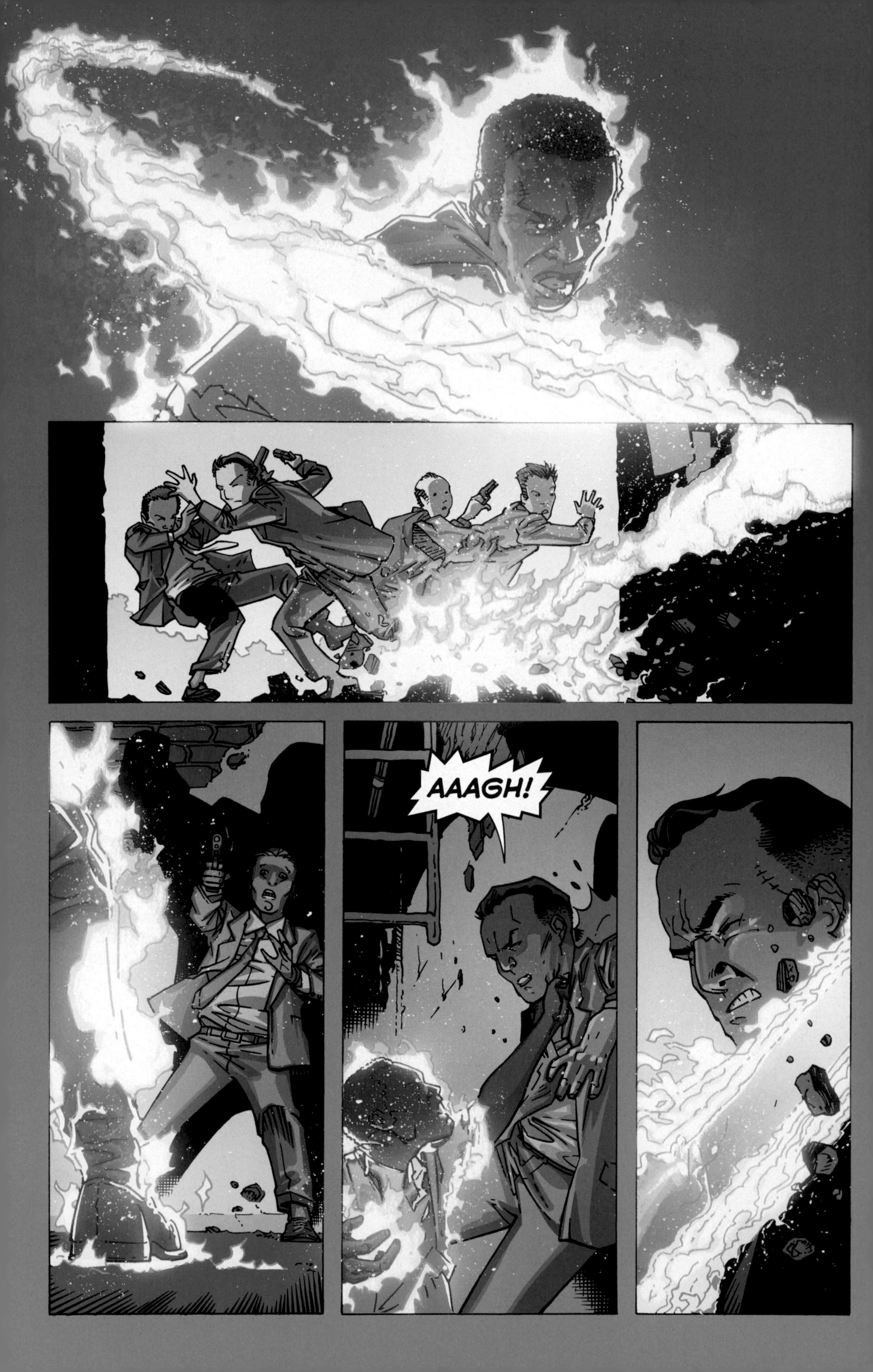
AAAGH!

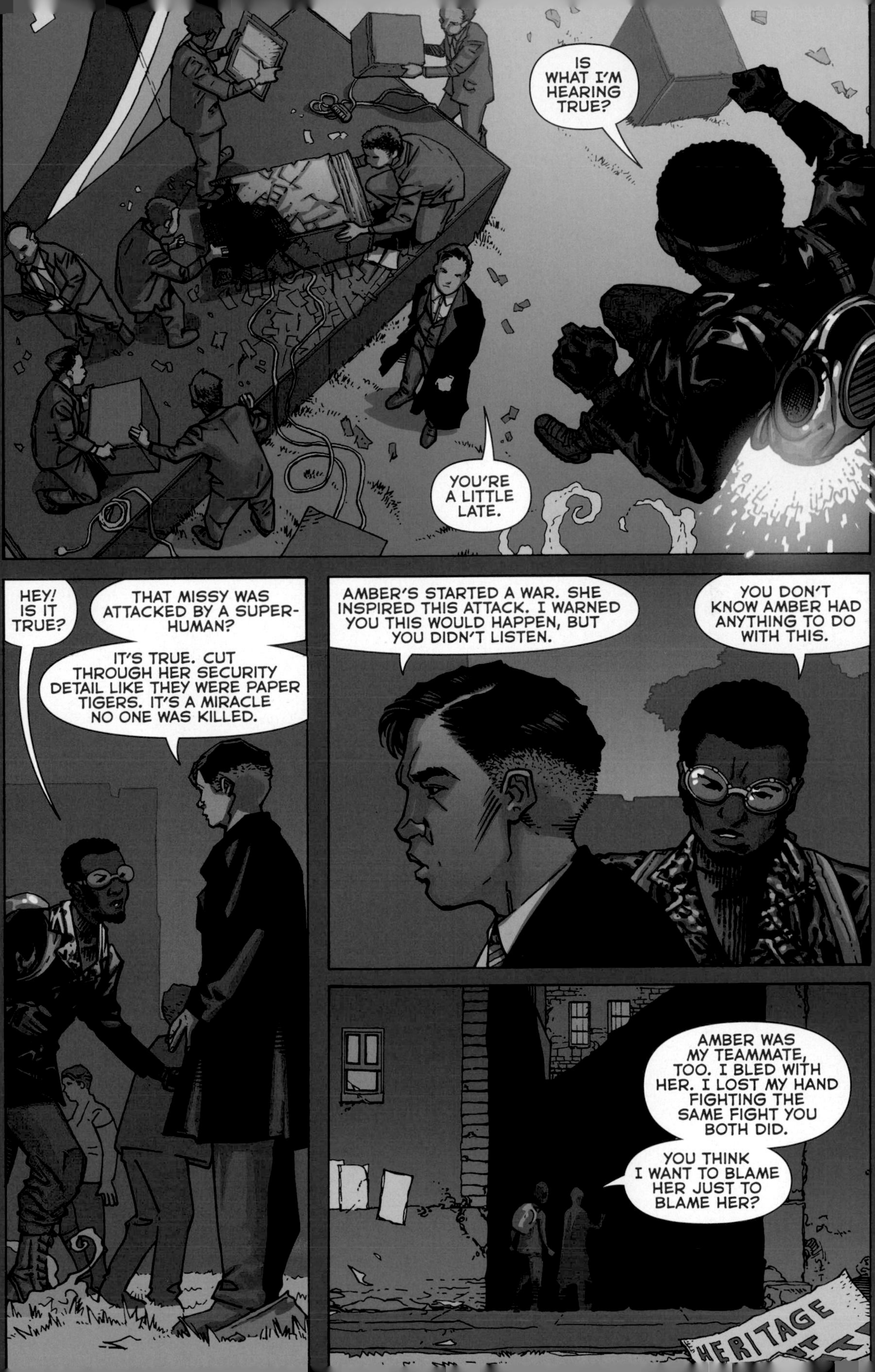
IS WHAT I'M HEARING TRUE?
YOU'RE A LITTLE LATE.
HEY! IS IT TRUE?
THAT MISSY WAS ATTACKED BY A SUPER-HUMAN?
IT'S TRUE. CUT THROUGH HER SECURITY DETAIL LIKE THEY WERE PAPER TIGERS. IT'S A MIRACLE NO ONE WAS KILLED.
AMBER'S STARTED A WAR. SHE INSPIRED THIS ATTACK. I WARNED YOU THIS WOULD HAPPEN, BUT YOU DIDN'T LISTEN.
YOU DON'T KNOW AMBER HAD ANYTHING TO DO WITH THIS.
AMBER WAS MY TEAMMATE, TOO. I BLED WITH HER. I LOST MY HAND FIGHTING THE SAME FIGHT YOU BOTH DID.
YOU THINK I WANT TO BLAME HER JUST TO BLAME HER?
HERITAGE

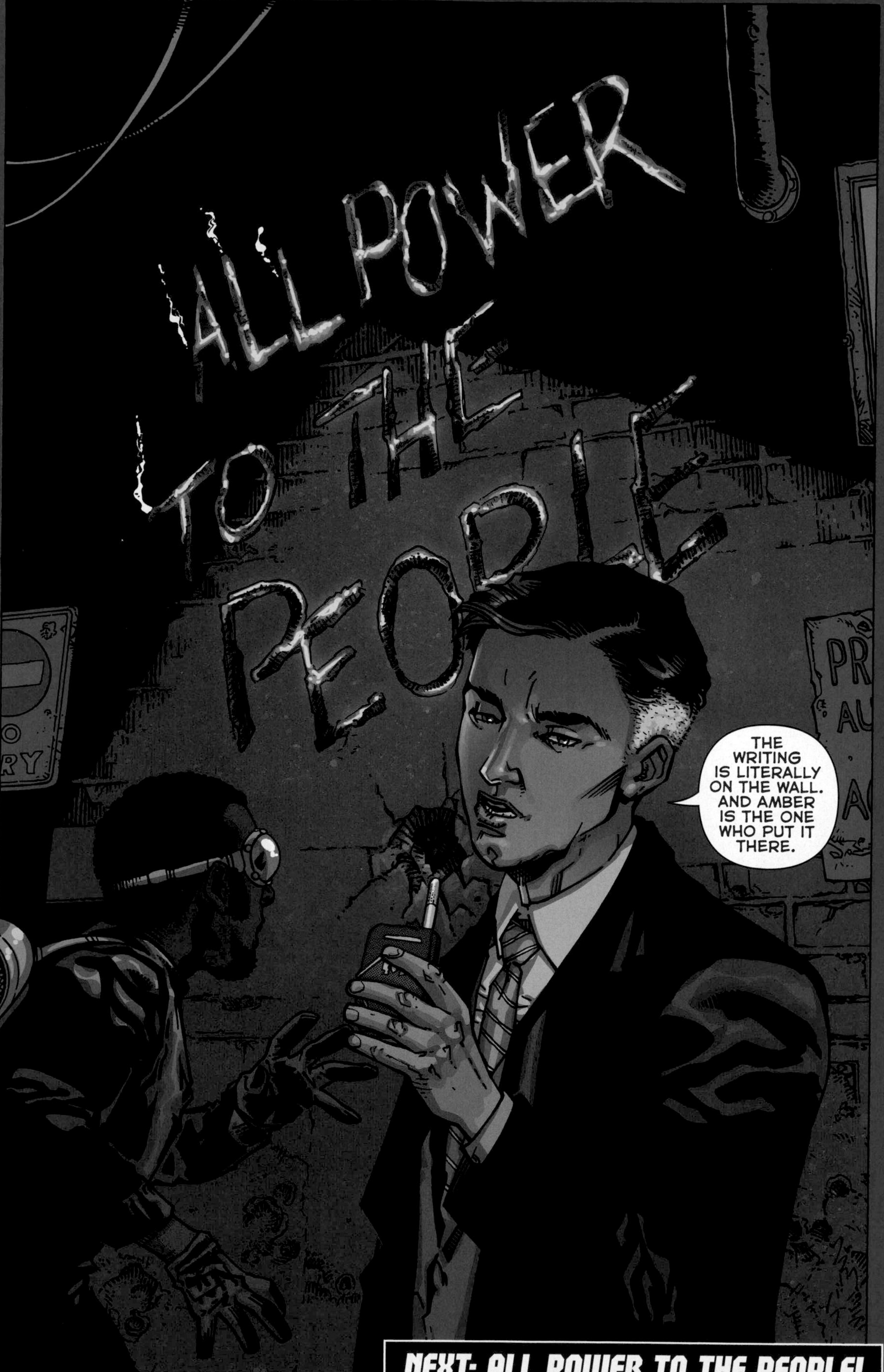
ALL POWER TO THE PEOPLE
THE WRITING IS LITERALLY ON THE WALL. AND AMBER IS THE ONE WHO PUT IT THERE.
NEXT: ALL POWER TO THE PEOPLE!

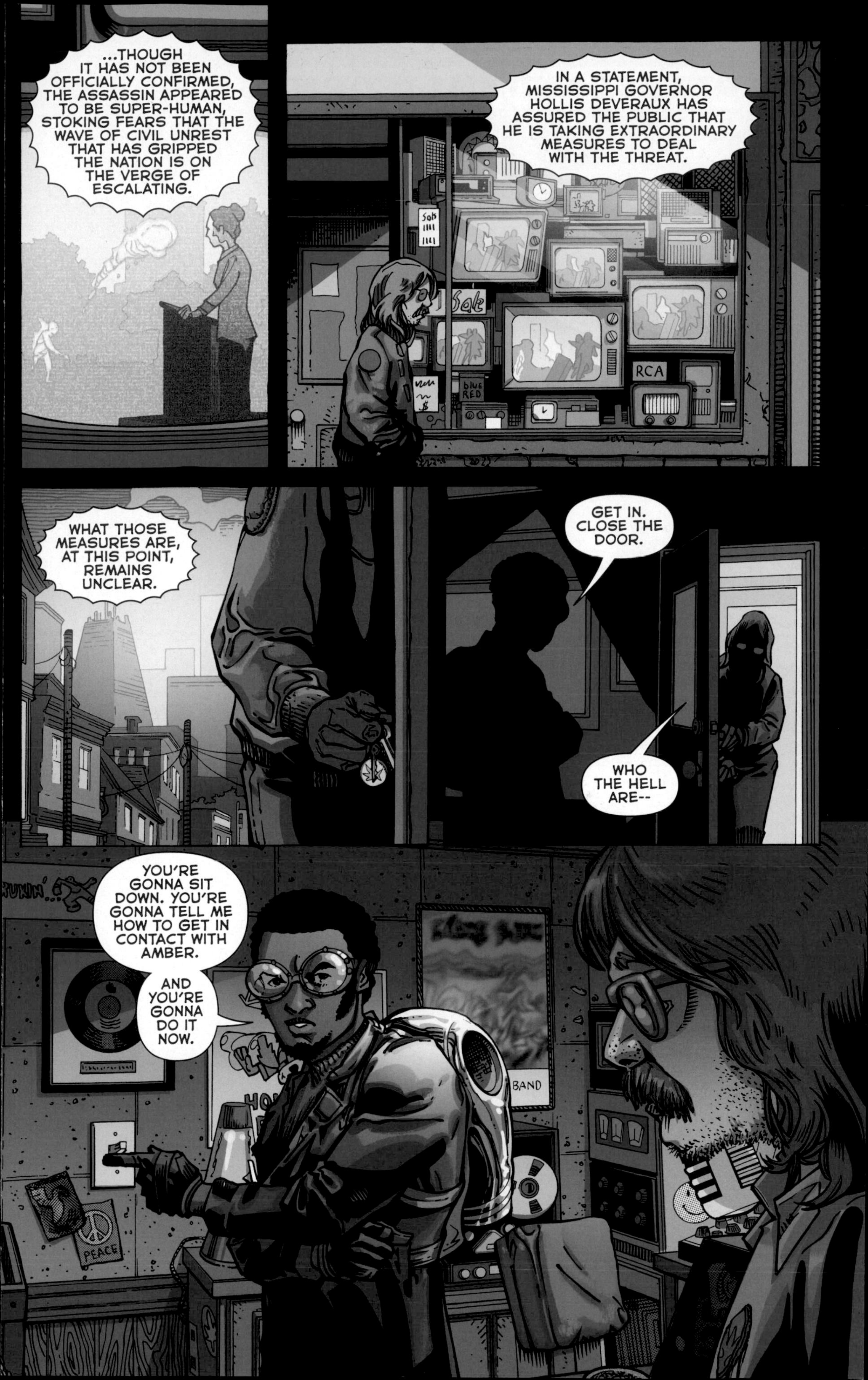
...THOUGH IT HAS NOT BEEN OFFICIALLY CONFIRMED, THE ASSASSIN APPEARED TO BE SUPER-HUMAN, STOKING FEARS THAT THE WAVE OF CIVIL UNREST THAT HAS GRIPPED THE NATION IS ON THE VERGE OF ESCALATING.
IN A STATEMENT, MISSISSIPPI GOVERNOR HOLLIS DEVERAUX HAS ASSURED THE PUBLIC THAT HE IS TAKING EXTRAORDINARY MEASURES TO DEAL WITH THE THREAT.
Sale
RCA
blue RED
WHAT THOSE MEASURES ARE, AT THIS POINT, REMAINS UNCLEAR.
GET IN. CLOSE THE DOOR.
WHO THE HELL ARE--
YOU'RE GONNA SIT DOWN. YOU'RE GONNA TELL ME HOW TO GET IN CONTACT WITH AMBER.
AND YOU'RE GONNA DO IT NOW.
BAND
PEACE

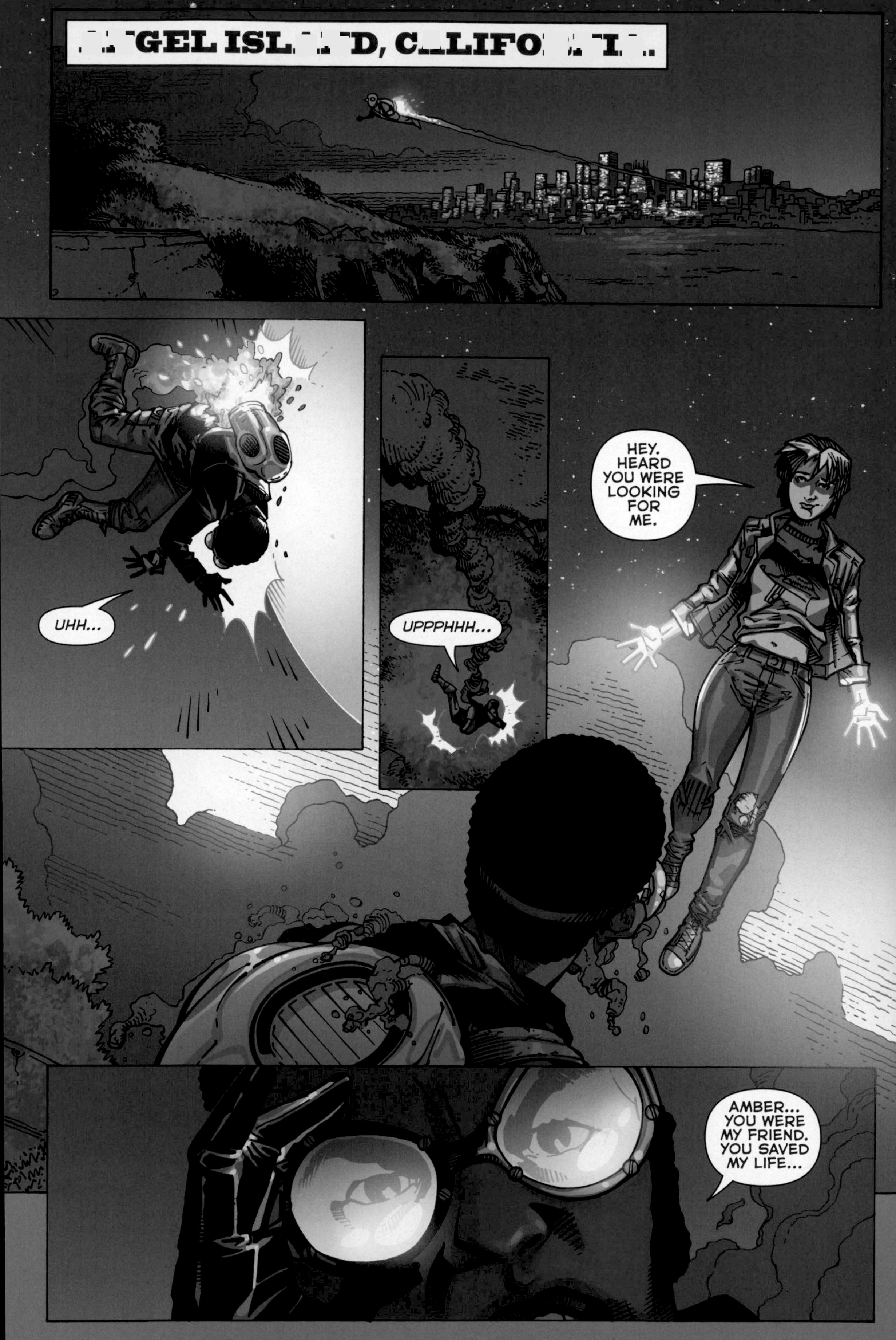
ANGEL ISLAND, CALIFORNIA.
UHH...
UPPHHH...
HEY. HEARD YOU WERE LOOKING FOR ME.
AMBER... YOU WERE MY FRIEND. YOU SAVED MY LIFE...

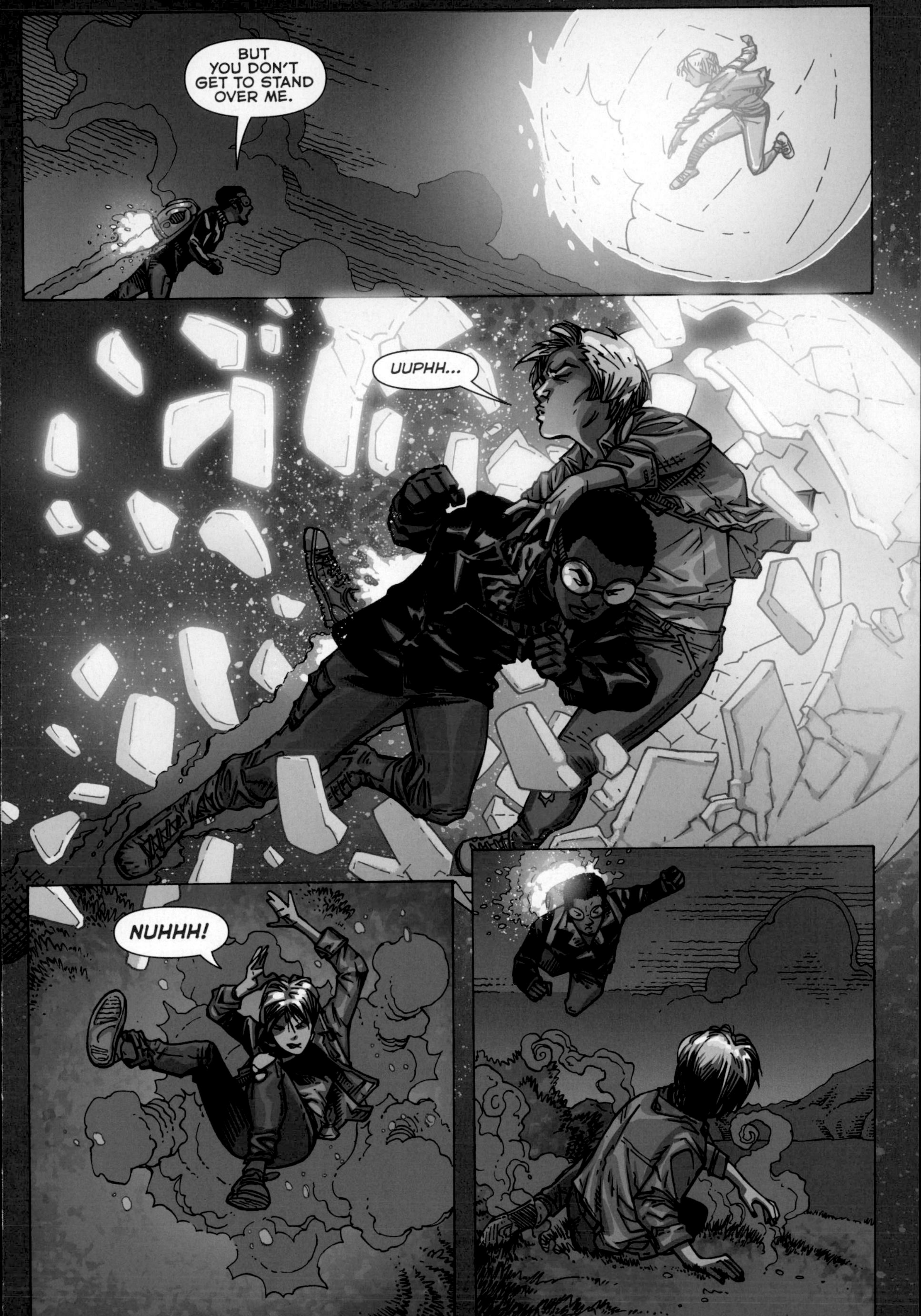
BUT YOU DON'T GET TO STAND OVER ME.
UUPHH...
NUHHH!

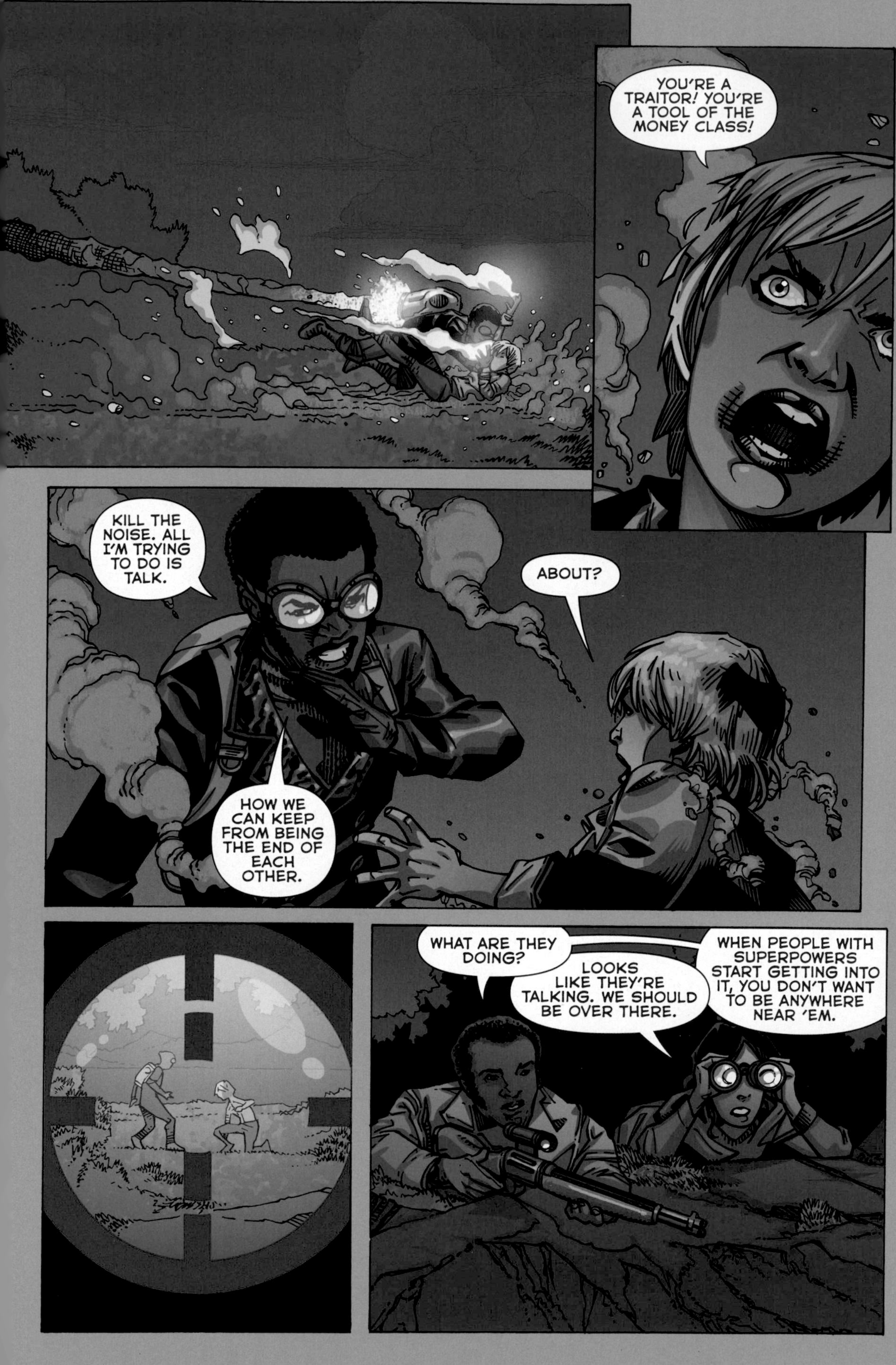
YOU'RE A TRAITOR! YOU'RE A TOOL OF THE MONEY CLASS!
KILL THE NOISE. ALL I'M TRYING TO DO IS TALK.
ABOUT?
HOW WE CAN KEEP FROM BEING THE END OF EACH OTHER.
WHAT ARE THEY DOING?
LOOKS LIKE THEY'RE TALKING. WE SHOULD BE OVER THERE.
WHEN PEOPLE WITH SUPERPOWERS START GETTING INTO IT, YOU DON'T WANT TO BE ANYWHERE NEAR 'EM.

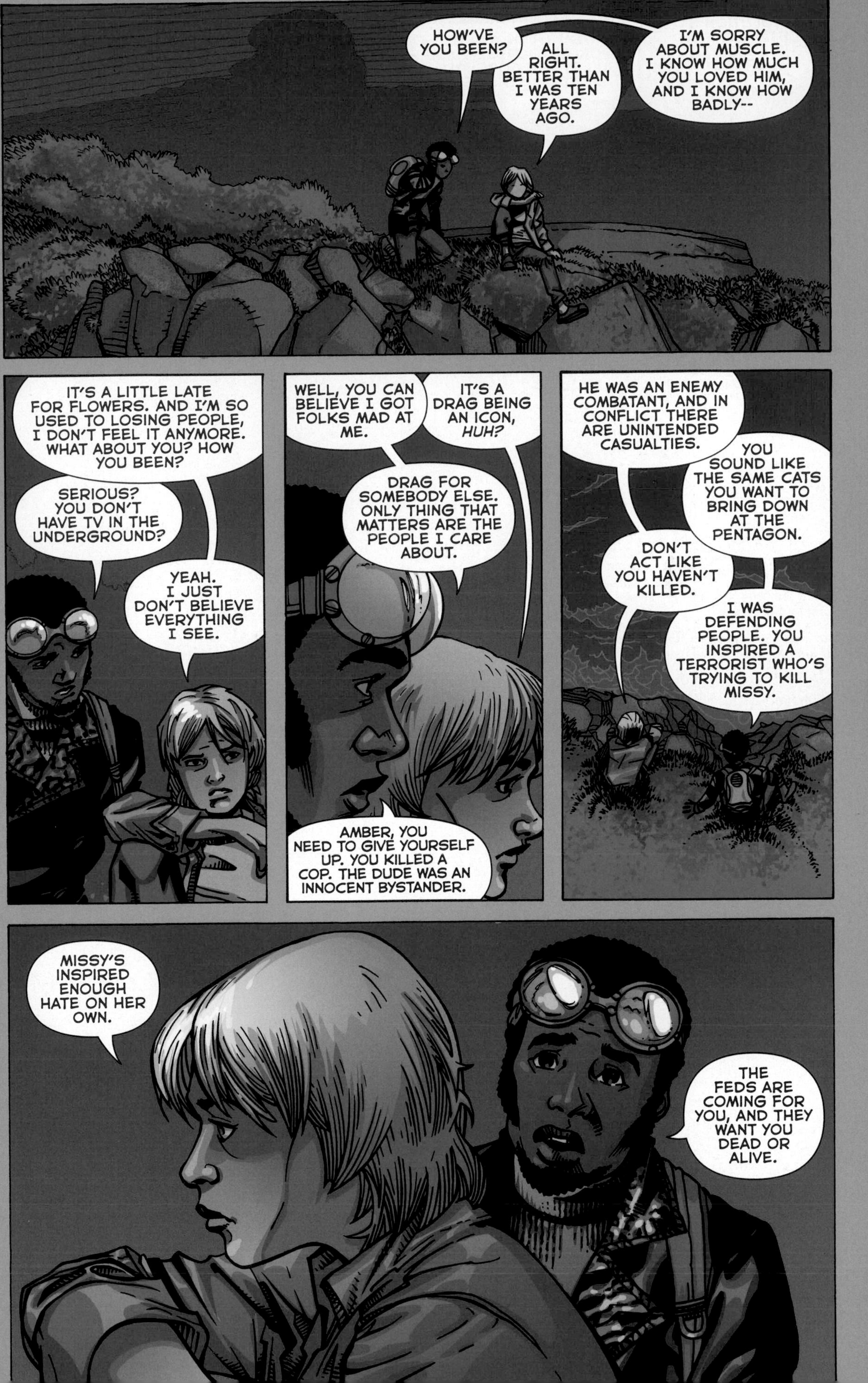
HOW'VE YOU BEEN?
ALL RIGHT. BETTER THAN I WAS TEN YEARS AGO.
I'M SORRY ABOUT MUSCLE. I KNOW HOW MUCH YOU LOVED HIM, AND I KNOW HOW BADLY--
IT'S A LITTLE LATE FOR FLOWERS. AND I'M SO USED TO LOSING PEOPLE, I DON'T FEEL IT ANYMORE. WHAT ABOUT YOU? HOW YOU BEEN?
SERIOUS? YOU DON'T HAVE TV IN THE UNDERGROUND?
YEAH. I JUST DON'T BELIEVE EVERYTHING I SEE.
WELL, YOU CAN BELIEVE I GOT FOLKS MAD AT ME.
IT'S A DRAG BEING AN ICON, HUH?
DRAG FOR SOMEBODY ELSE. ONLY THING THAT MATTERS ARE THE PEOPLE I CARE ABOUT.
AMBER, YOU NEED TO GIVE YOURSELF UP. YOU KILLED A COP. THE DUDE WAS AN INNOCENT BYSTANDER.
HE WAS AN ENEMY COMBATANT, AND IN CONFLICT THERE ARE UNINTENDED CASUALTIES.
YOU SOUND LIKE THE SAME CATS YOU WANT TO BRING DOWN AT THE PENTAGON.
DON'T ACT LIKE YOU HAVEN'T KILLED.
I WAS DEFENDING PEOPLE. YOU INSPIRED A TERRORIST WHO'S TRYING TO KILL MISSY.
MISSY'S INSPIRED ENOUGH HATE ON HER OWN.
THE FEDS ARE COMING FOR YOU, AND THEY WANT YOU DEAD OR ALIVE.

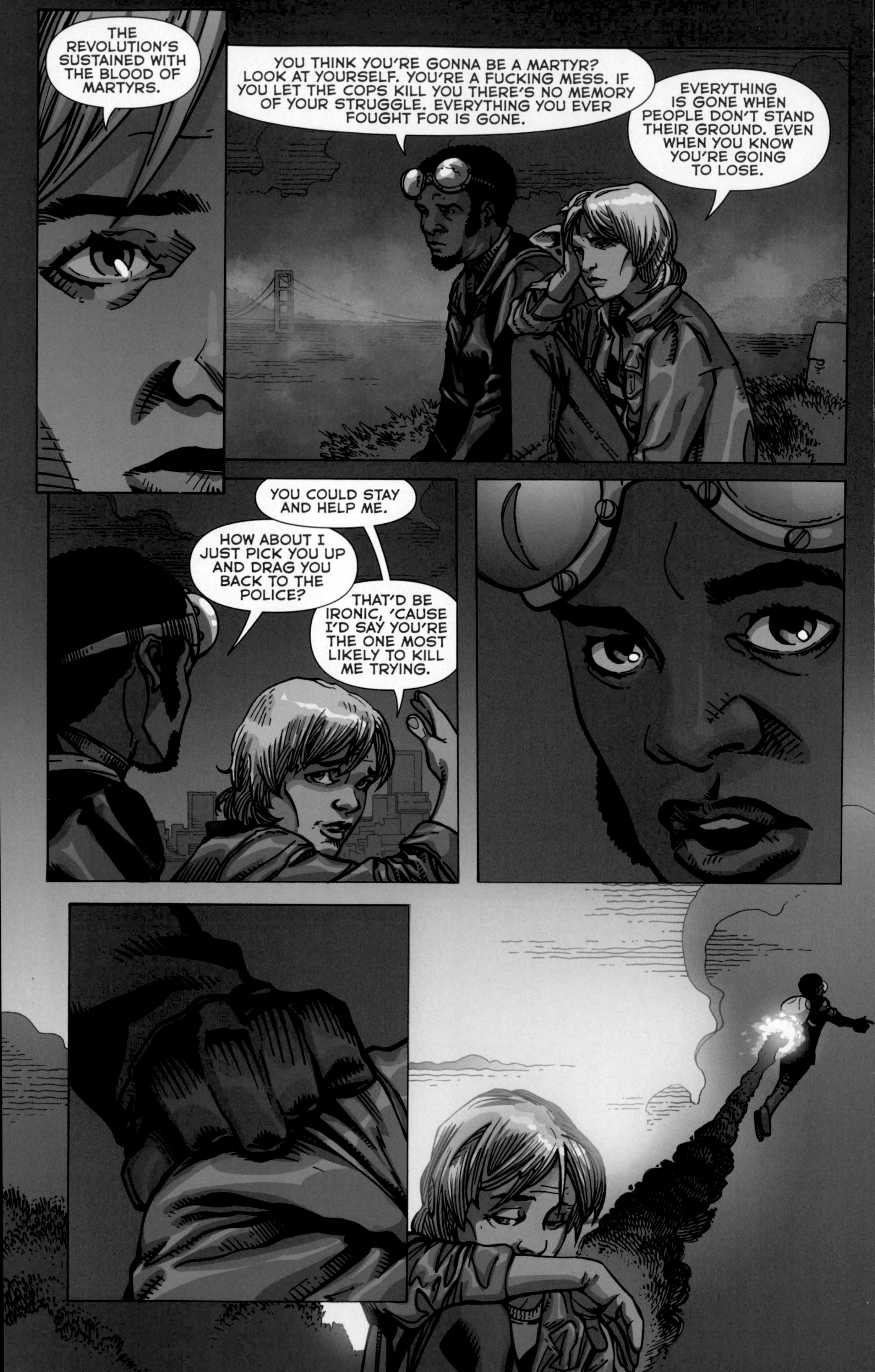
THE REVOLUTION'S SUSTAINED WITH THE BLOOD OF MARTYRS.
YOU THINK YOU'RE GONNA BE A MARTYR? LOOK AT YOURSELF. YOU'RE A FUCKING MESS. IF YOU LET THE COPS KILL YOU THERE'S NO MEMORY OF YOUR STRUGGLE. EVERYTHING YOU EVER FOUGHT FOR IS GONE.
EVERYTHING IS GONE WHEN PEOPLE DON'T STAND THEIR GROUND. EVEN WHEN YOU KNOW YOU'RE GOING TO LOSE.
YOU COULD STAY AND HELP ME.
HOW ABOUT I JUST PICK YOU UP AND DRAG YOU BACK TO THE POLICE?
THAT'D BE IRONIC, 'CAUSE I'D SAY YOU'RE THE ONE MOST LIKELY TO KILL ME TRYING.

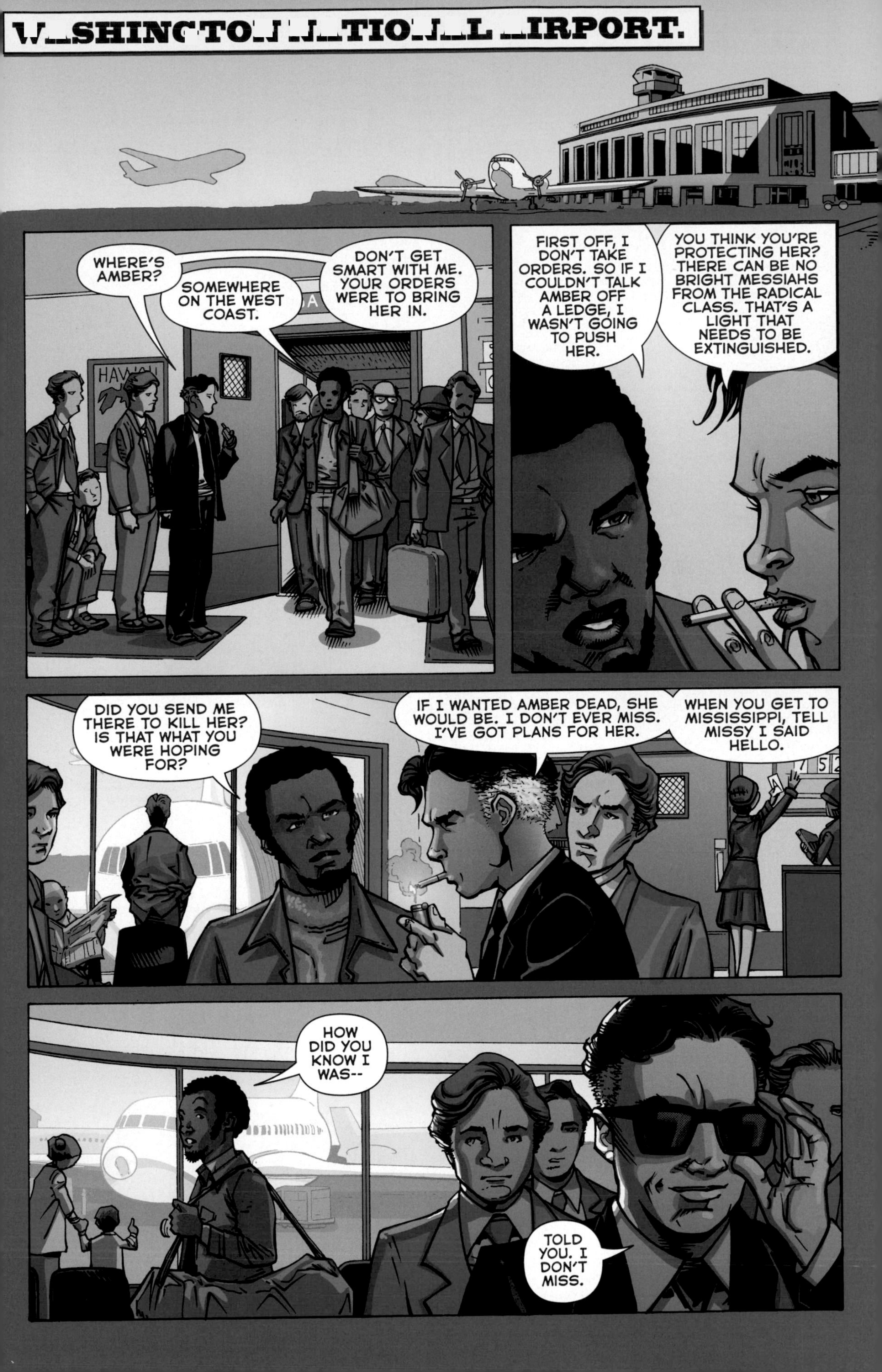

V[redacted]SHINGTO[redacted]TIO[redacted]L [redacted]IRPORT.
WHERE'S AMBER?
SOMEWHERE ON THE WEST COAST.
DON'T GET SMART WITH ME. YOUR ORDERS WERE TO BRING HER IN.
FIRST OFF, I DON'T TAKE ORDERS. SO IF I COULDN'T TALK AMBER OFF A LEDGE, I WASN'T GOING TO PUSH HER.
YOU THINK YOU'RE PROTECTING HER? THERE CAN BE NO BRIGHT MESSIAHS FROM THE RADICAL CLASS. THAT'S A LIGHT THAT NEEDS TO BE EXTINGUISHED.
DID YOU SEND ME THERE TO KILL HER? IS THAT WHAT YOU WERE HOPING FOR?
IF I WANTED AMBER DEAD, SHE WOULD BE. I DON'T EVER MISS. I'VE GOT PLANS FOR HER.
WHEN YOU GET TO MISSISSIPPI, TELL MISSY I SAID HELLO.
HOW DID YOU KNOW I WAS--
TOLD YOU. I DON'T MISS.

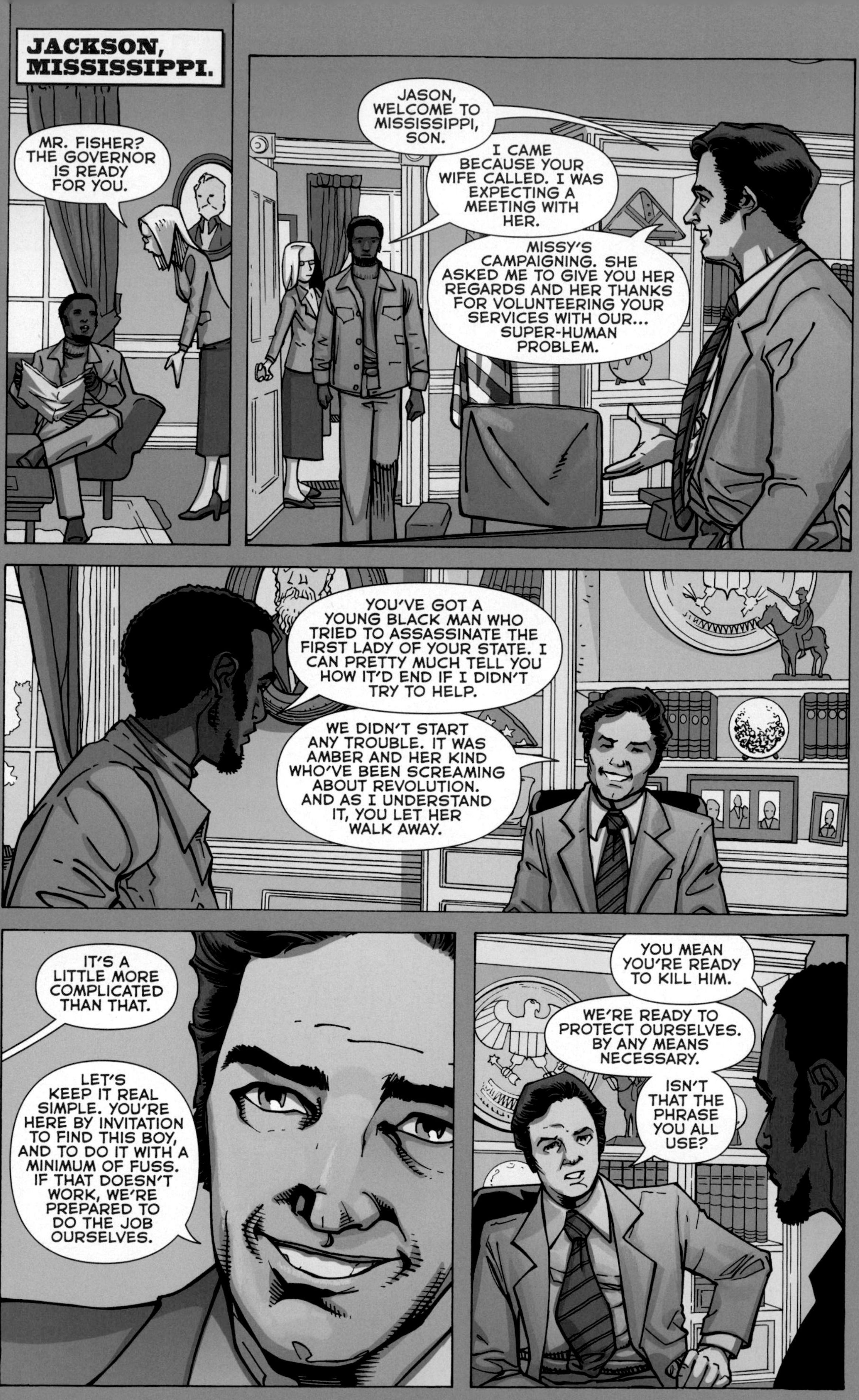
JACKSON, MISSISSIPPI.
MR. FISHER? THE GOVERNOR IS READY FOR YOU.
JASON, WELCOME TO MISSISSIPPI, SON.
I CAME BECAUSE YOUR WIFE CALLED. I WAS EXPECTING A MEETING WITH HER.
MISSY'S CAMPAIGNING. SHE ASKED ME TO GIVE YOU HER REGARDS AND HER THANKS FOR VOLUNTEERING YOUR SERVICES WITH OUR... SUPER-HUMAN PROBLEM.
YOU'VE GOT A YOUNG BLACK MAN WHO TRIED TO ASSASSINATE THE FIRST LADY OF YOUR STATE. I CAN PRETTY MUCH TELL YOU HOW IT'D END IF I DIDN'T TRY TO HELP.
WE DIDN'T START ANY TROUBLE. IT WAS AMBER AND HER KIND WHO'VE BEEN SCREAMING ABOUT REVOLUTION. AND AS I UNDERSTAND IT, YOU LET HER WALK AWAY.
IT'S A LITTLE MORE COMPLICATED THAN THAT.
LET'S KEEP IT REAL SIMPLE. YOU'RE HERE BY INVITATION TO FIND THIS BOY, AND TO DO IT WITH A MINIMUM OF FUSS. IF THAT DOESN'T WORK, WE'RE PREPARED TO DO THE JOB OURSELVES.
YOU MEAN YOU'RE READY TO KILL HIM.
WE'RE READY TO PROTECT OURSELVES. BY ANY MEANS NECESSARY.
ISN'T THAT THE PHRASE YOU ALL USE?

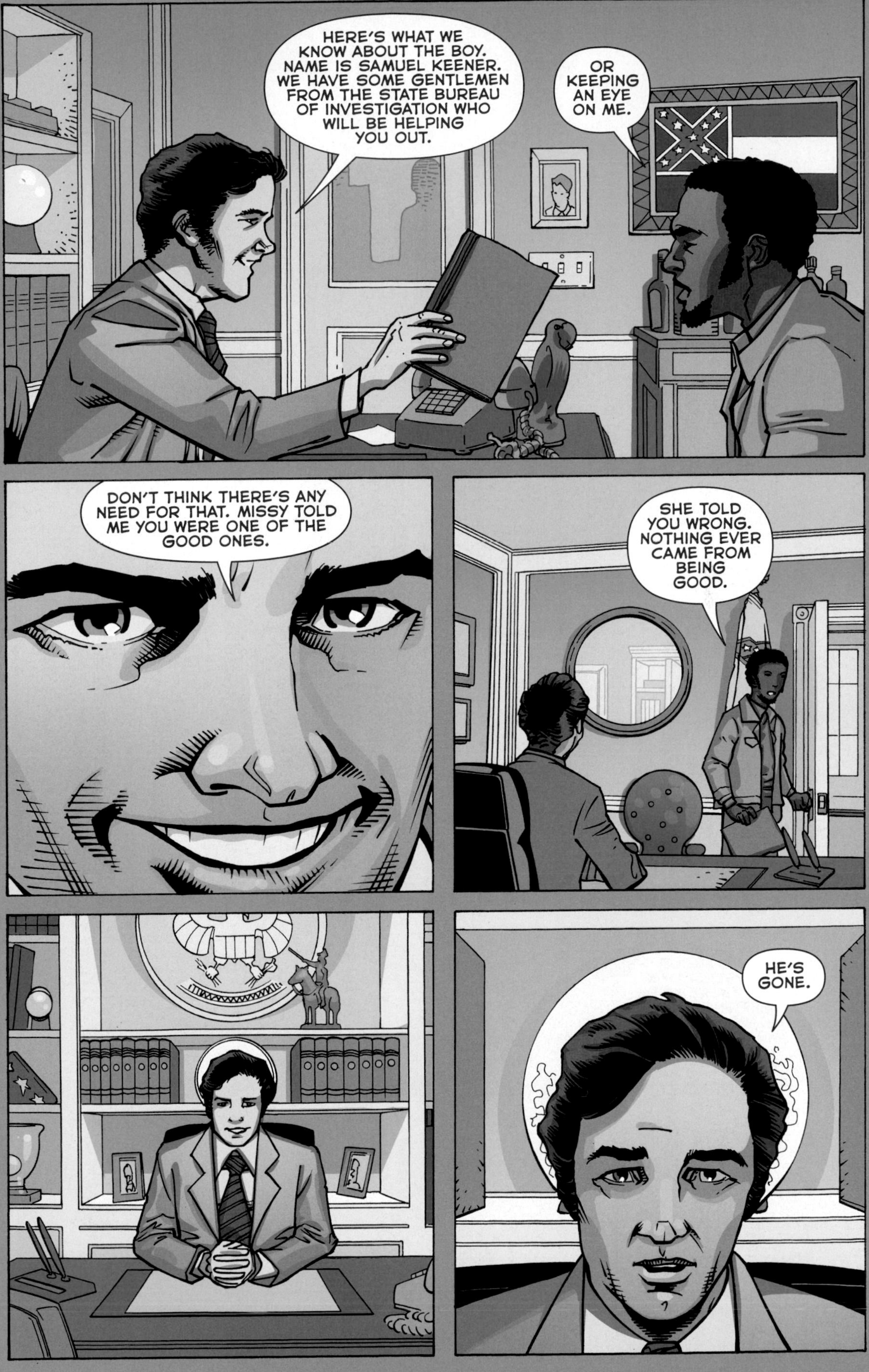
HERE'S WHAT WE KNOW ABOUT THE BOY. NAME IS SAMUEL KEENER. WE HAVE SOME GENTLEMEN FROM THE STATE BUREAU OF INVESTIGATION WHO WILL BE HELPING YOU OUT.
OR KEEPING AN EYE ON ME.
DON'T THINK THERE'S ANY NEED FOR THAT. MISSY TOLD ME YOU WERE ONE OF THE GOOD ONES.
SHE TOLD YOU WRONG. NOTHING EVER CAME FROM BEING GOOD.
HE'S GONE.

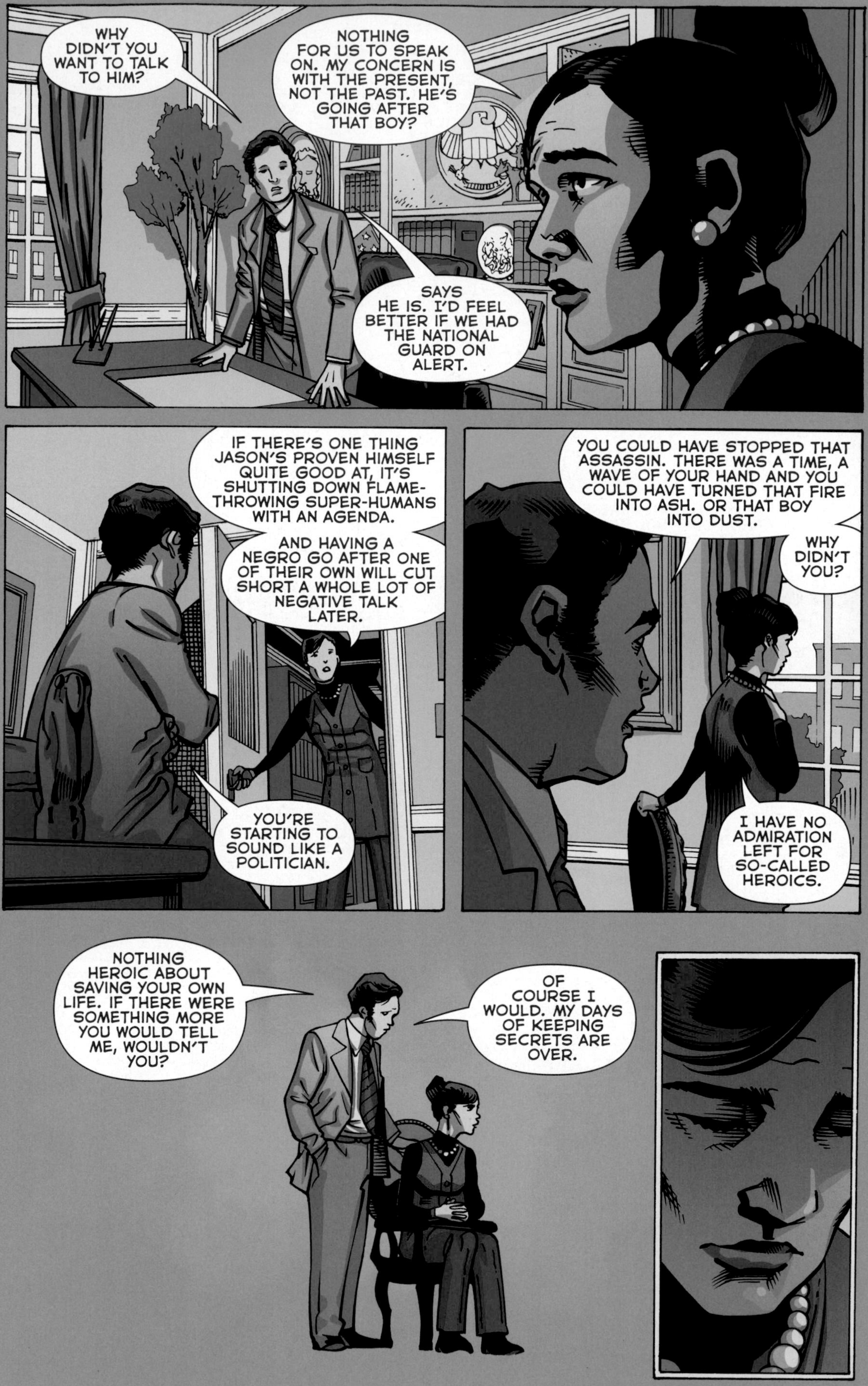
WHY DIDN'T YOU WANT TO TALK TO HIM?
NOTHING FOR US TO SPEAK ON. MY CONCERN IS WITH THE PRESENT, NOT THE PAST. HE'S GOING AFTER THAT BOY?
SAYS HE IS. I'D FEEL BETTER IF WE HAD THE NATIONAL GUARD ON ALERT.
IF THERE'S ONE THING JASON'S PROVEN HIMSELF QUITE GOOD AT, IT'S SHUTTING DOWN FLAME-THROWING SUPER-HUMANS WITH AN AGENDA.
AND HAVING A NEGRO GO AFTER ONE OF THEIR OWN WILL CUT SHORT A WHOLE LOT OF NEGATIVE TALK LATER.
YOU'RE STARTING TO SOUND LIKE A POLITICIAN.
YOU COULD HAVE STOPPED THAT ASSASSIN. THERE WAS A TIME, A WAVE OF YOUR HAND AND YOU COULD HAVE TURNED THAT FIRE INTO ASH. OR THAT BOY INTO DUST.
WHY DIDN'T YOU?
I HAVE NO ADMIRATION LEFT FOR SO-CALLED HEROICS.
NOTHING HEROIC ABOUT SAVING YOUR OWN LIFE. IF THERE WERE SOMETHING MORE YOU WOULD TELL ME, WOULDN'T YOU?
OF COURSE I WOULD. MY DAYS OF KEEPING SECRETS ARE OVER.

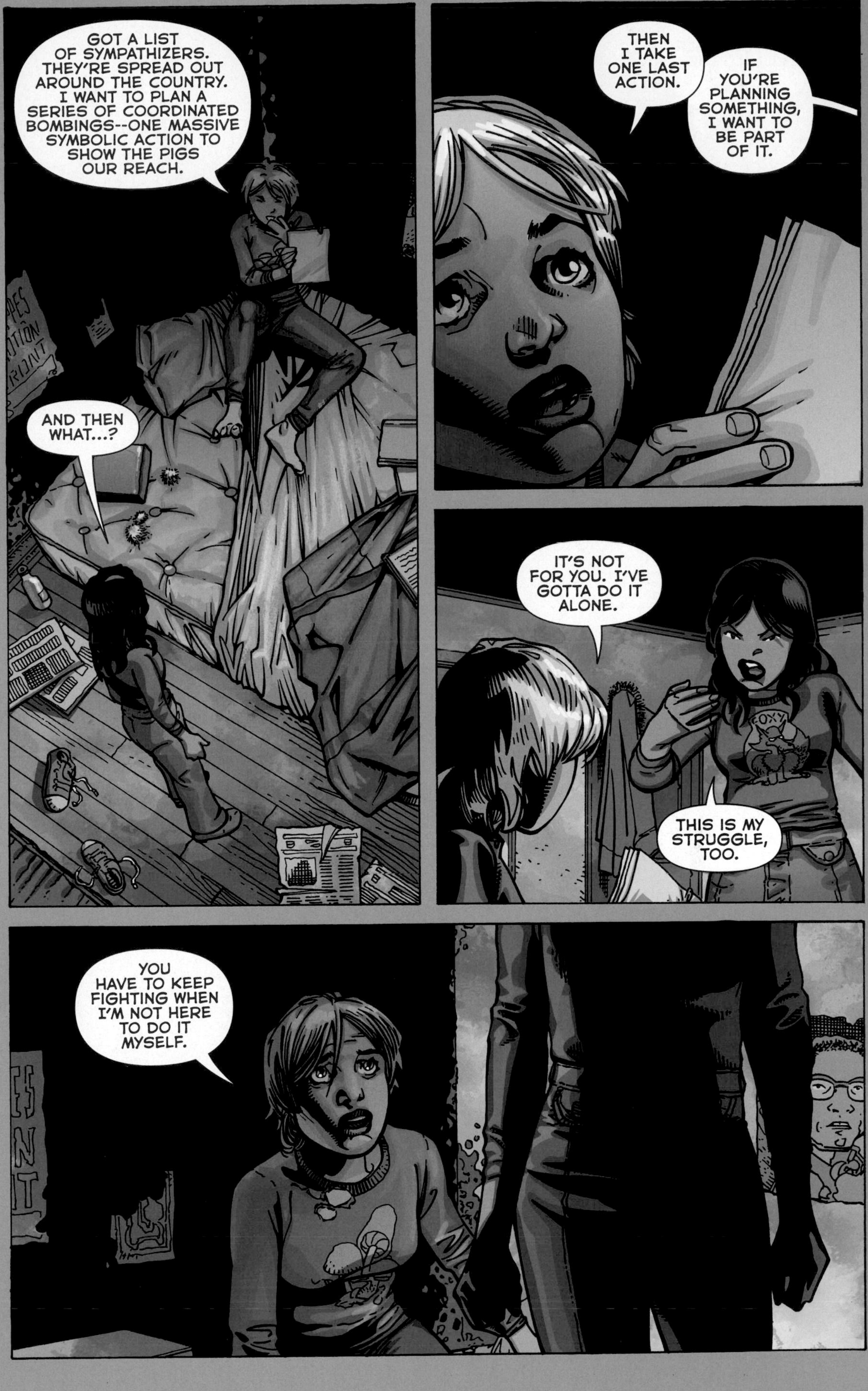
GOT A LIST OF SYMPATHIZERS. THEY'RE SPREAD OUT AROUND THE COUNTRY. I WANT TO PLAN A SERIES OF COORDINATED BOMBINGS--ONE MASSIVE SYMBOLIC ACTION TO SHOW THE PIGS OUR REACH.
AND THEN WHAT...?
THEN I TAKE ONE LAST ACTION.
IF YOU'RE PLANNING SOMETHING, I WANT TO BE PART OF IT.
IT'S NOT FOR YOU. I'VE GOTTA DO IT ALONE.
THIS IS MY STRUGGLE, TOO.
YOU HAVE TO KEEP FIGHTING WHEN I'M NOT HERE TO DO IT MYSELF.

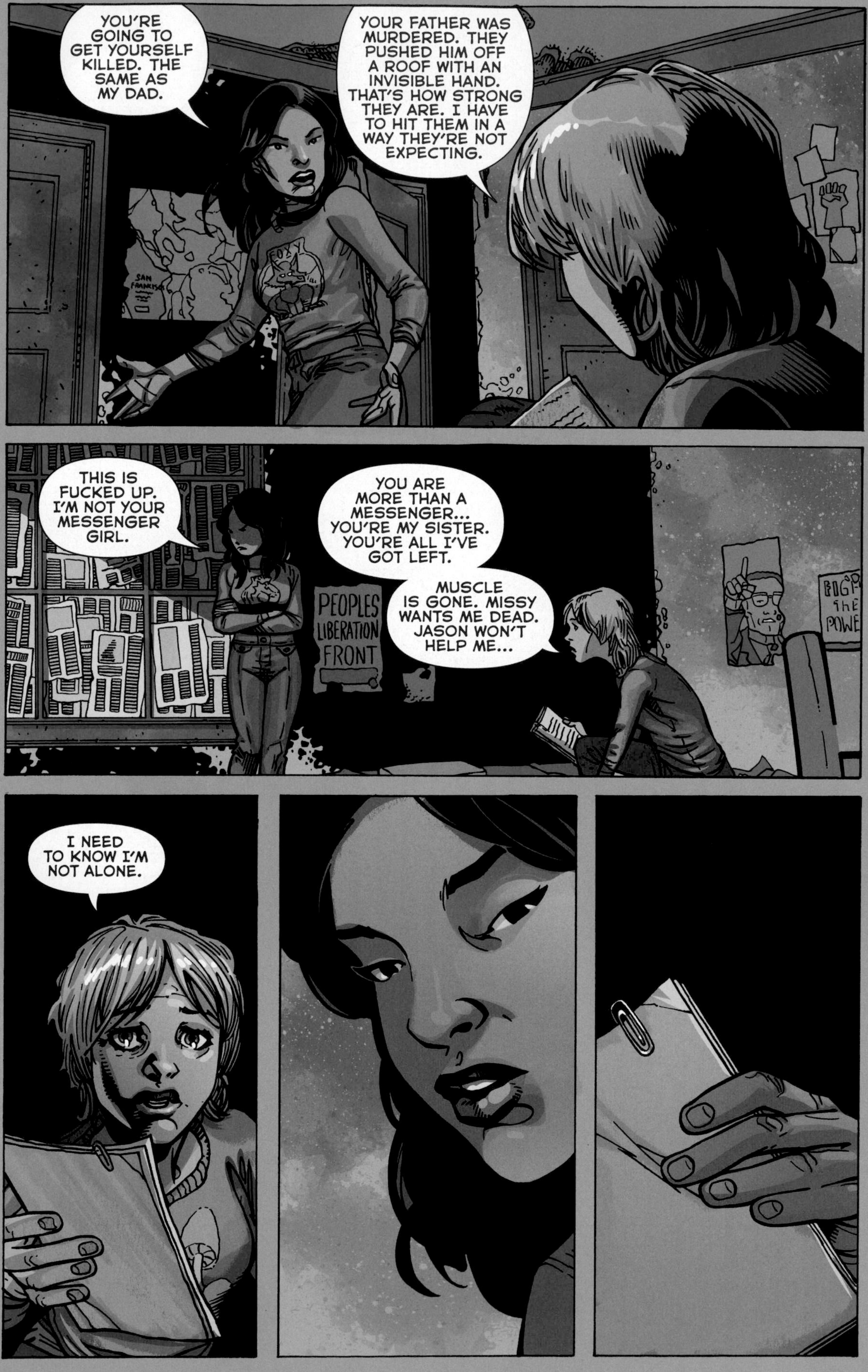
YOU'RE GOING TO GET YOURSELF KILLED. THE SAME AS MY DAD.
YOUR FATHER WAS MURDERED. THEY PUSHED HIM OFF A ROOF WITH AN INVISIBLE HAND. THAT'S HOW STRONG THEY ARE. I HAVE TO HIT THEM IN A WAY THEY'RE NOT EXPECTING.
THIS IS FUCKED UP. I'M NOT YOUR MESSENGER GIRL.
YOU ARE MORE THAN A MESSENGER... YOU'RE MY SISTER. YOU'RE ALL I'VE GOT LEFT.
MUSCLE IS GONE. MISSY WANTS ME DEAD. JASON WON'T HELP ME...
PEOPLES LIBERATION FRONT
I NEED TO KNOW I'M NOT ALONE.

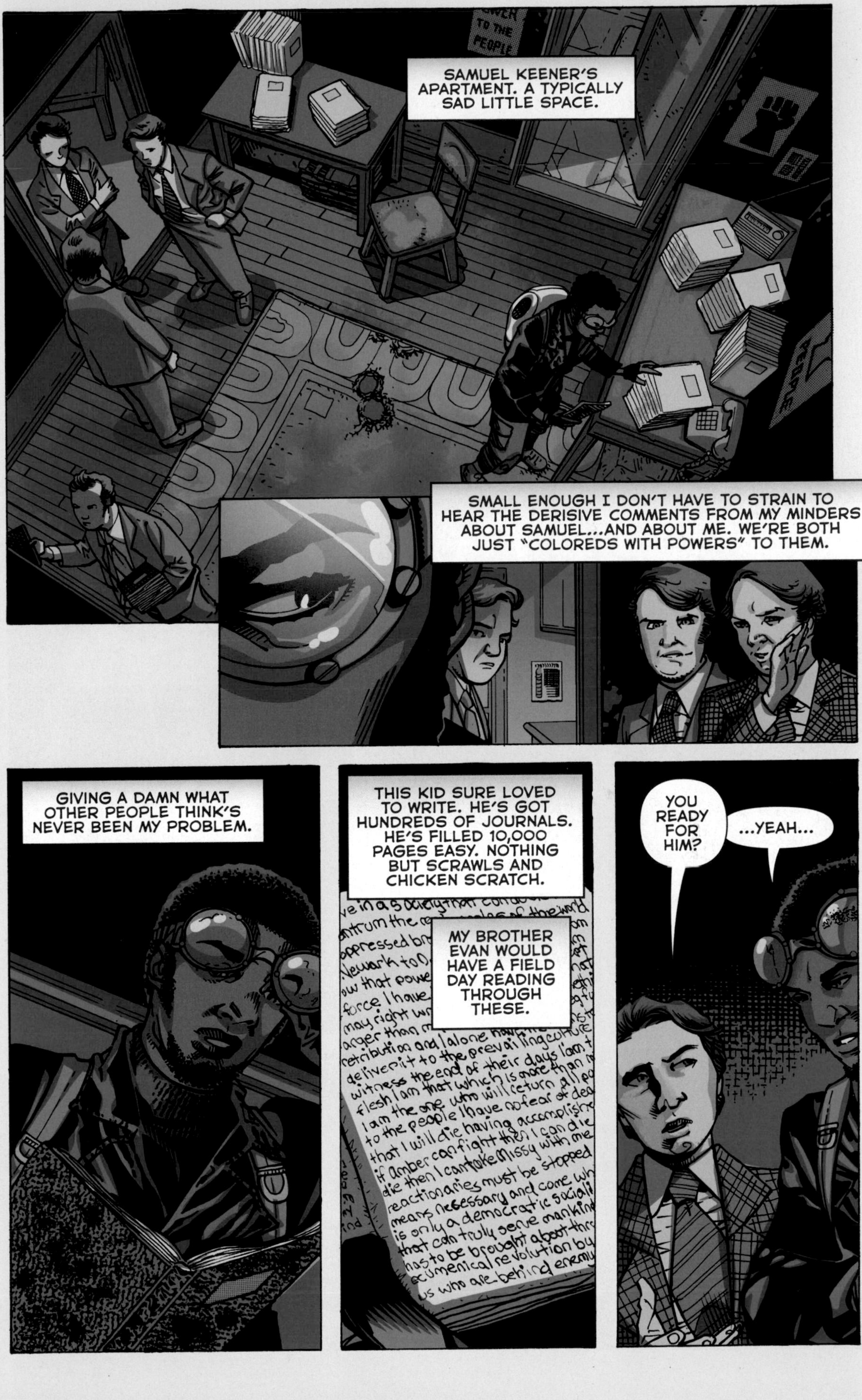
TO THE PEOPLE
SAMUEL KEENER'S APARTMENT. A TYPICALLY SAD LITTLE SPACE.
SMALL ENOUGH I DON'T HAVE TO STRAIN TO HEAR THE DERISIVE COMMENTS FROM MY MINDERS ABOUT SAMUEL...AND ABOUT ME. WE'RE BOTH JUST "COLOREDS WITH POWERS" TO THEM.
GIVING A DAMN WHAT OTHER PEOPLE THINK'S NEVER BEEN MY PROBLEM.
THIS KID SURE LOVED TO WRITE. HE'S GOT HUNDREDS OF JOURNALS. HE'S FILLED 10,000 PAGES EASY. NOTHING BUT SCRAWLS AND CHICKEN SCRATCH.
MY BROTHER EVAN WOULD HAVE A FIELD DAY READING THROUGH THESE.
YOU READY FOR HIM?
...YEAH...

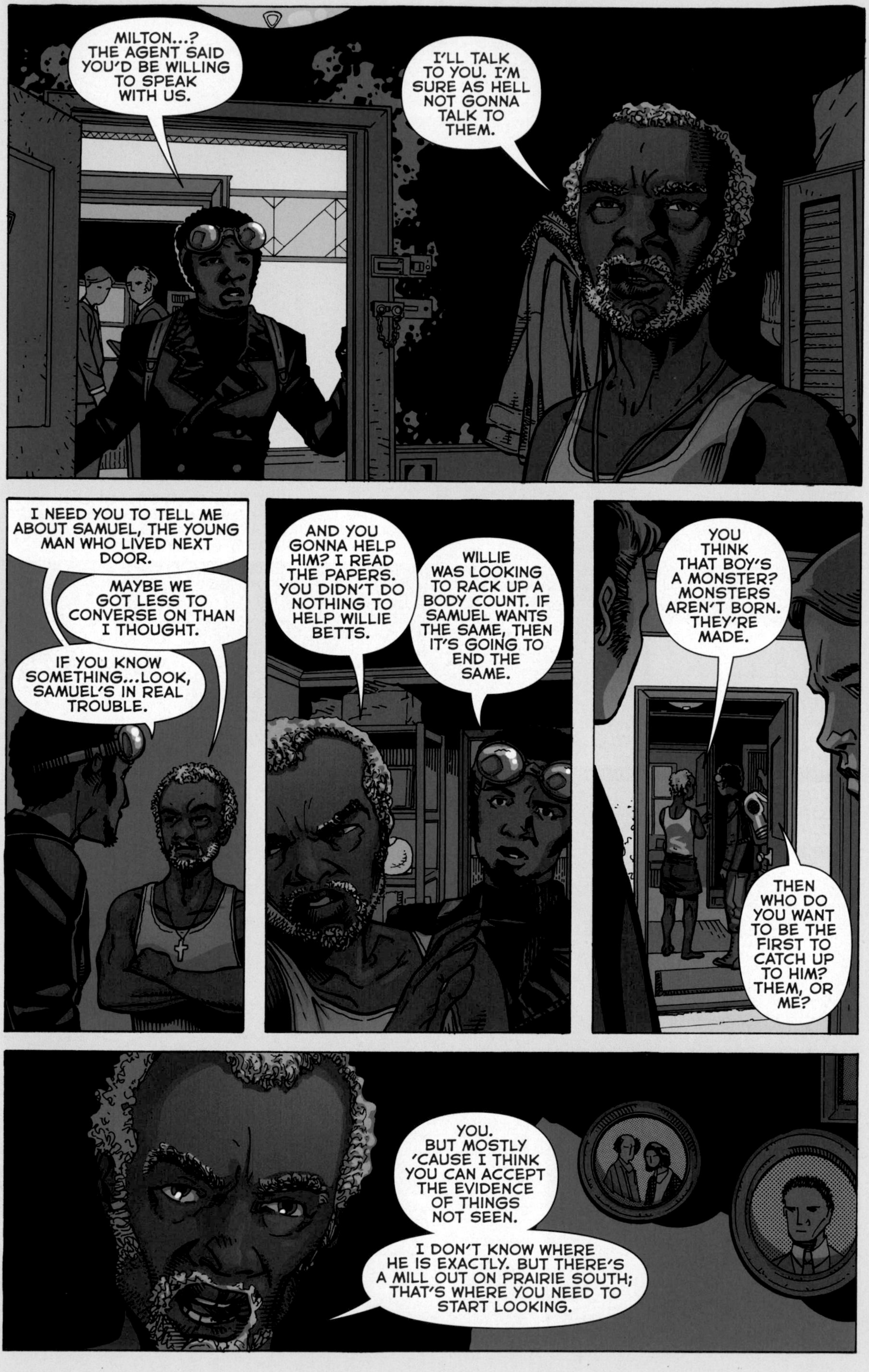
MILTON...? THE AGENT SAID YOU'D BE WILLING TO SPEAK WITH US.
I'LL TALK TO YOU. I'M SURE AS HELL NOT GONNA TALK TO THEM.
I NEED YOU TO TELL ME ABOUT SAMUEL, THE YOUNG MAN WHO LIVED NEXT DOOR.
MAYBE WE GOT LESS TO CONVERSE ON THAN I THOUGHT.
IF YOU KNOW SOMETHING...LOOK, SAMUEL'S IN REAL TROUBLE.
AND YOU GONNA HELP HIM? I READ THE PAPERS. YOU DIDN'T DO NOTHING TO HELP WILLIE BETTS.
WILLIE WAS LOOKING TO RACK UP A BODY COUNT. IF SAMUEL WANTS THE SAME, THEN IT'S GOING TO END THE SAME.
YOU THINK THAT BOY'S A MONSTER? MONSTERS AREN'T BORN. THEY'RE MADE.
THEN WHO DO YOU WANT TO BE THE FIRST TO CATCH UP TO HIM? THEM, OR ME?
YOU. BUT MOSTLY 'CAUSE I THINK YOU CAN ACCEPT THE EVIDENCE OF THINGS NOT SEEN.
I DON'T KNOW WHERE HE IS EXACTLY. BUT THERE'S A MILL OUT ON PRAIRIE SOUTH; THAT'S WHERE YOU NEED TO START LOOKING.

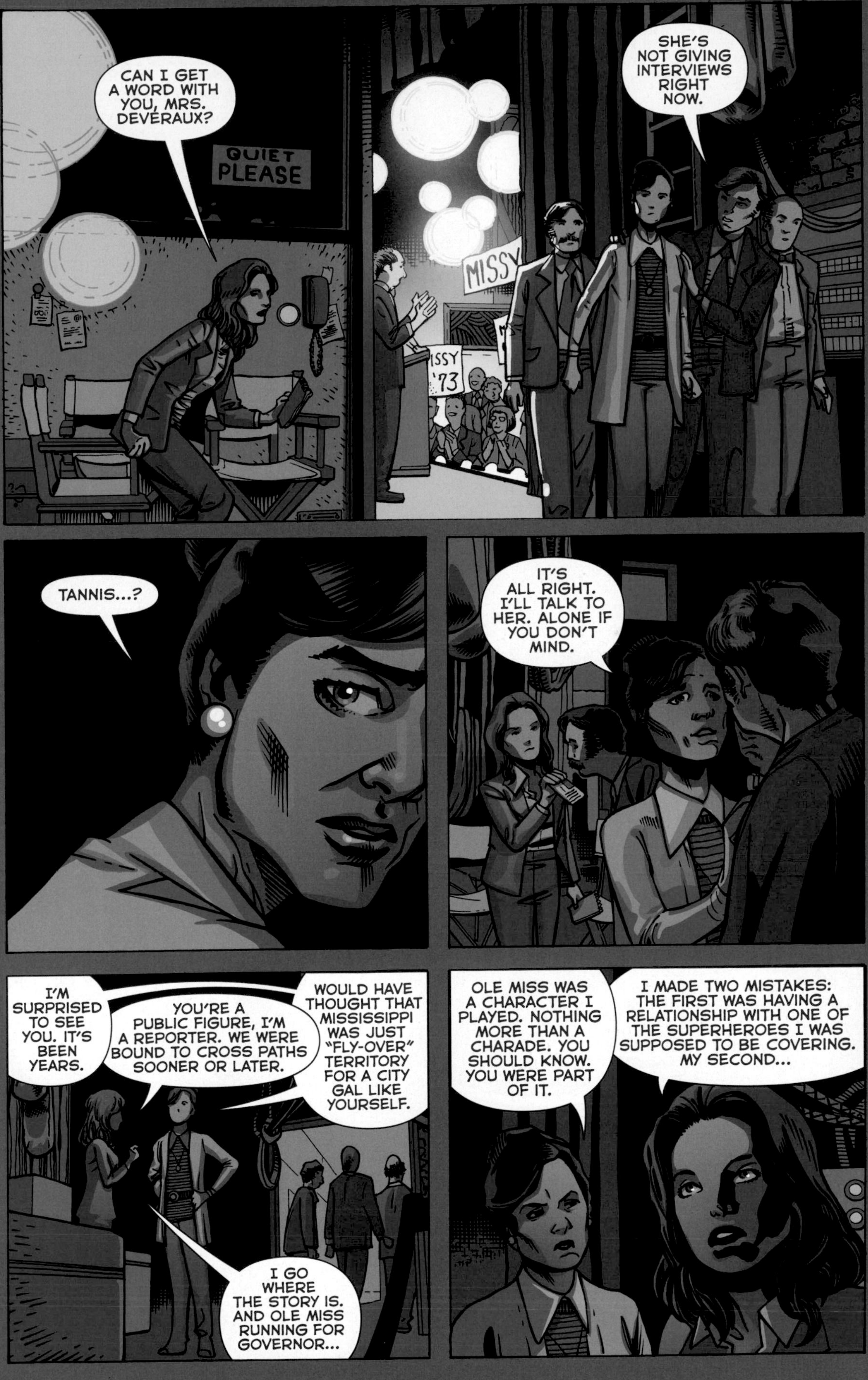

QUIET PLEASE
CAN I GET A WORD WITH YOU, MRS. DEVERAUX?
MISSY
ISSY '73
SHE'S NOT GIVING INTERVIEWS RIGHT NOW.
TANNIS...?
IT'S ALL RIGHT. I'LL TALK TO HER. ALONE IF YOU DON'T MIND.
I'M SURPRISED TO SEE YOU. IT'S BEEN YEARS.
YOU'RE A PUBLIC FIGURE, I'M A REPORTER. WE WERE BOUND TO CROSS PATHS SOONER OR LATER.
WOULD HAVE THOUGHT THAT MISSISSIPPI WAS JUST "FLY-OVER" TERRITORY FOR A CITY GAL LIKE YOURSELF.
I GO WHERE THE STORY IS. AND OLE MISS RUNNING FOR GOVERNOR...
OLE MISS WAS A CHARACTER I PLAYED. NOTHING MORE THAN A CHARADE. YOU SHOULD KNOW. YOU WERE PART OF IT.
I MADE TWO MISTAKES: THE FIRST WAS HAVING A RELATIONSHIP WITH ONE OF THE SUPERHEROES I WAS SUPPOSED TO BE COVERING. MY SECOND...

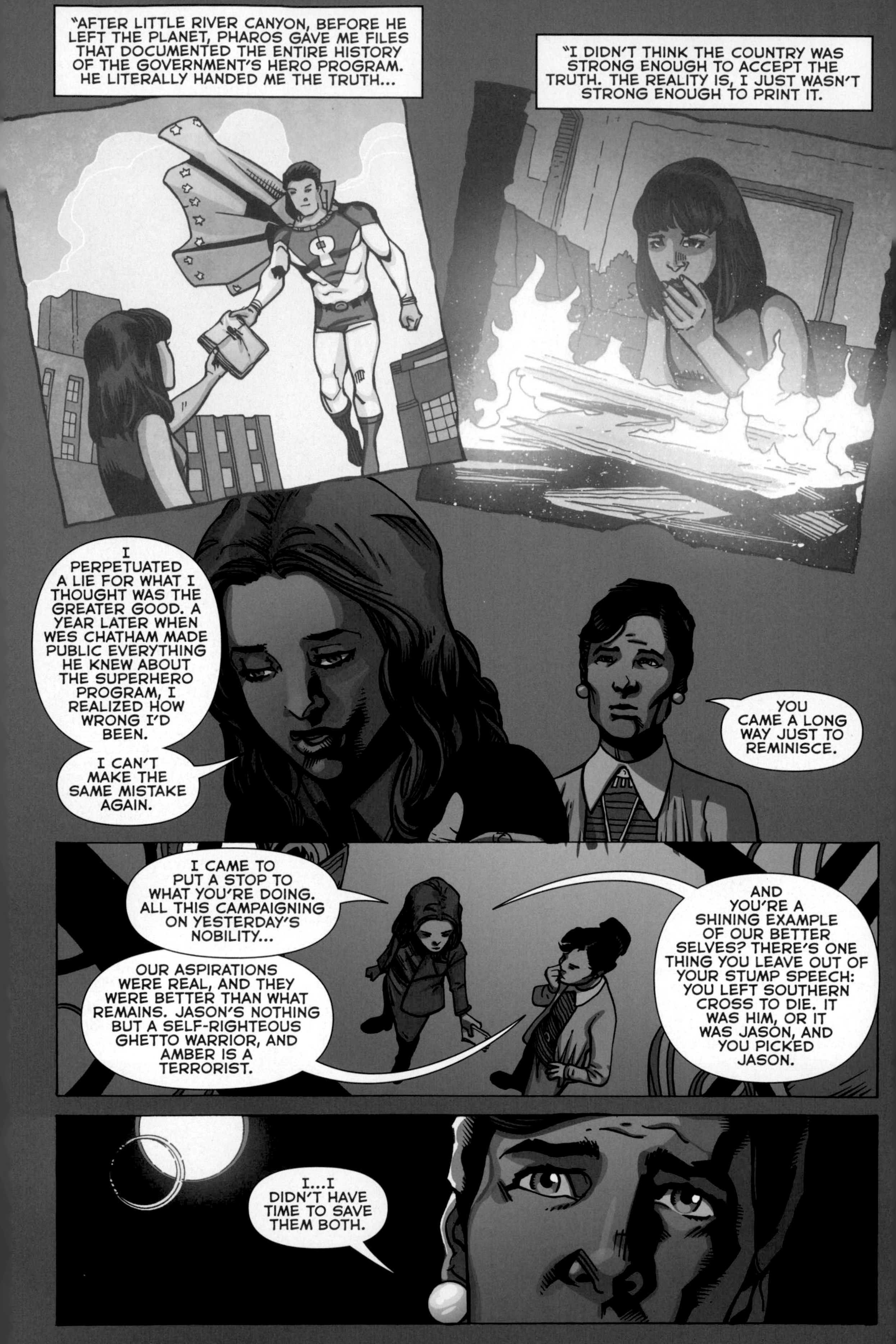
"AFTER LITTLE RIVER CANYON, BEFORE HE LEFT THE PLANET, PHAROS GAVE ME FILES THAT DOCUMENTED THE ENTIRE HISTORY OF THE GOVERNMENT'S HERO PROGRAM. HE LITERALLY HANDED ME THE TRUTH...
"I DIDN'T THINK THE COUNTRY WAS STRONG ENOUGH TO ACCEPT THE TRUTH. THE REALITY IS, I JUST WASN'T STRONG ENOUGH TO PRINT IT.
I PERPETUATED A LIE FOR WHAT I THOUGHT WAS THE GREATER GOOD. A YEAR LATER WHEN WES CHATHAM MADE PUBLIC EVERYTHING HE KNEW ABOUT THE SUPERHERO PROGRAM, I REALIZED HOW WRONG I'D BEEN.
I CAN'T MAKE THE SAME MISTAKE AGAIN.
YOU CAME A LONG WAY JUST TO REMINISCE.
I CAME TO PUT A STOP TO WHAT YOU'RE DOING. ALL THIS CAMPAIGNING ON YESTERDAY'S NOBILITY...
OUR ASPIRATIONS WERE REAL, AND THEY WERE BETTER THAN WHAT REMAINS. JASON'S NOTHING BUT A SELF-RIGHTEOUS GHETTO WARRIOR, AND AMBER IS A TERRORIST.
AND YOU'RE A SHINING EXAMPLE OF OUR BETTER SELVES? THERE'S ONE THING YOU LEAVE OUT OF YOUR STUMP SPEECH: YOU LEFT SOUTHERN CROSS TO DIE. IT WAS HIM, OR IT WAS JASON, AND YOU PICKED JASON.
I...I DIDN'T HAVE TIME TO SAVE THEM BOTH.

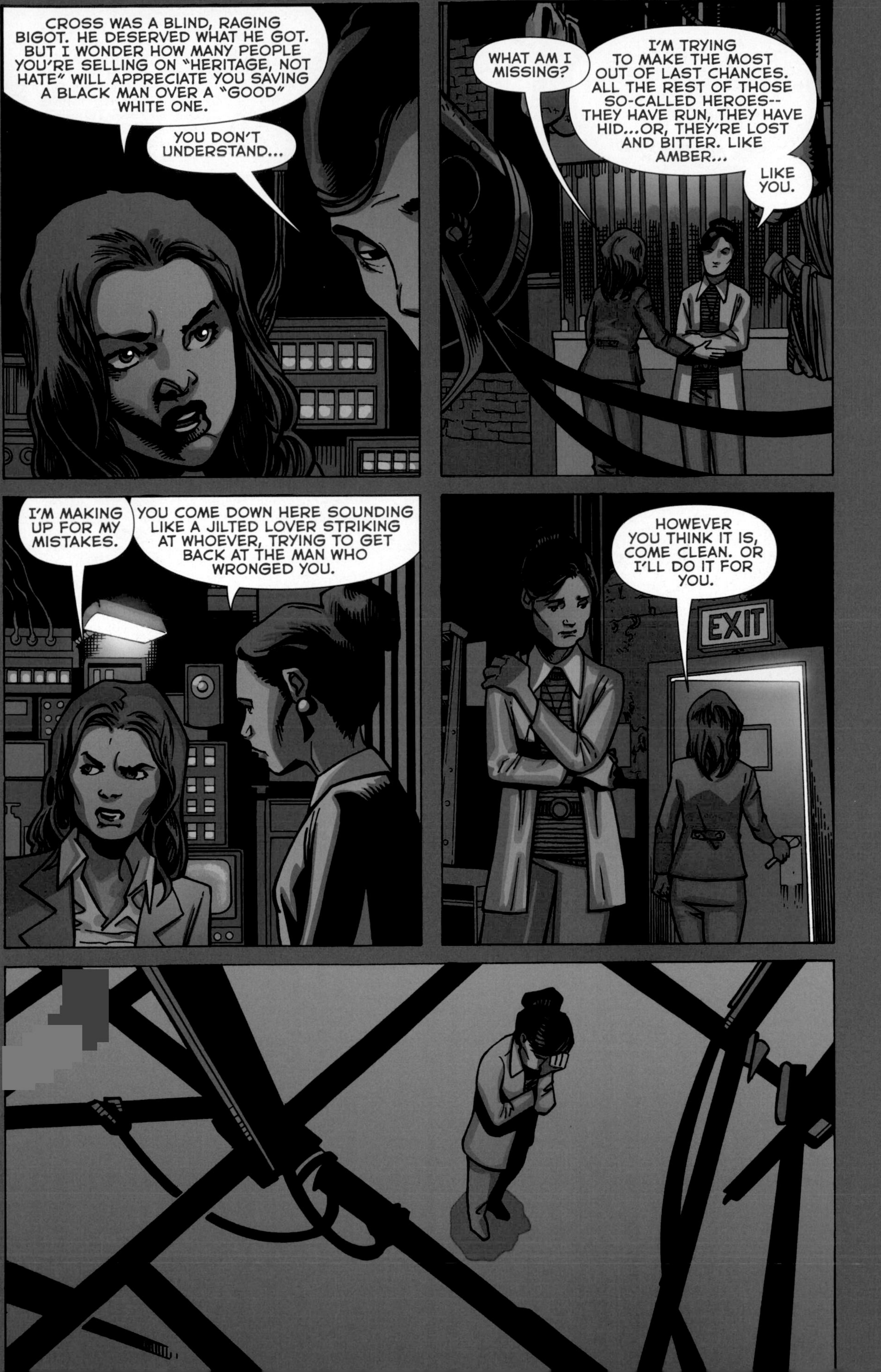
CROSS WAS A BLIND, RAGING BIGOT. HE DESERVED WHAT HE GOT. BUT I WONDER HOW MANY PEOPLE YOU'RE SELLING ON "HERITAGE, NOT HATE" WILL APPRECIATE YOU SAVING A BLACK MAN OVER A "GOOD" WHITE ONE.
YOU DON'T UNDERSTAND...
WHAT AM I MISSING?
I'M TRYING TO MAKE THE MOST OUT OF LAST CHANCES. ALL THE REST OF THOSE SO-CALLED HEROES-- THEY HAVE RUN, THEY HAVE HID...OR, THEY'RE LOST AND BITTER. LIKE AMBER...
LIKE YOU.
I'M MAKING UP FOR MY MISTAKES.
YOU COME DOWN HERE SOUNDING LIKE A JILTED LOVER STRIKING AT WHOEVER, TRYING TO GET BACK AT THE MAN WHO WRONGED YOU.
HOWEVER YOU THINK IT IS, COME CLEAN. OR I'LL DO IT FOR YOU.
EXIT

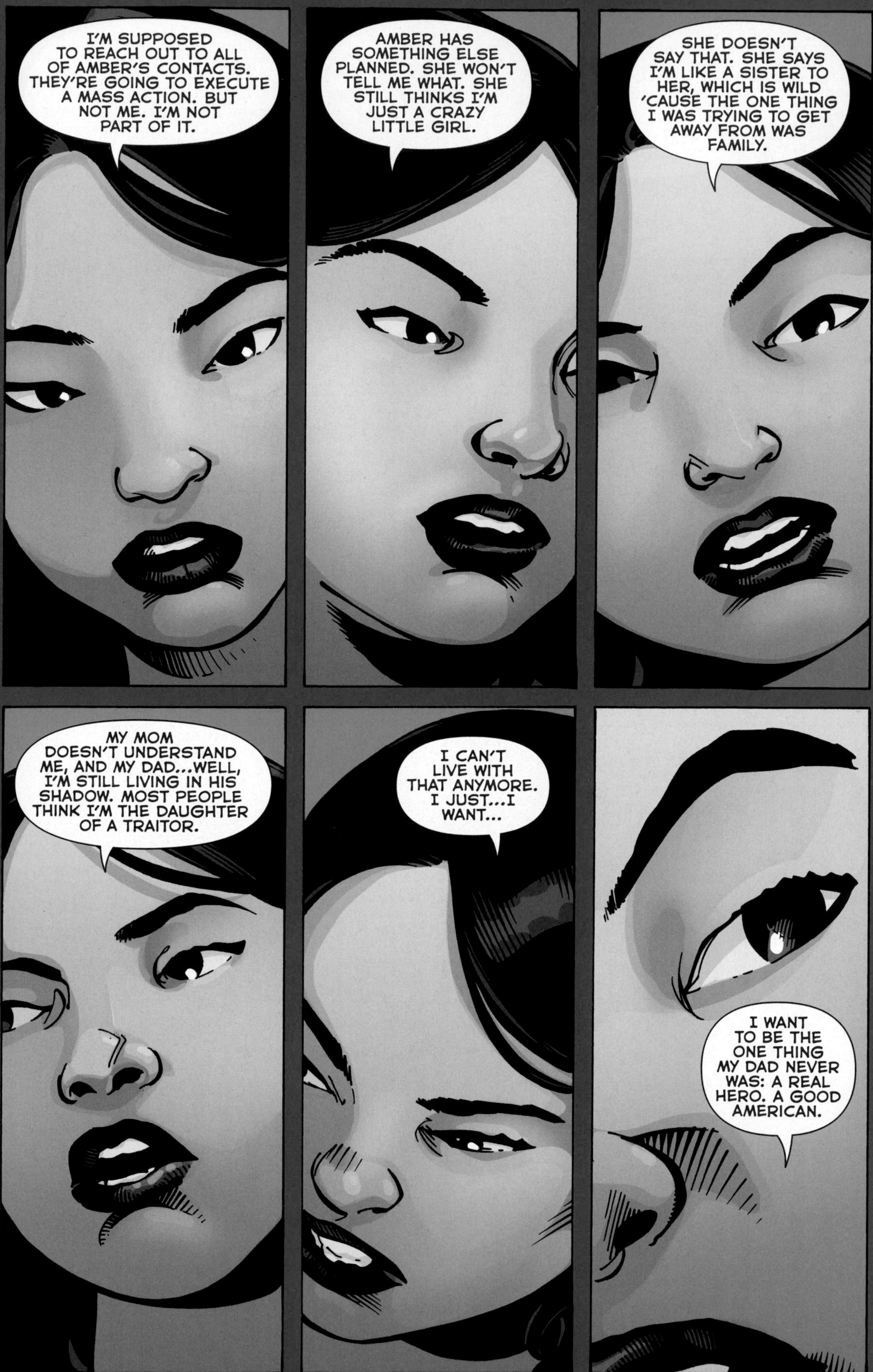
I'M SUPPOSED TO REACH OUT TO ALL OF AMBER'S CONTACTS. THEY'RE GOING TO EXECUTE A MASS ACTION. BUT NOT ME. I'M NOT PART OF IT.
AMBER HAS SOMETHING ELSE PLANNED. SHE WON'T TELL ME WHAT. SHE STILL THINKS I'M JUST A CRAZY LITTLE GIRL.
SHE DOESN'T SAY THAT. SHE SAYS I'M LIKE A SISTER TO HER, WHICH IS WILD 'CAUSE THE ONE THING I WAS TRYING TO GET AWAY FROM WAS FAMILY.
MY MOM DOESN'T UNDERSTAND ME, AND MY DAD...WELL, I'M STILL LIVING IN HIS SHADOW. MOST PEOPLE THINK I'M THE DAUGHTER OF A TRAITOR.
I CAN'T LIVE WITH THAT ANYMORE. I JUST...I WANT...
I WANT TO BE THE ONE THING MY DAD NEVER WAS: A REAL HERO. A GOOD AMERICAN.

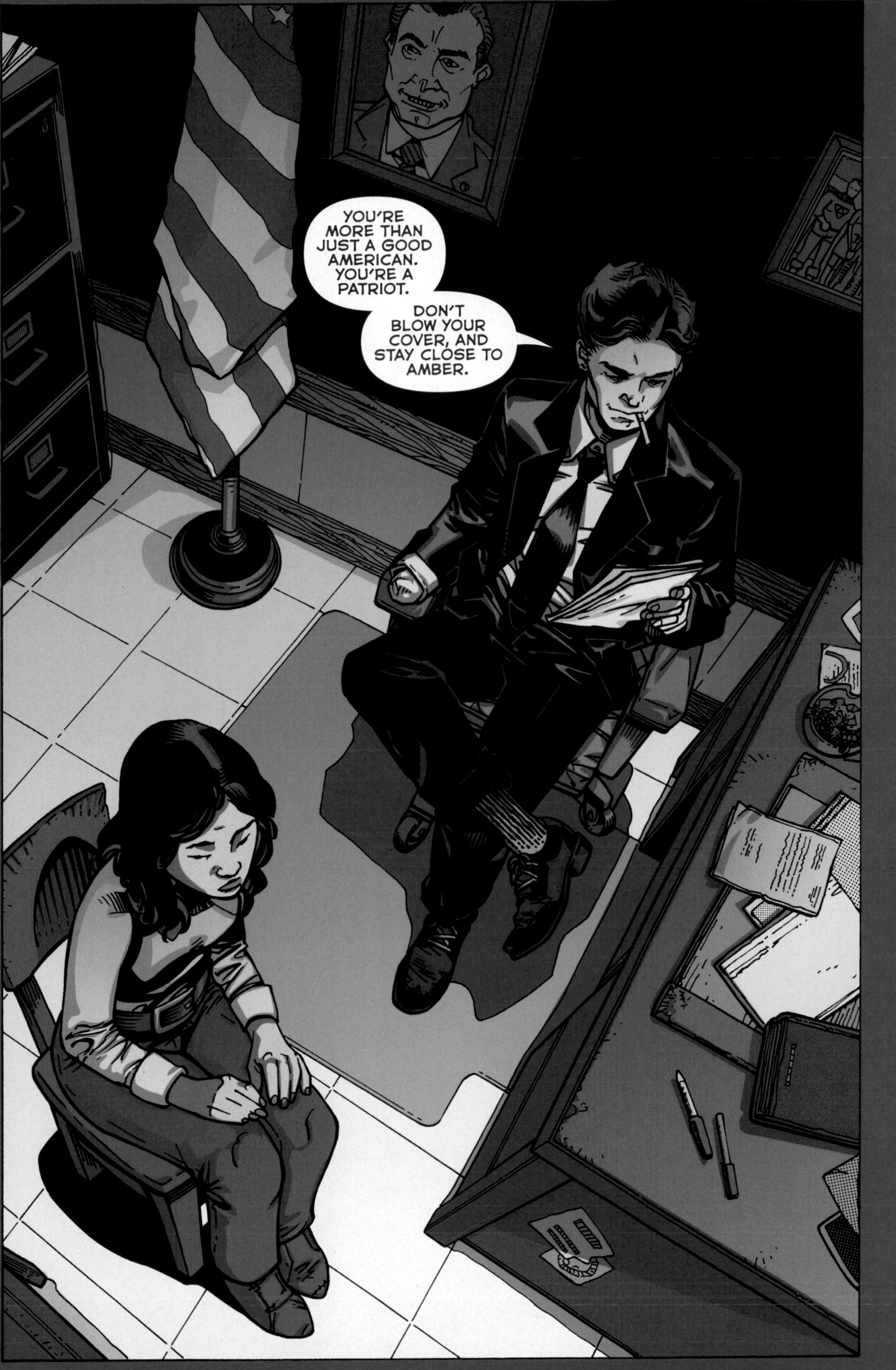
YOU'RE MORE THAN JUST A GOOD AMERICAN. YOU'RE A PATRIOT.
DON'T BLOW YOUR COVER, AND STAY CLOSE TO AMBER.

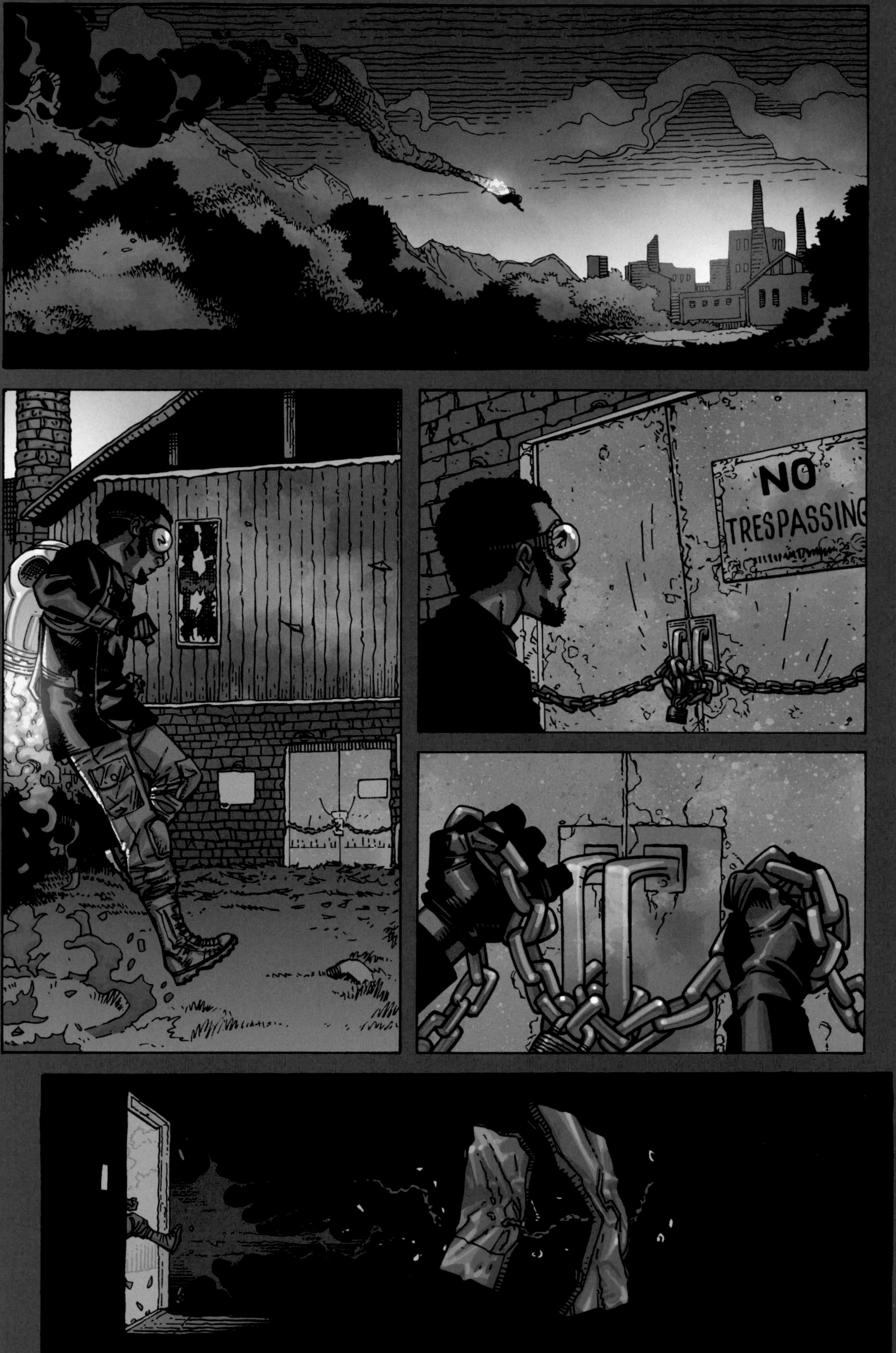
NO
TRESPASSING

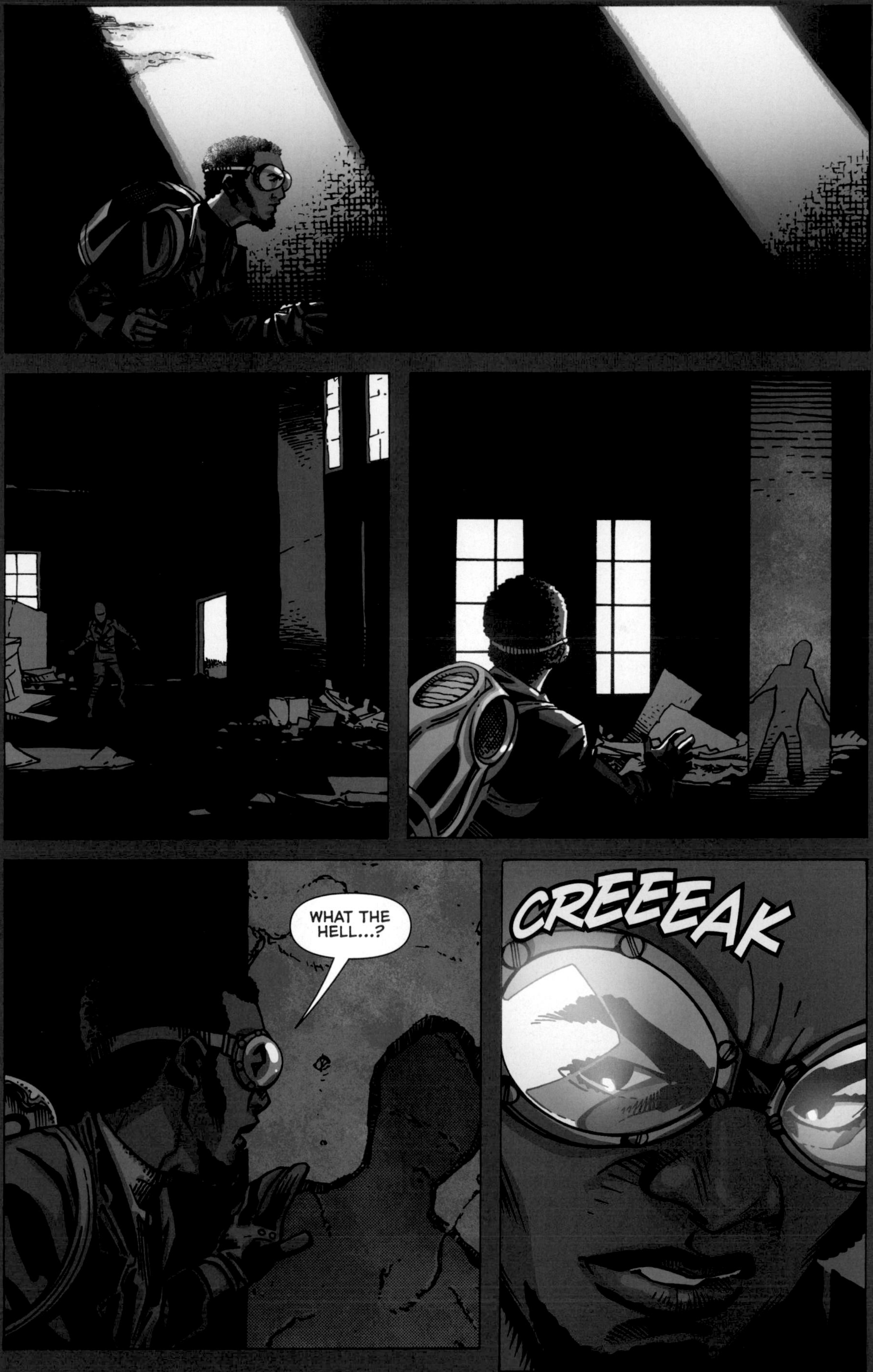
WHAT THE HELL...?
CREEEAK

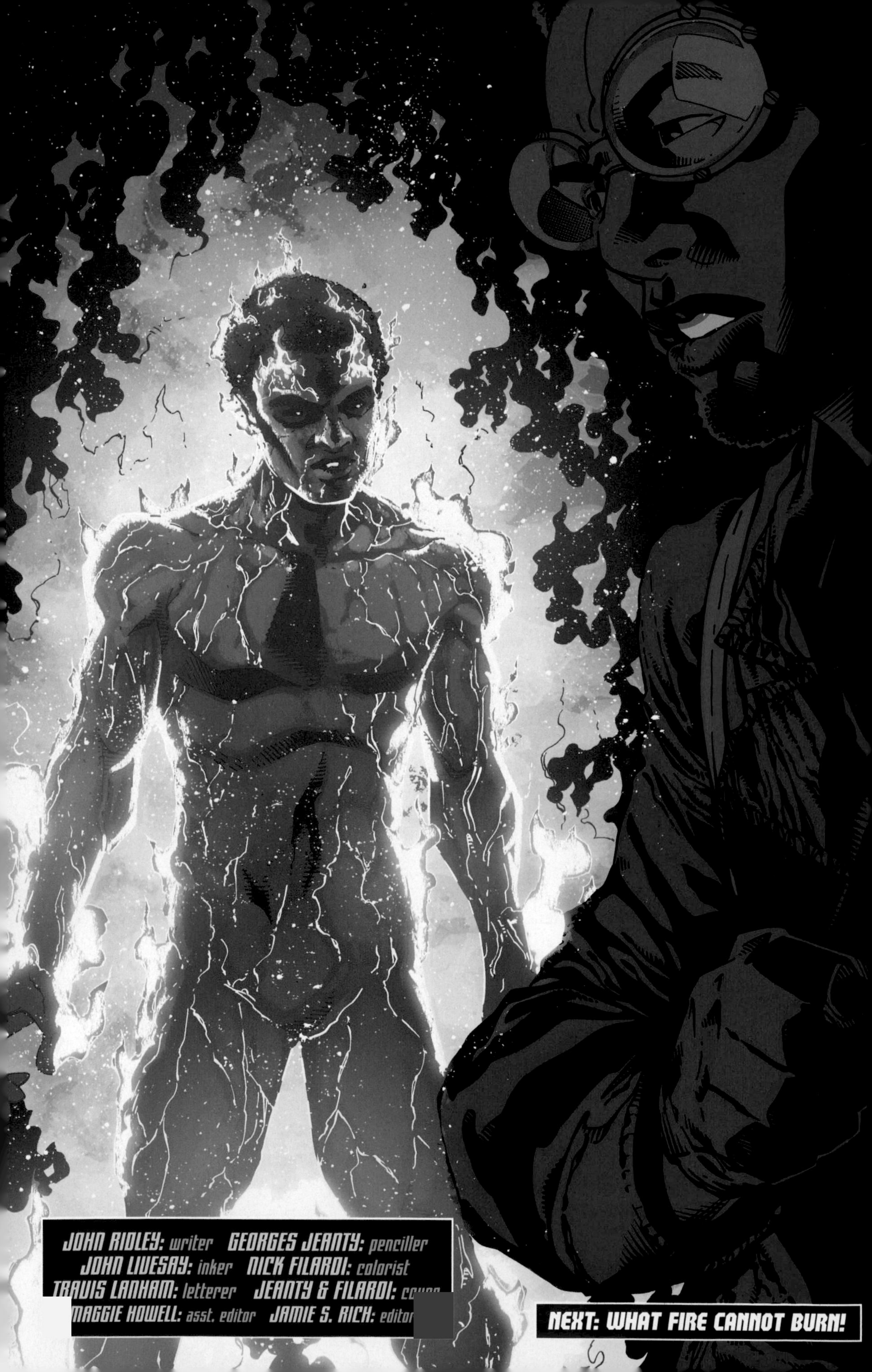
JOHN RIDLEY: writer GEORGES JEANTY: penciller
JOHN LIVESAY: inker NICK FILARDI: colorist
TRAVIS LANHAM: letterer JEANTY & FILARDI: cove
MAGGIE HOWELL: asst. editor JAMIE S. RICH: edito
NEXT: WHAT FIRE CANNOT BURN!

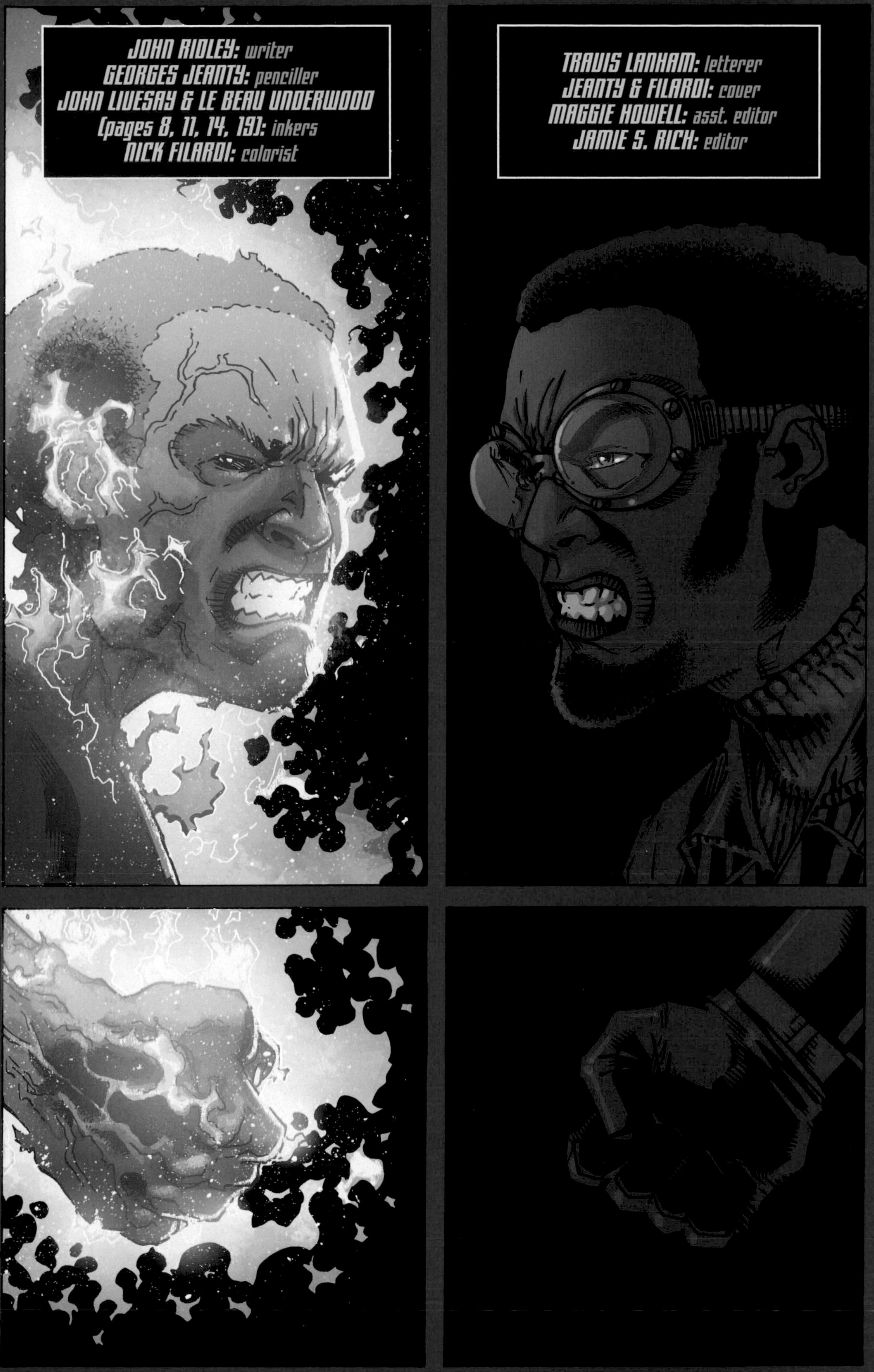
JOHN RIDLEY: writer
GEORGES JEANTY: penciller
JOHN LIVESAY & LE BEAU UNDERWOOD
(pages 8, 11, 14, 19): inkers
NICK FILARDI: colorist
TRAVIS LANHAM: letterer
JEANTY & FILARDI: cover
MAGGIE HOWELL: asst. editor
JAMIE S. RICH: editor

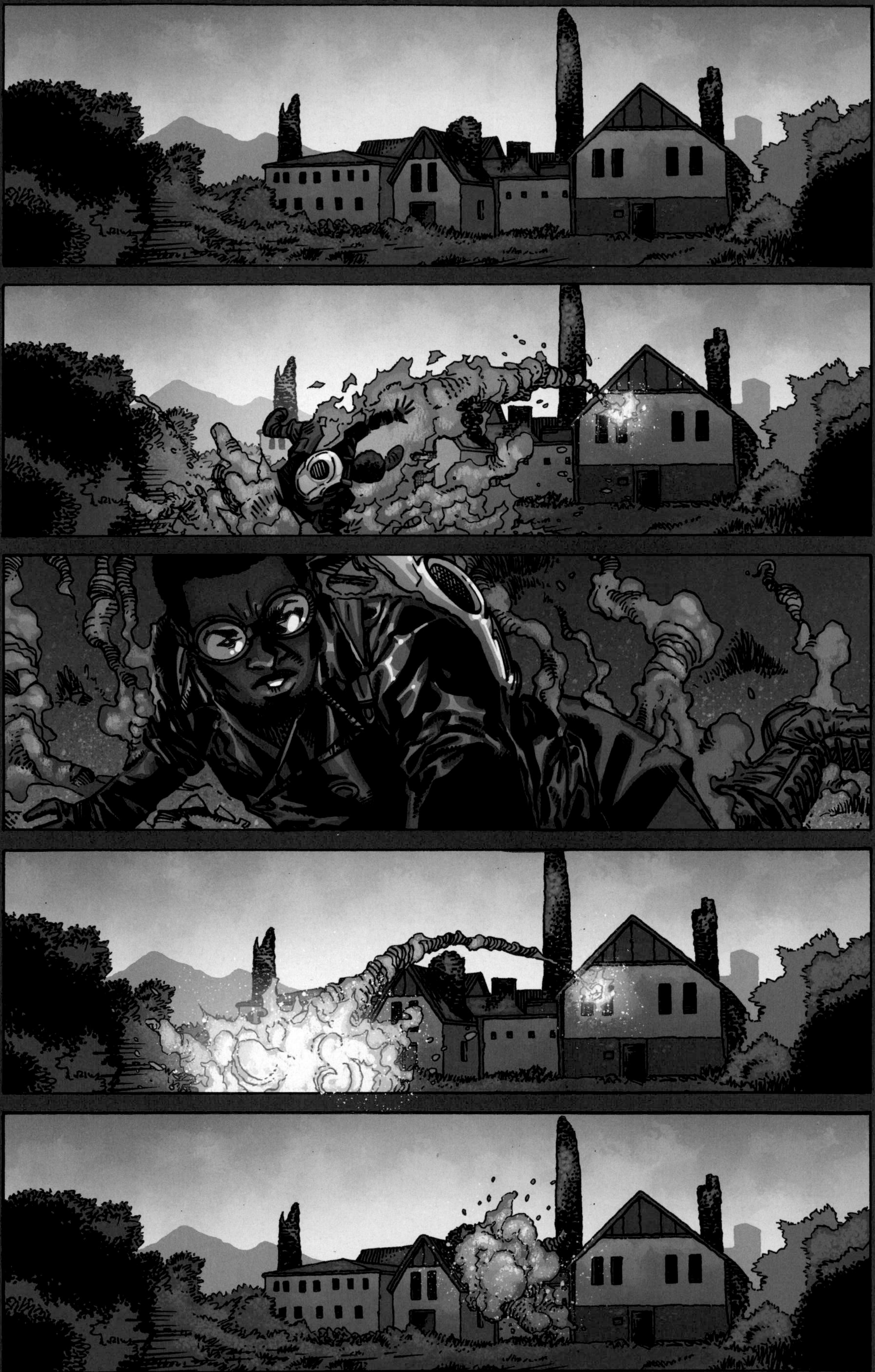

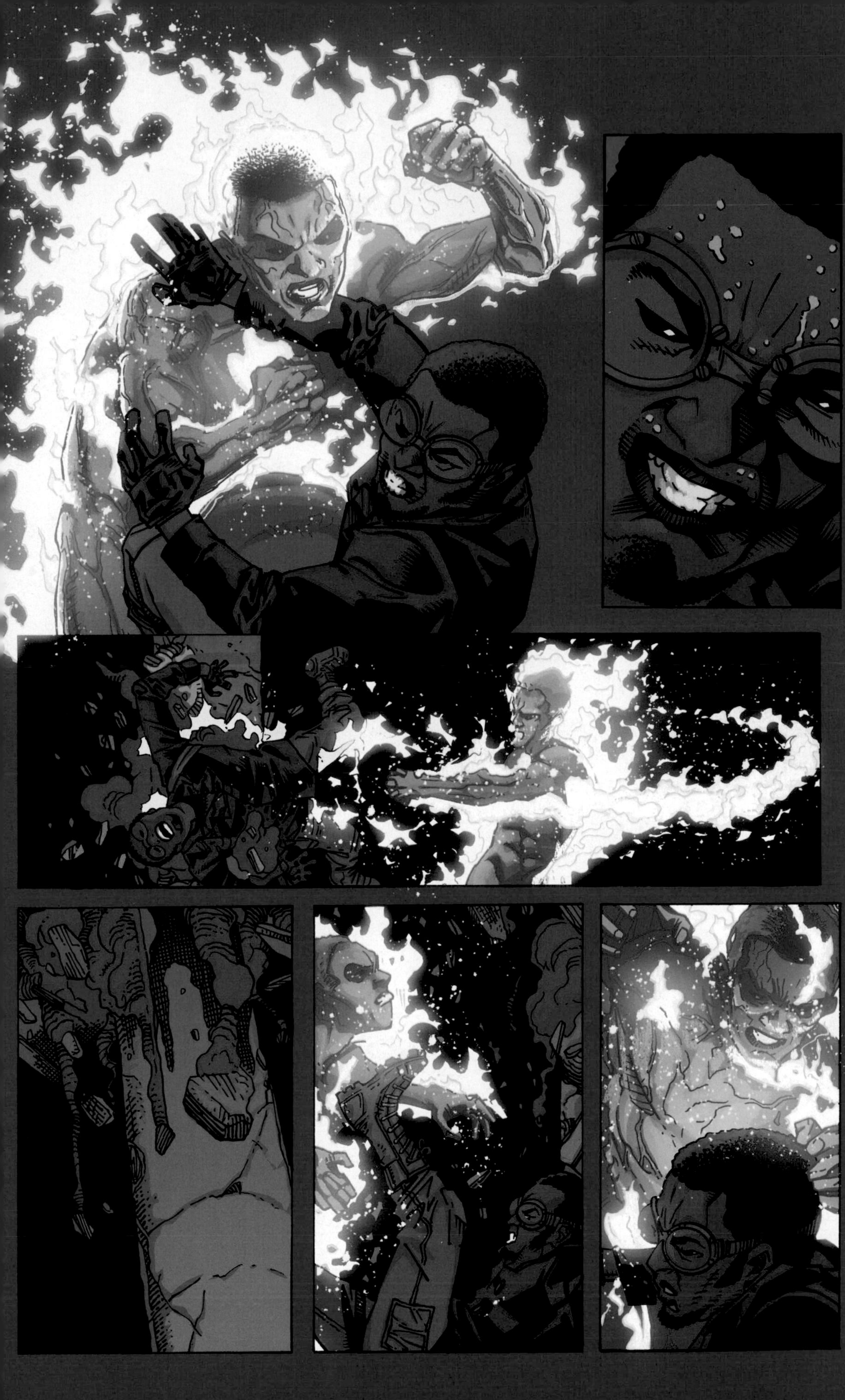

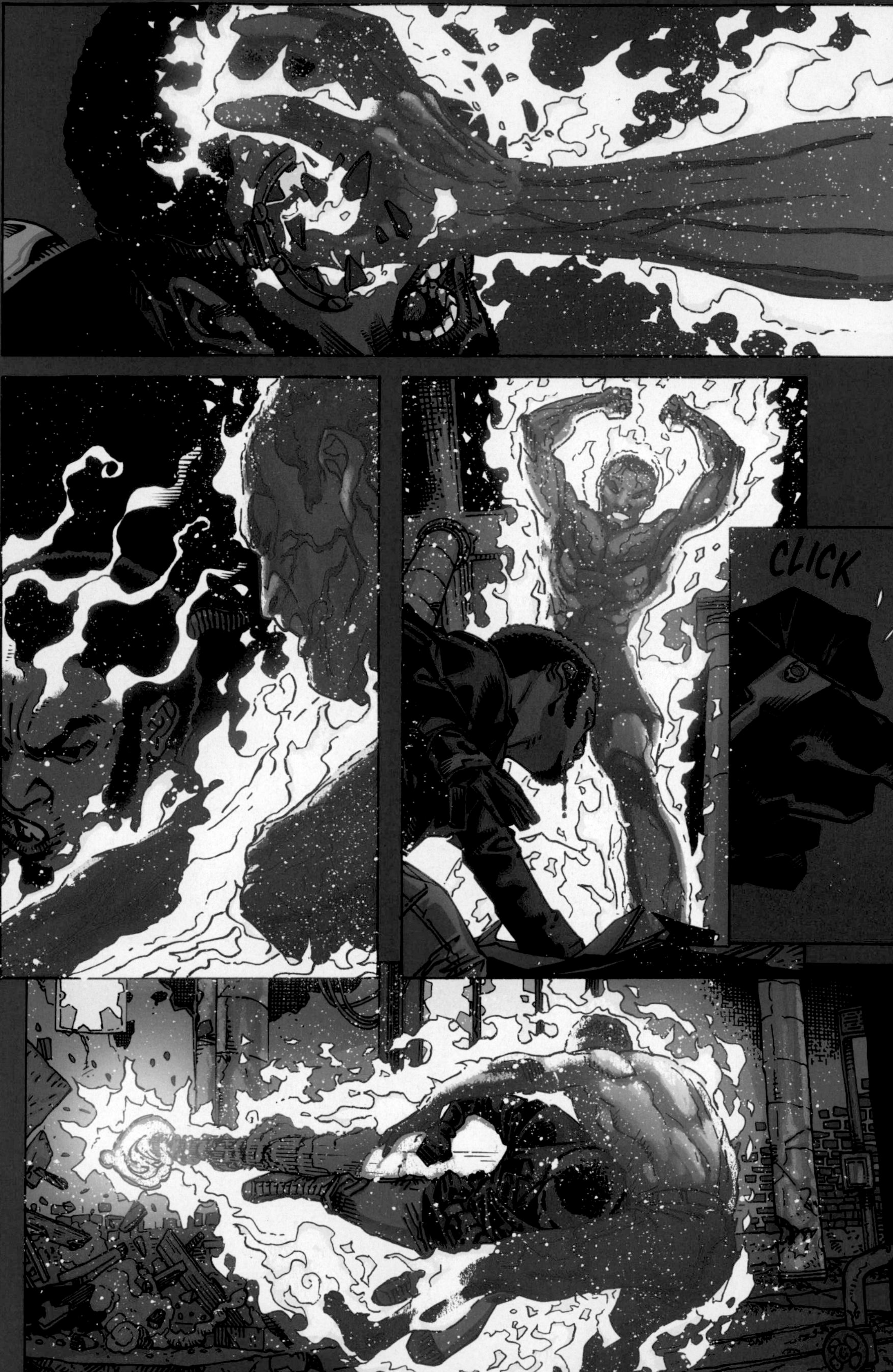
CLICK

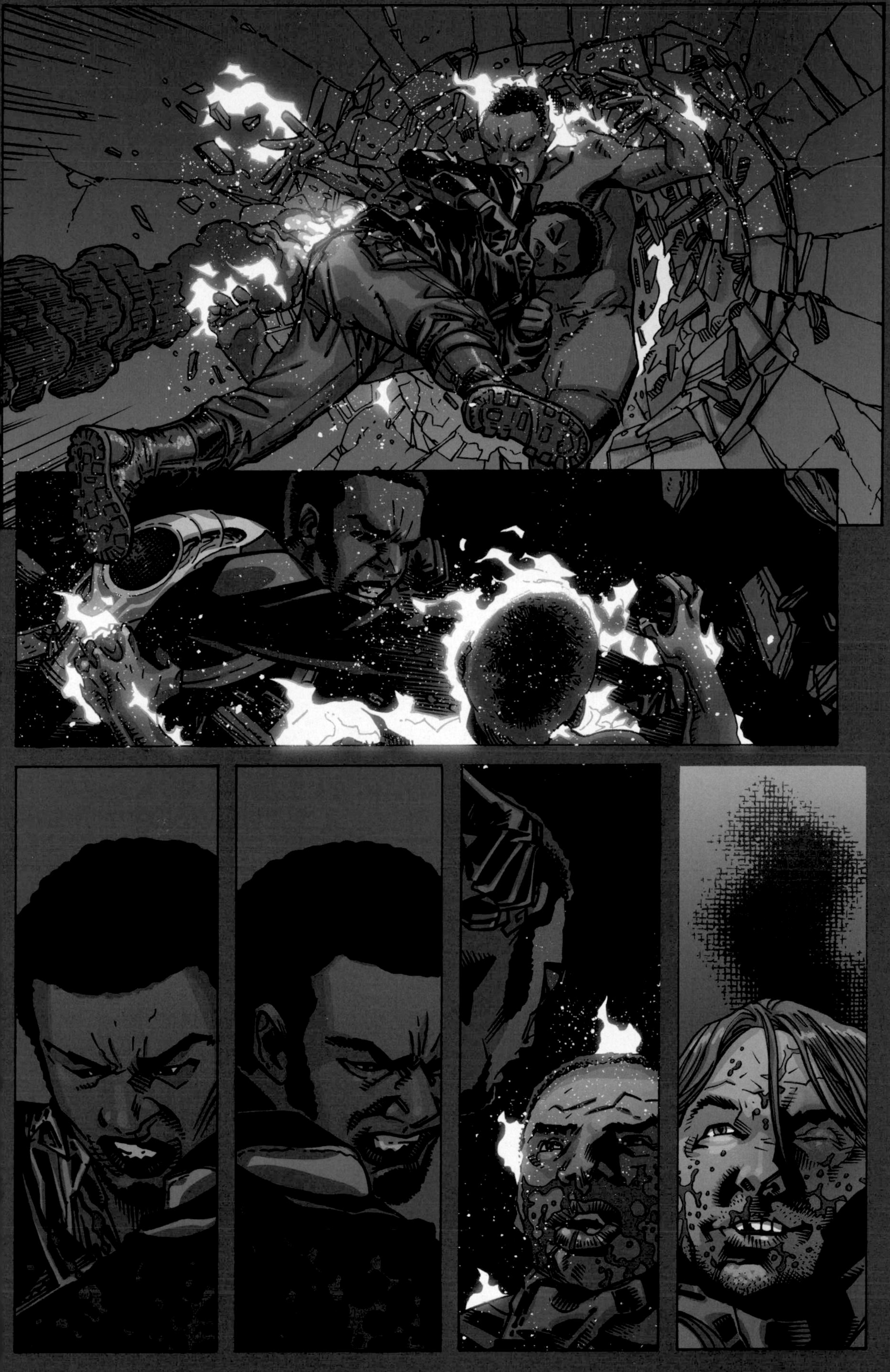

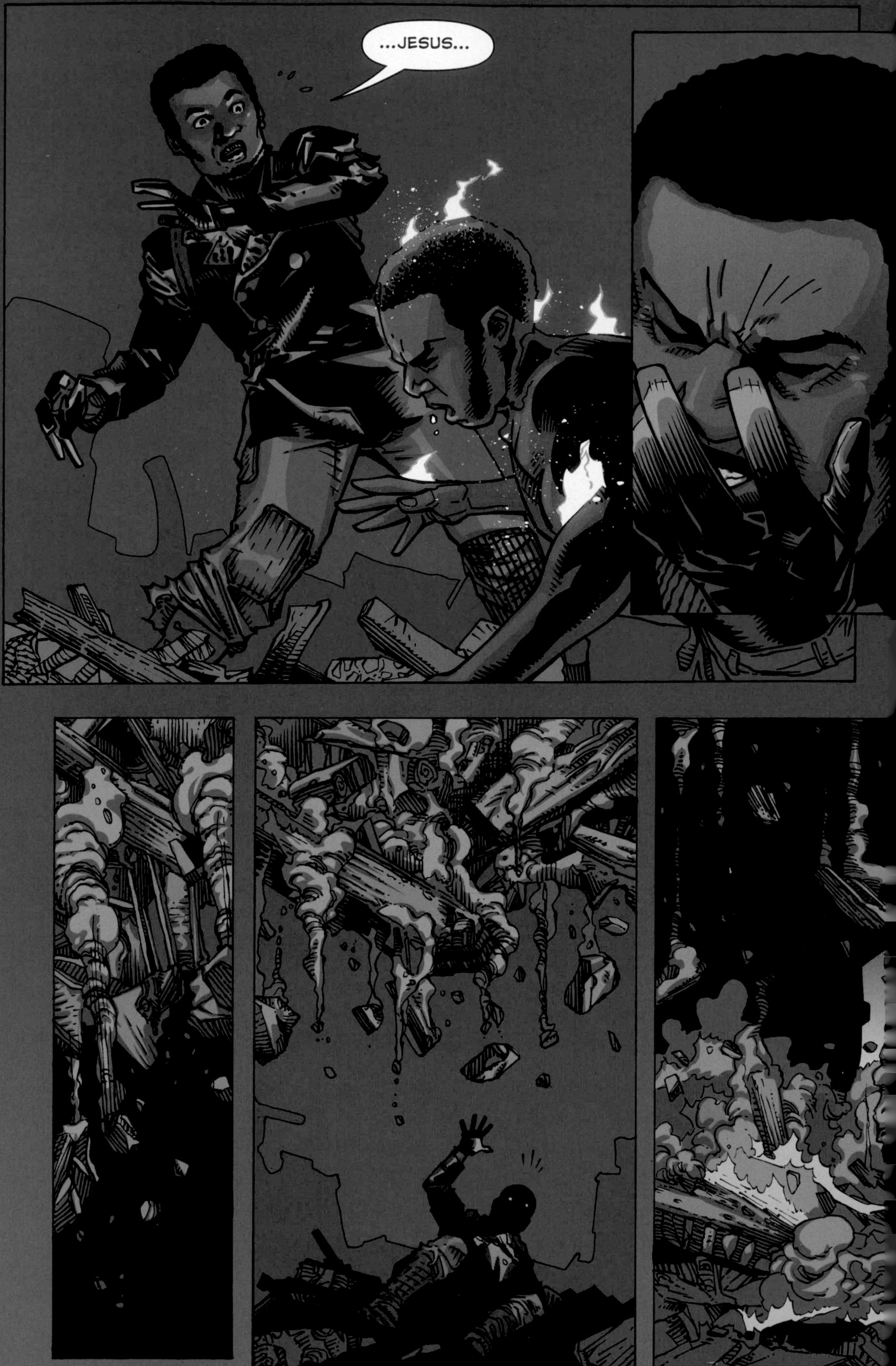
...JESUS...

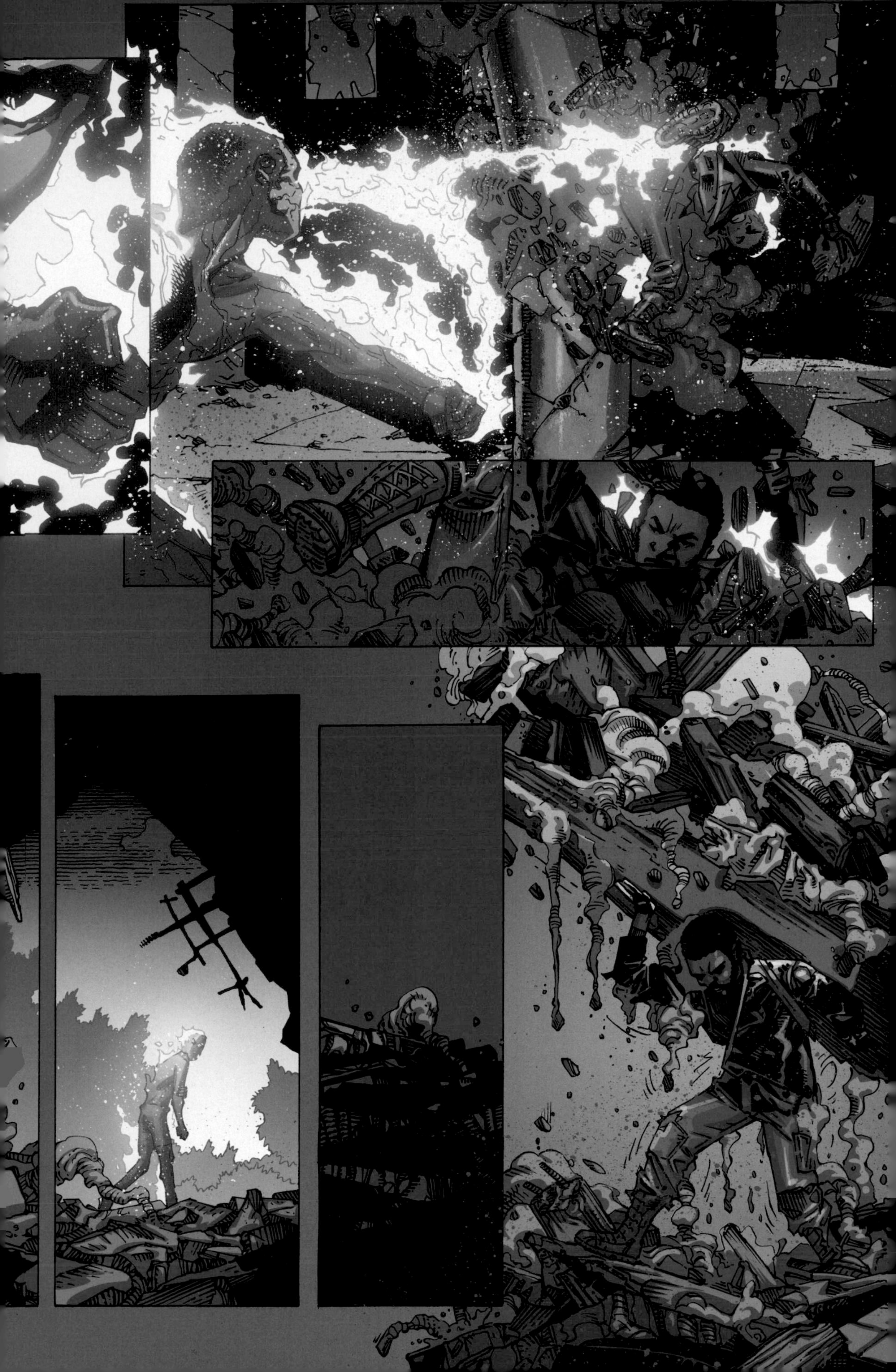

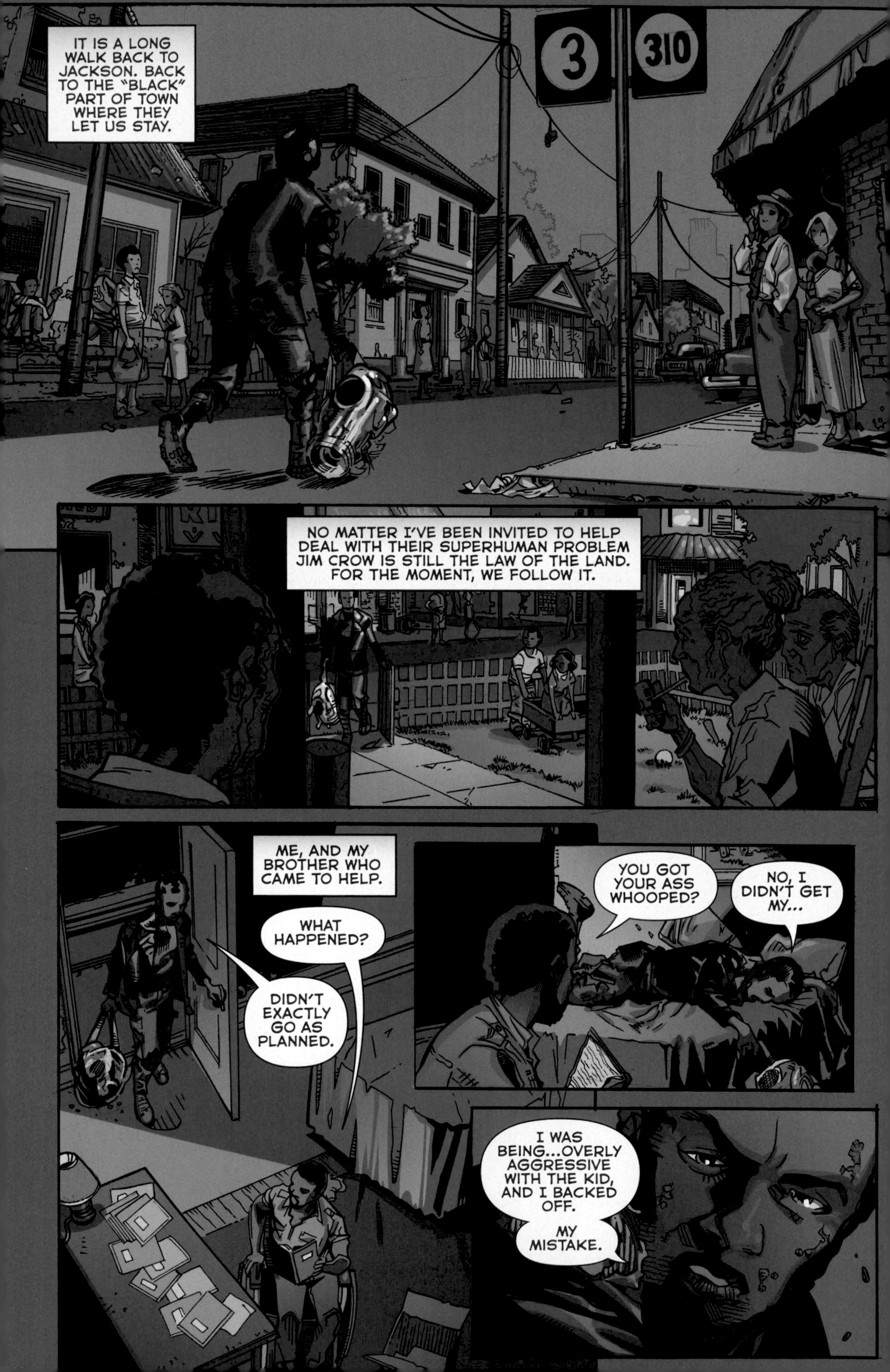
IT IS A LONG WALK BACK TO JACKSON. BACK TO THE "BLACK" PART OF TOWN WHERE THEY LET US STAY.
3
310
NO MATTER I'VE BEEN INVITED TO HELP DEAL WITH THEIR SUPERHUMAN PROBLEM JIM CROW IS STILL THE LAW OF THE LAND. FOR THE MOMENT, WE FOLLOW IT.
ME, AND MY BROTHER WHO CAME TO HELP.
WHAT HAPPENED?
DIDN'T EXACTLY GO AS PLANNED.
YOU GOT YOUR ASS WHOOPED?
NO, I DIDN'T GET MY...
I WAS BEING...OVERLY AGGRESSIVE WITH THE KID, AND I BACKED OFF.
MY MISTAKE.

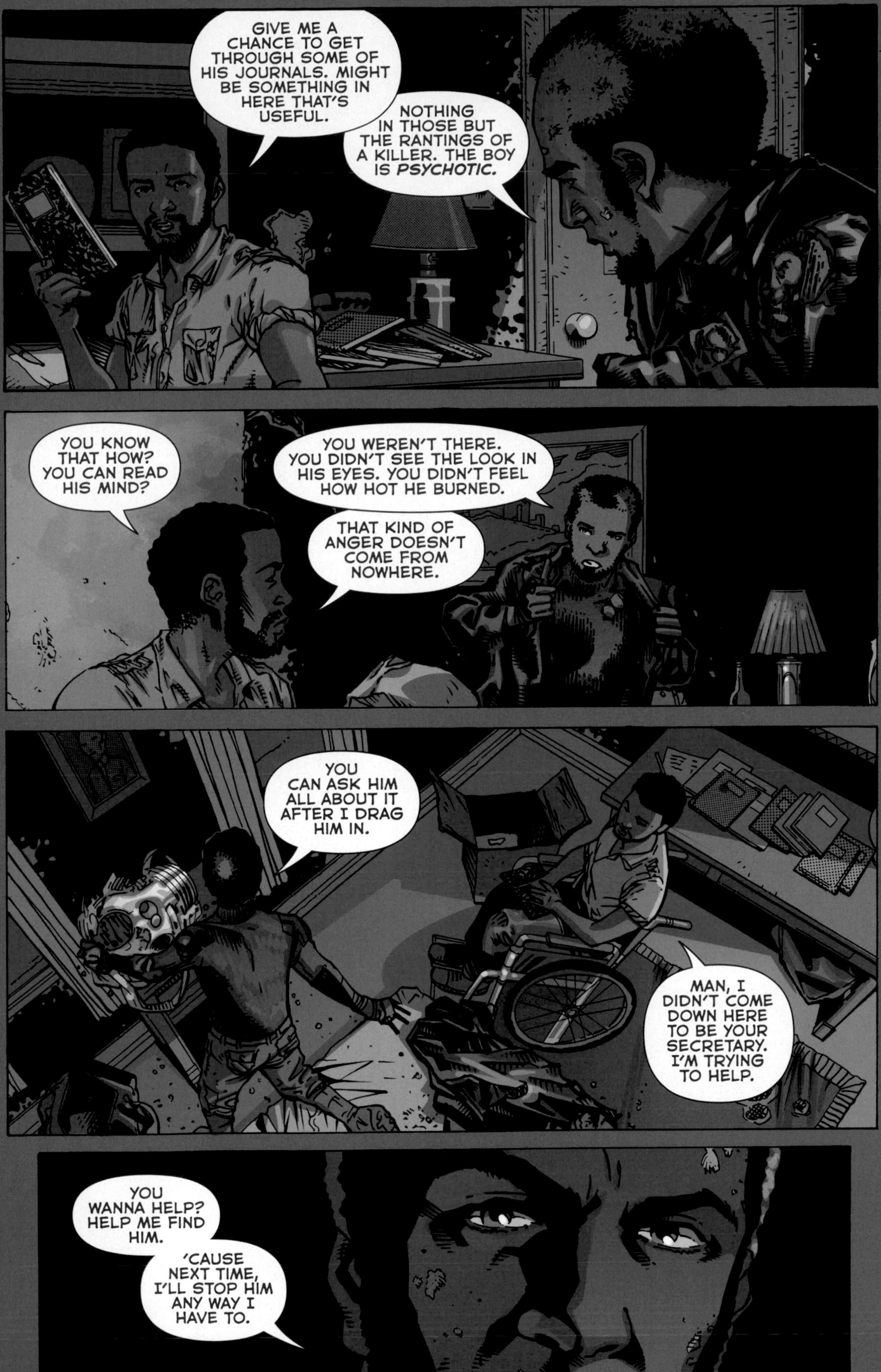
GIVE ME A CHANCE TO GET THROUGH SOME OF HIS JOURNALS. MIGHT BE SOMETHING IN HERE THAT'S USEFUL.
NOTHING IN THOSE BUT THE RANTINGS OF A KILLER. THE BOY IS *PSYCHOTIC.*
YOU KNOW THAT HOW? YOU CAN READ HIS MIND?
YOU WEREN'T THERE. YOU DIDN'T SEE THE LOOK IN HIS EYES. YOU DIDN'T FEEL HOW HOT HE BURNED.
THAT KIND OF ANGER DOESN'T COME FROM NOWHERE.
YOU CAN ASK HIM ALL ABOUT IT AFTER I DRAG HIM IN.
MAN, I DIDN'T COME DOWN HERE TO BE YOUR SECRETARY. I'M TRYING TO HELP.
YOU WANNA HELP? HELP ME FIND HIM.
'CAUSE NEXT TIME, I'LL STOP HIM ANY WAY I HAVE TO.

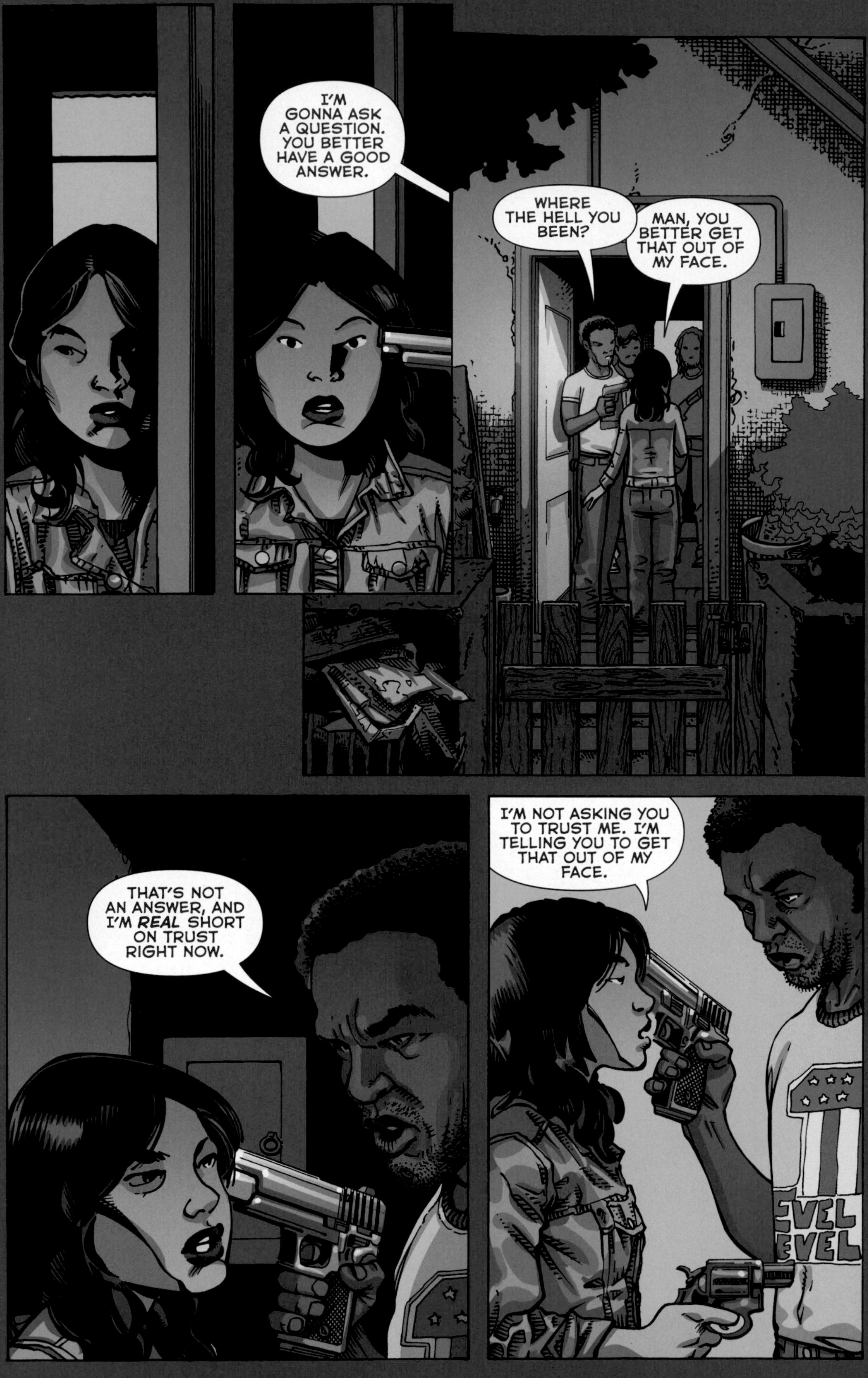
I'M GONNA ASK A QUESTION. YOU BETTER HAVE A GOOD ANSWER.
WHERE THE HELL YOU BEEN?
MAN, YOU BETTER GET THAT OUT OF MY FACE.
THAT'S NOT AN ANSWER, AND I'M *REAL* SHORT ON TRUST RIGHT NOW.
I'M NOT ASKING YOU TO TRUST ME. I'M TELLING YOU TO GET THAT OUT OF MY FACE.
EVEL
EVEL

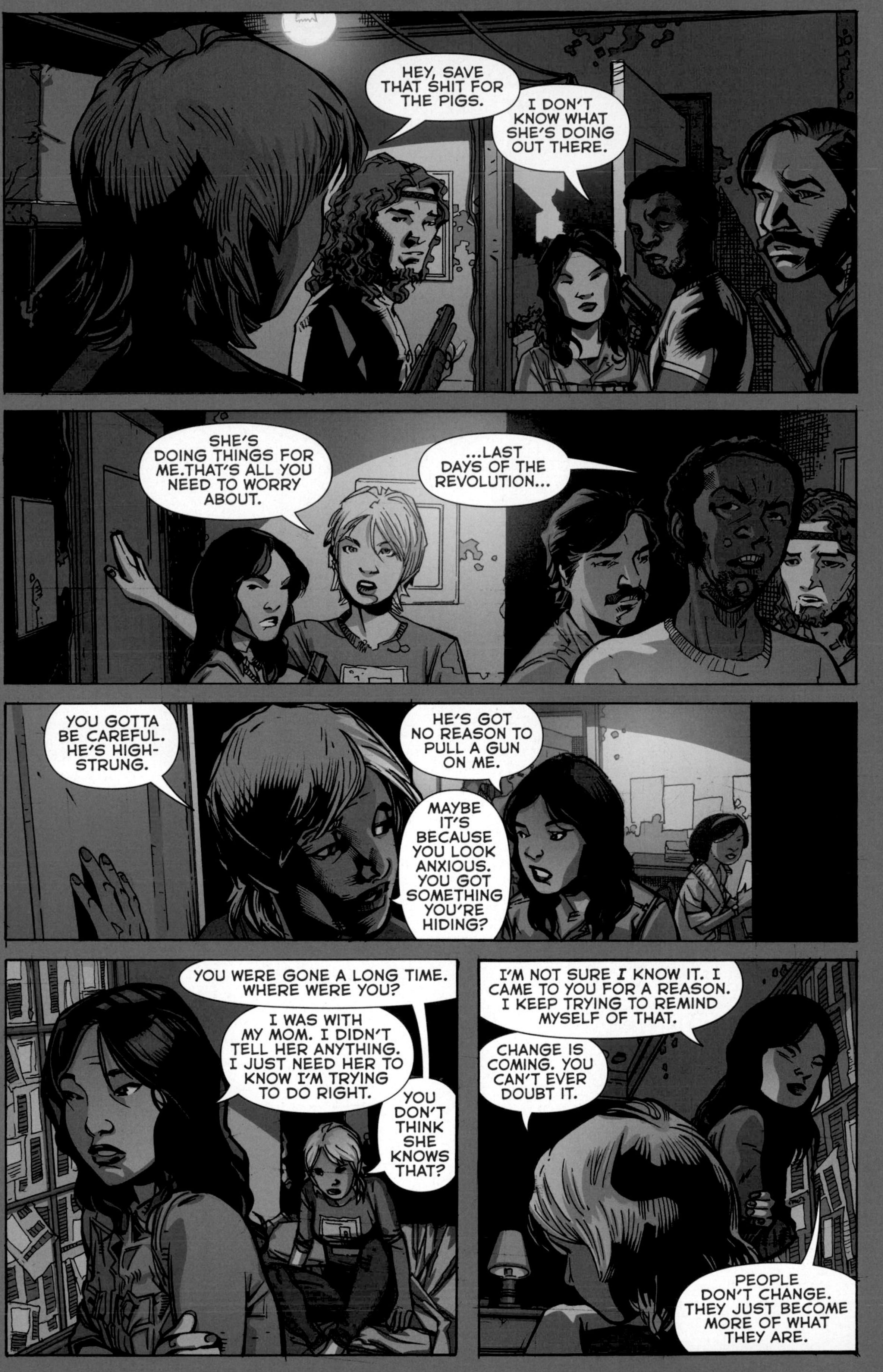
HEY, SAVE THAT SHIT FOR THE PIGS.
I DON'T KNOW WHAT SHE'S DOING OUT THERE.
SHE'S DOING THINGS FOR ME. THAT'S ALL YOU NEED TO WORRY ABOUT.
...LAST DAYS OF THE REVOLUTION...
YOU GOTTA BE CAREFUL. HE'S HIGH-STRUNG.
HE'S GOT NO REASON TO PULL A GUN ON ME.
MAYBE IT'S BECAUSE YOU LOOK ANXIOUS. YOU GOT SOMETHING YOU'RE HIDING?
YOU WERE GONE A LONG TIME. WHERE WERE YOU?
I WAS WITH MY MOM. I DIDN'T TELL HER ANYTHING. I JUST NEED HER TO KNOW I'M TRYING TO DO RIGHT.
YOU DON'T THINK SHE KNOWS THAT?
I'M NOT SURE *I* KNOW IT. I CAME TO YOU FOR A REASON. I KEEP TRYING TO REMIND MYSELF OF THAT.
CHANGE IS COMING. YOU CAN'T EVER DOUBT IT.
PEOPLE DON'T CHANGE. THEY JUST BECOME MORE OF WHAT THEY ARE.

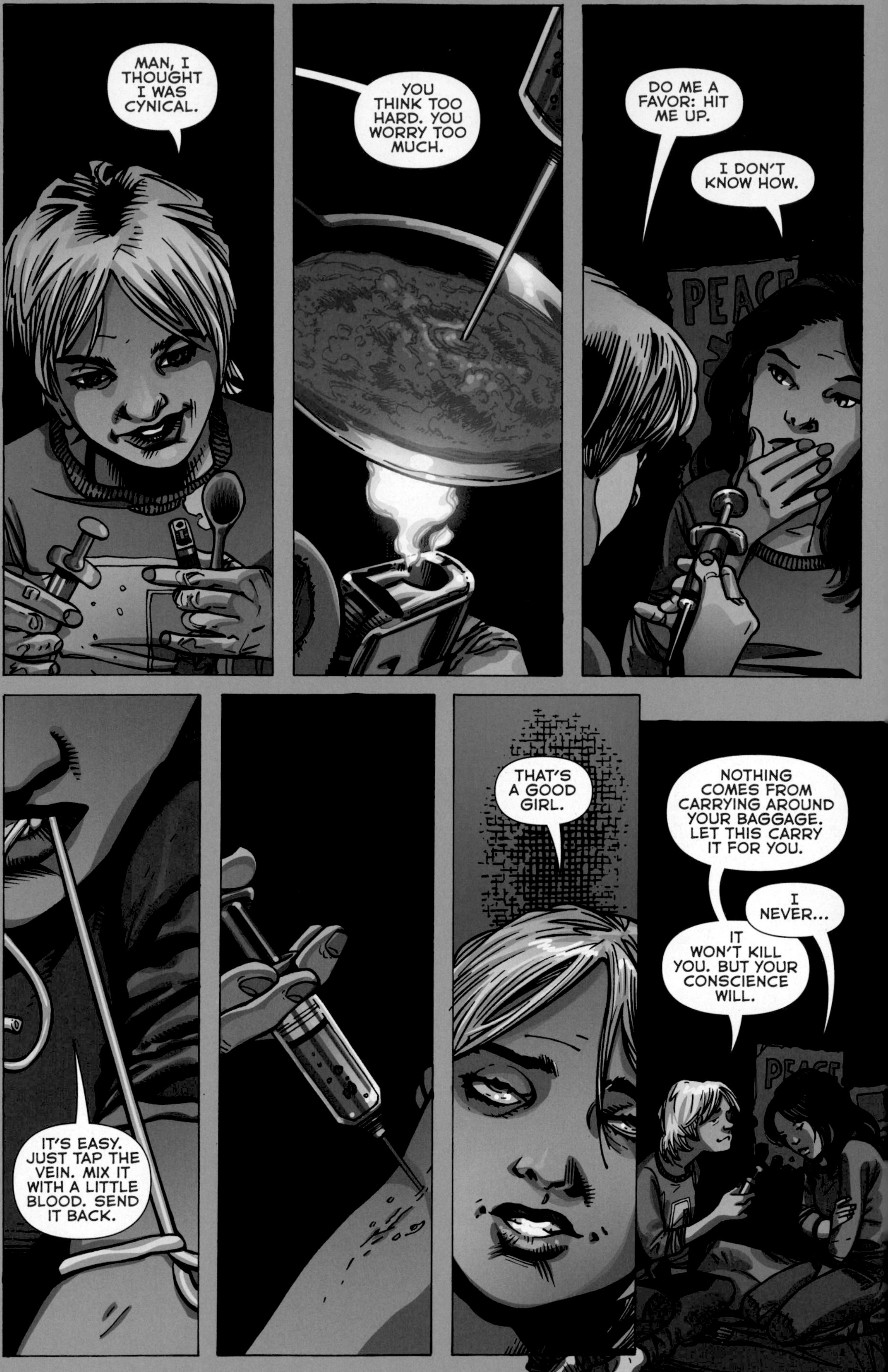
MAN, I THOUGHT I WAS CYNICAL.
YOU THINK TOO HARD. YOU WORRY TOO MUCH.
DO ME A FAVOR: HIT ME UP.
I DON'T KNOW HOW.
PEACE
IT'S EASY. JUST TAP THE VEIN. MIX IT WITH A LITTLE BLOOD. SEND IT BACK.
THAT'S A GOOD GIRL.
NOTHING COMES FROM CARRYING AROUND YOUR BAGGAGE. LET THIS CARRY IT FOR YOU.
I NEVER...
IT WON'T KILL YOU. BUT YOUR CONSCIENCE WILL.

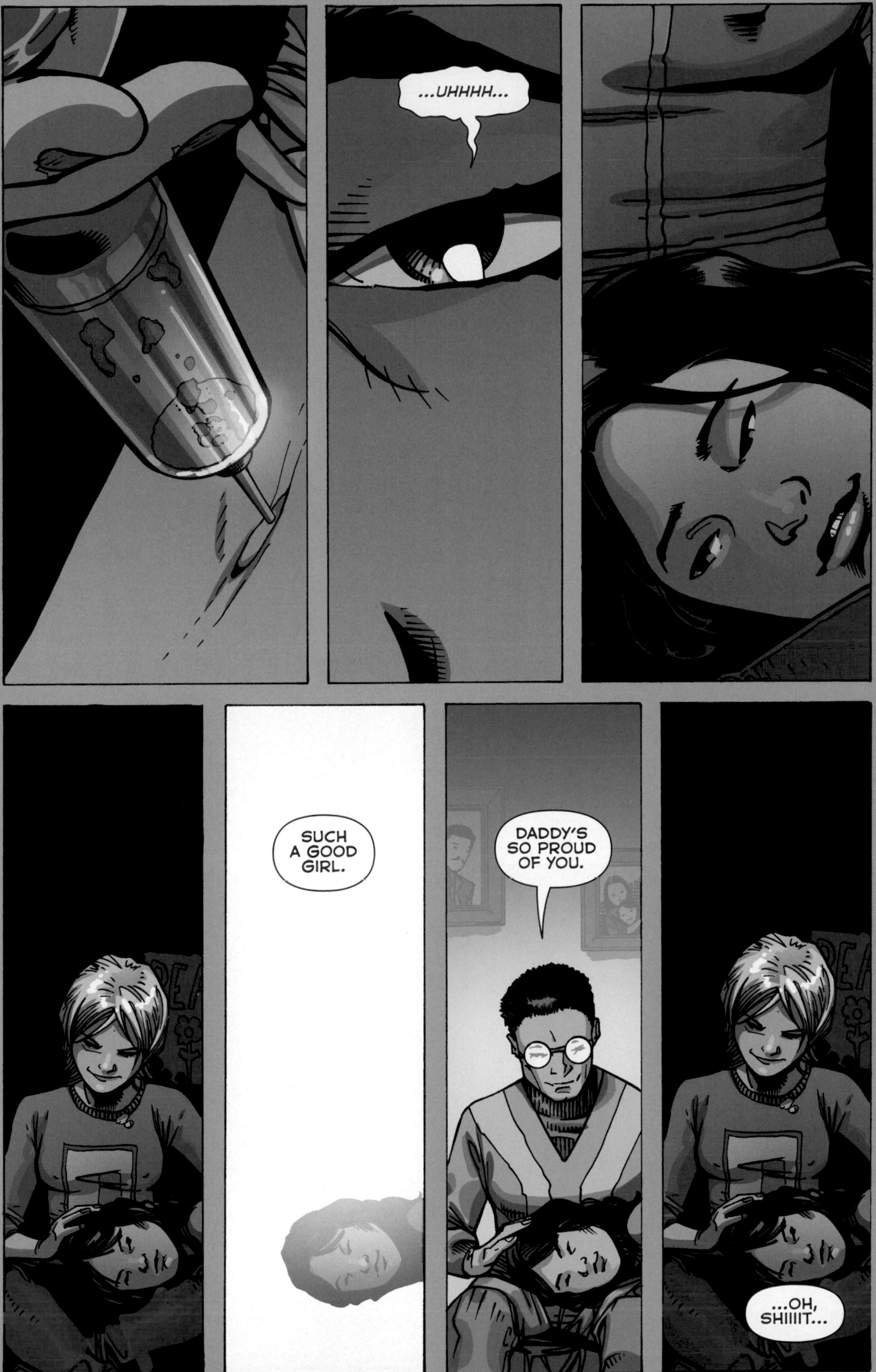
...UHHHH...
SUCH A GOOD GIRL.
DADDY'S SO PROUD OF YOU.
...OH, SHIIIIT...

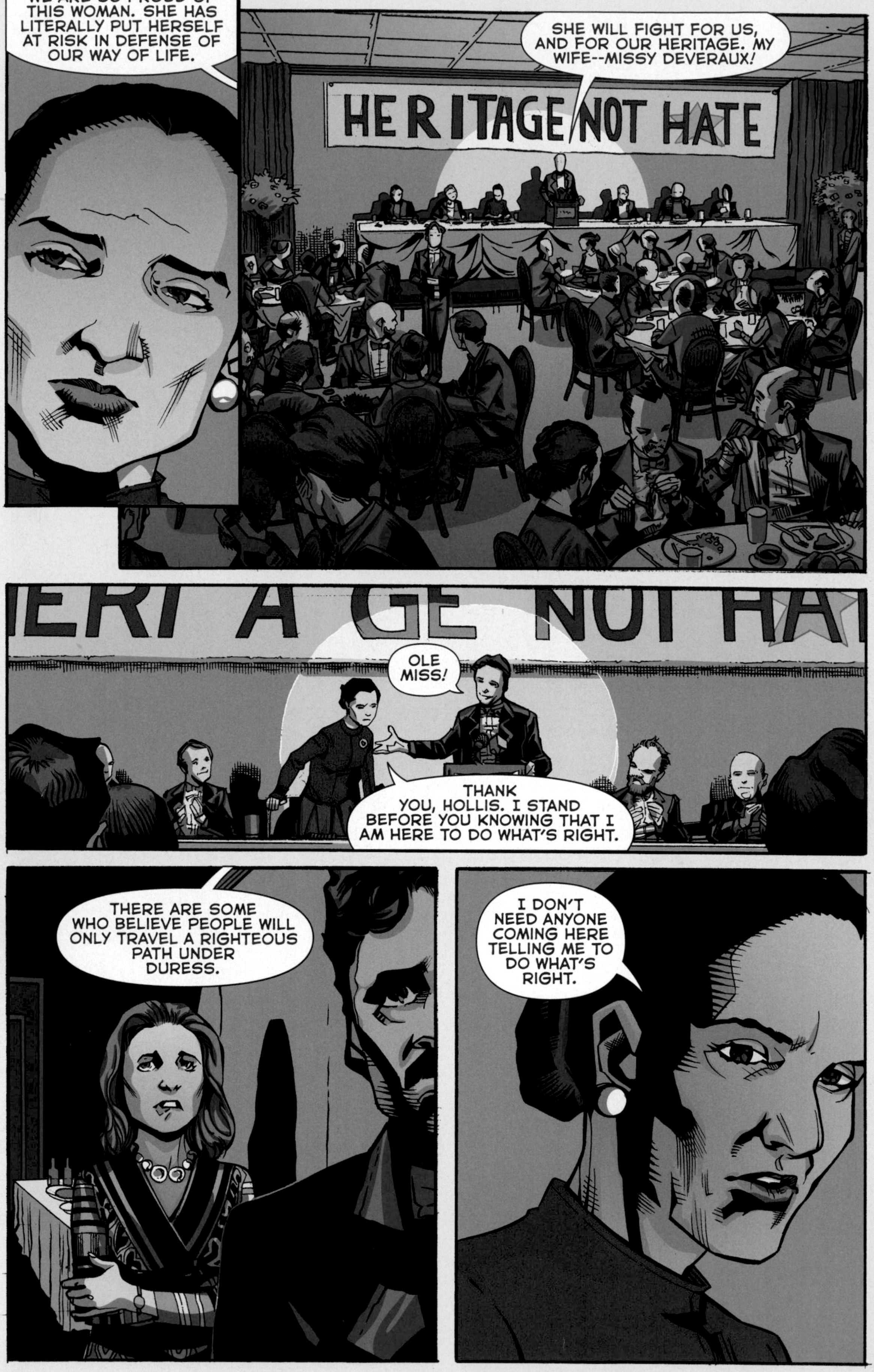
WE ARE SO PROUD OF THIS WOMAN. SHE HAS LITERALLY PUT HERSELF AT RISK IN DEFENSE OF OUR WAY OF LIFE.
SHE WILL FIGHT FOR US, AND FOR OUR HERITAGE. MY WIFE--MISSY DEVERAUX!
HERITAGE NOT HATE
OLE MISS!
THANK YOU, HOLLIS. I STAND BEFORE YOU KNOWING THAT I AM HERE TO DO WHAT'S RIGHT.
THERE ARE SOME WHO BELIEVE PEOPLE WILL ONLY TRAVEL A RIGHTEOUS PATH UNDER DURESS.
I DON'T NEED ANYONE COMING HERE TELLING ME TO DO WHAT'S RIGHT.

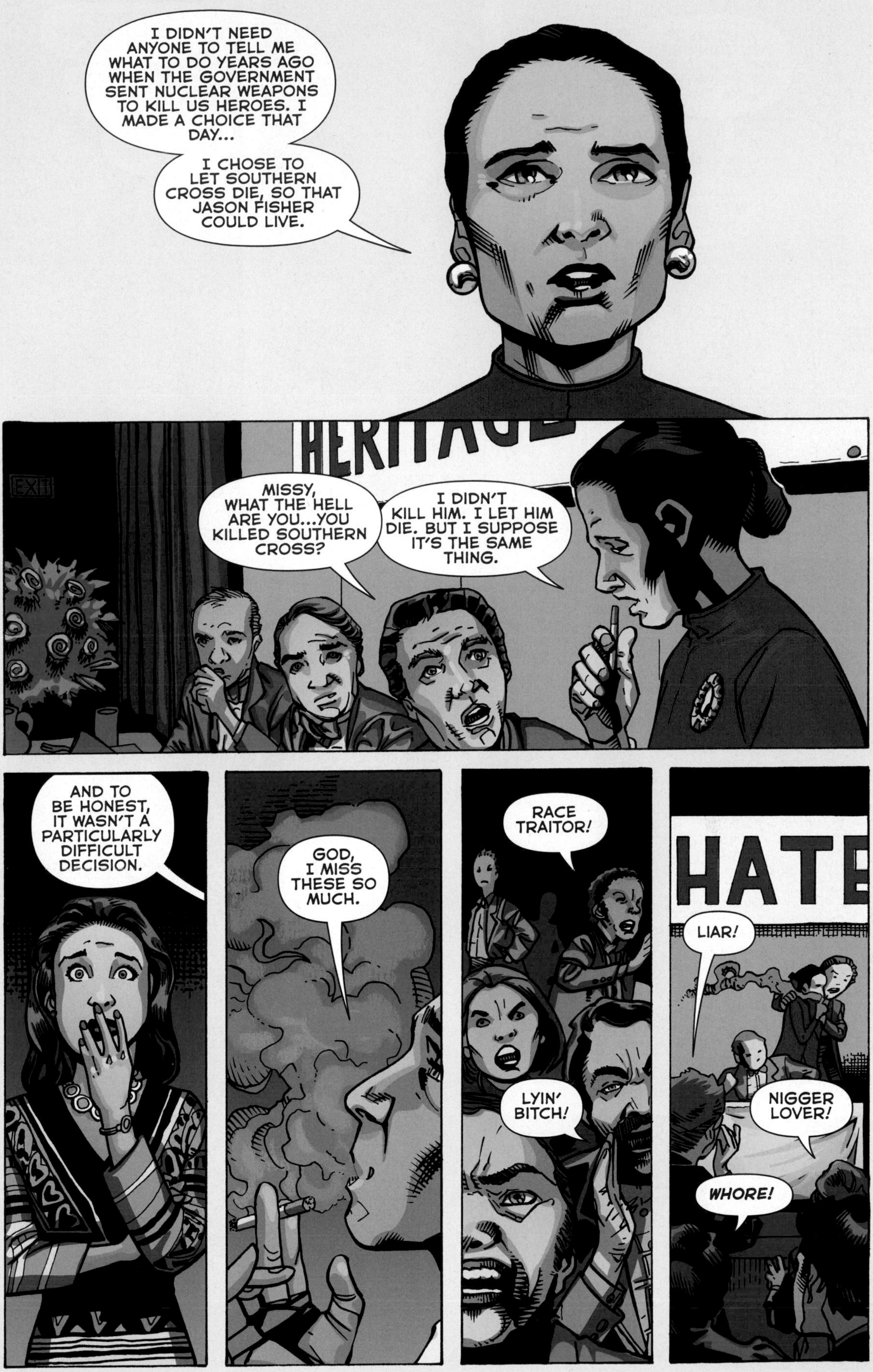
I DIDN'T NEED ANYONE TO TELL ME WHAT TO DO YEARS AGO WHEN THE GOVERNMENT SENT NUCLEAR WEAPONS TO KILL US HEROES. I MADE A CHOICE THAT DAY...
I CHOSE TO LET SOUTHERN CROSS DIE, SO THAT JASON FISHER COULD LIVE.
HERITAGE
EXIT
MISSY, WHAT THE HELL ARE YOU...YOU KILLED SOUTHERN CROSS?
I DIDN'T KILL HIM. I LET HIM DIE. BUT I SUPPOSE IT'S THE SAME THING.
AND TO BE HONEST, IT WASN'T A PARTICULARLY DIFFICULT DECISION.
GOD, I MISS THESE SO MUCH.
RACE TRAITOR!
LYIN' BITCH!
HATE
LIAR!
NIGGER LOVER!
WHORE!

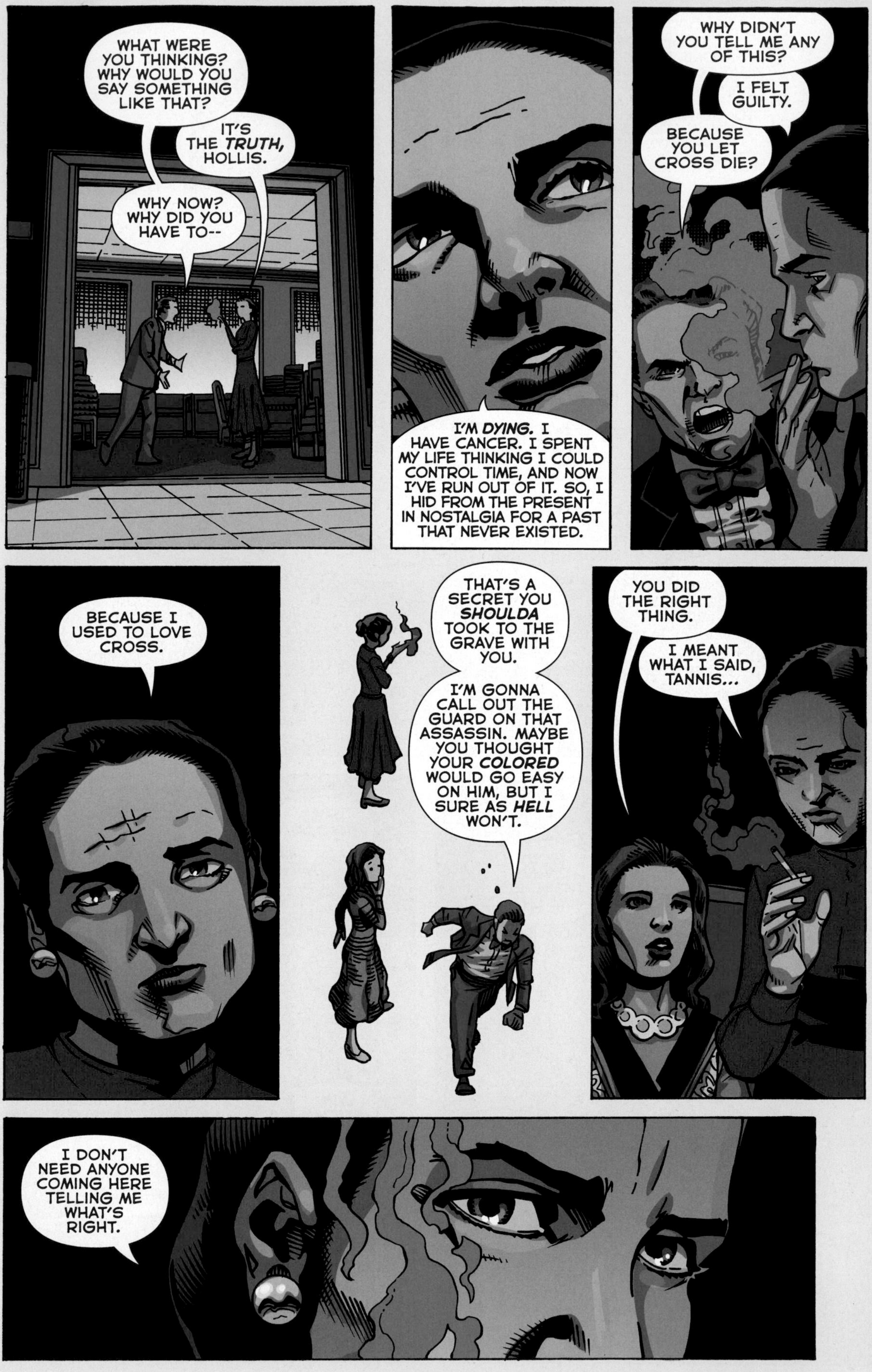
WHAT WERE YOU THINKING? WHY WOULD YOU SAY SOMETHING LIKE THAT?
IT'S THE *TRUTH,* HOLLIS.
WHY NOW? WHY DID YOU HAVE TO--
I'M *DYING.* I HAVE CANCER. I SPENT MY LIFE THINKING I COULD CONTROL TIME, AND NOW I'VE RUN OUT OF IT. SO, I HID FROM THE PRESENT IN NOSTALGIA FOR A PAST THAT NEVER EXISTED.
WHY DIDN'T YOU TELL ME ANY OF THIS?
I FELT GUILTY.
BECAUSE YOU LET CROSS DIE?
BECAUSE I USED TO LOVE CROSS.
THAT'S A SECRET YOU *SHOULDA* TOOK TO THE GRAVE WITH YOU.
I'M GONNA CALL OUT THE GUARD ON THAT ASSASSIN. MAYBE YOU THOUGHT YOUR *COLORED* WOULD GO EASY ON HIM, BUT I SURE AS *HELL* WON'T.
YOU DID THE RIGHT THING.
I MEANT WHAT I SAID, TANNIS...
I DON'T NEED ANYONE COMING HERE TELLING ME WHAT'S RIGHT.

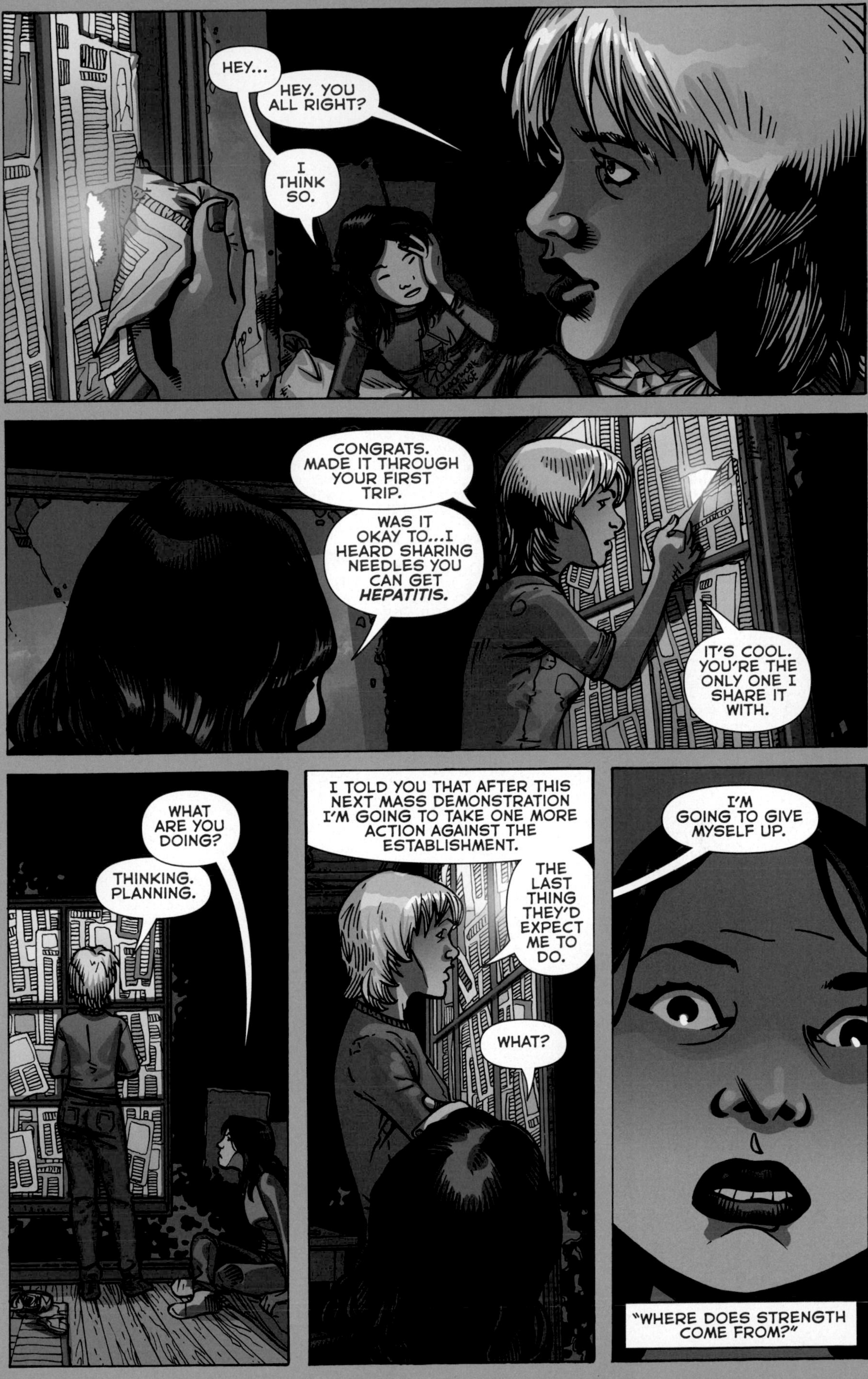
HEY...
HEY. YOU ALL RIGHT?
I THINK SO.
CONGRATS. MADE IT THROUGH YOUR FIRST TRIP.
WAS IT OKAY TO...I HEARD SHARING NEEDLES YOU CAN GET *HEPATITIS.*
IT'S COOL. YOU'RE THE ONLY ONE I SHARE IT WITH.
WHAT ARE YOU DOING?
THINKING. PLANNING.
I TOLD YOU THAT AFTER THIS NEXT MASS DEMONSTRATION I'M GOING TO TAKE ONE MORE ACTION AGAINST THE ESTABLISHMENT.
THE LAST THING THEY'D EXPECT ME TO DO.
WHAT?
I'M GOING TO GIVE MYSELF UP.
"WHERE DOES STRENGTH COME FROM?"

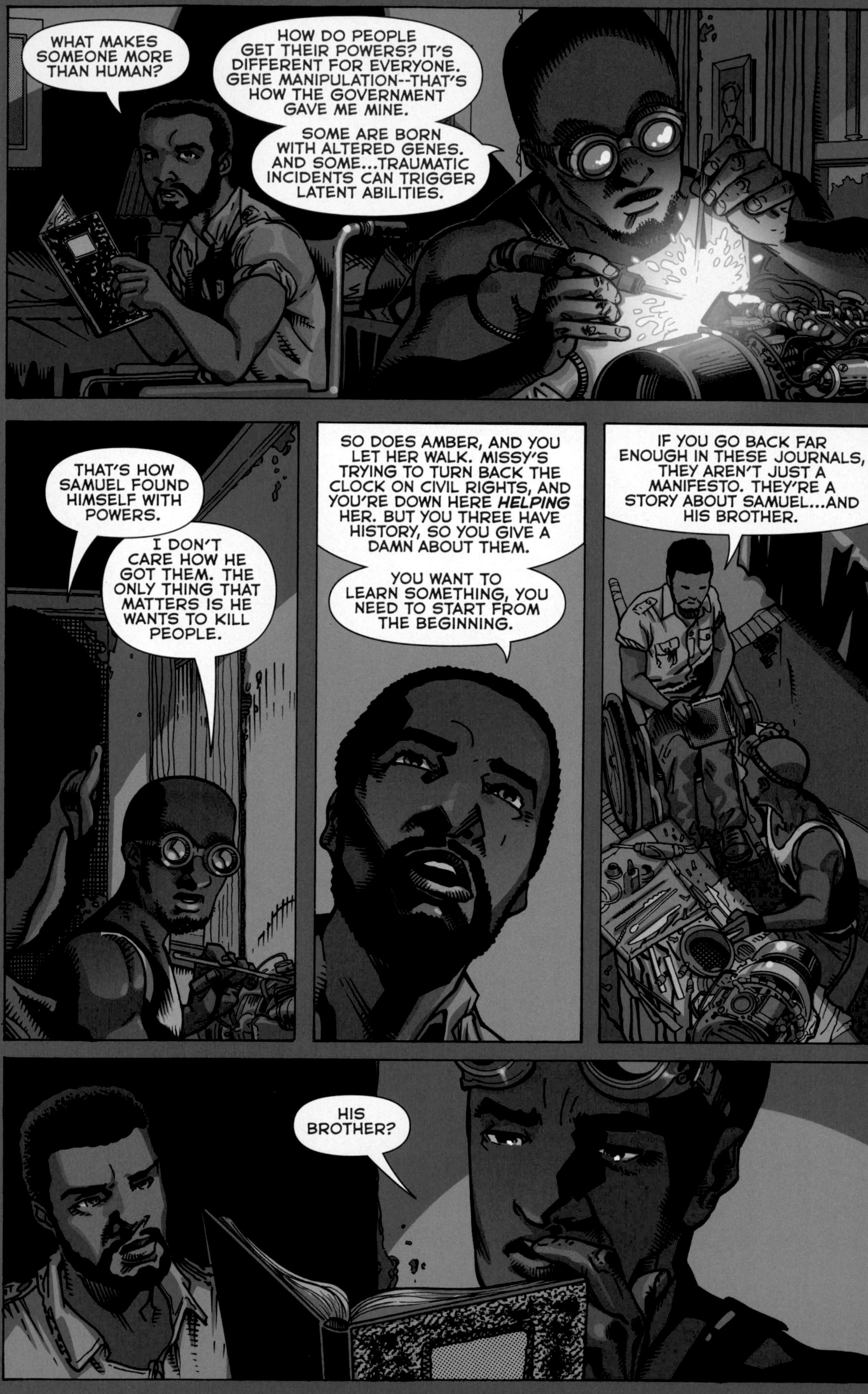
WHAT MAKES SOMEONE MORE THAN HUMAN?
HOW DO PEOPLE GET THEIR POWERS? IT'S DIFFERENT FOR EVERYONE. GENE MANIPULATION--THAT'S HOW THE GOVERNMENT GAVE ME MINE.
SOME ARE BORN WITH ALTERED GENES. AND SOME...TRAUMATIC INCIDENTS CAN TRIGGER LATENT ABILITIES.
THAT'S HOW SAMUEL FOUND HIMSELF WITH POWERS.
I DON'T CARE HOW HE GOT THEM. THE ONLY THING THAT MATTERS IS HE WANTS TO KILL PEOPLE.
SO DOES AMBER, AND YOU LET HER WALK. MISSY'S TRYING TO TURN BACK THE CLOCK ON CIVIL RIGHTS, AND YOU'RE DOWN HERE *HELPING* HER. BUT YOU THREE HAVE HISTORY, SO YOU GIVE A DAMN ABOUT THEM.
YOU WANT TO LEARN SOMETHING, YOU NEED TO START FROM THE BEGINNING.
IF YOU GO BACK FAR ENOUGH IN THESE JOURNALS, THEY AREN'T JUST A MANIFESTO. THEY'RE A STORY ABOUT SAMUEL...AND HIS BROTHER.
HIS BROTHER?

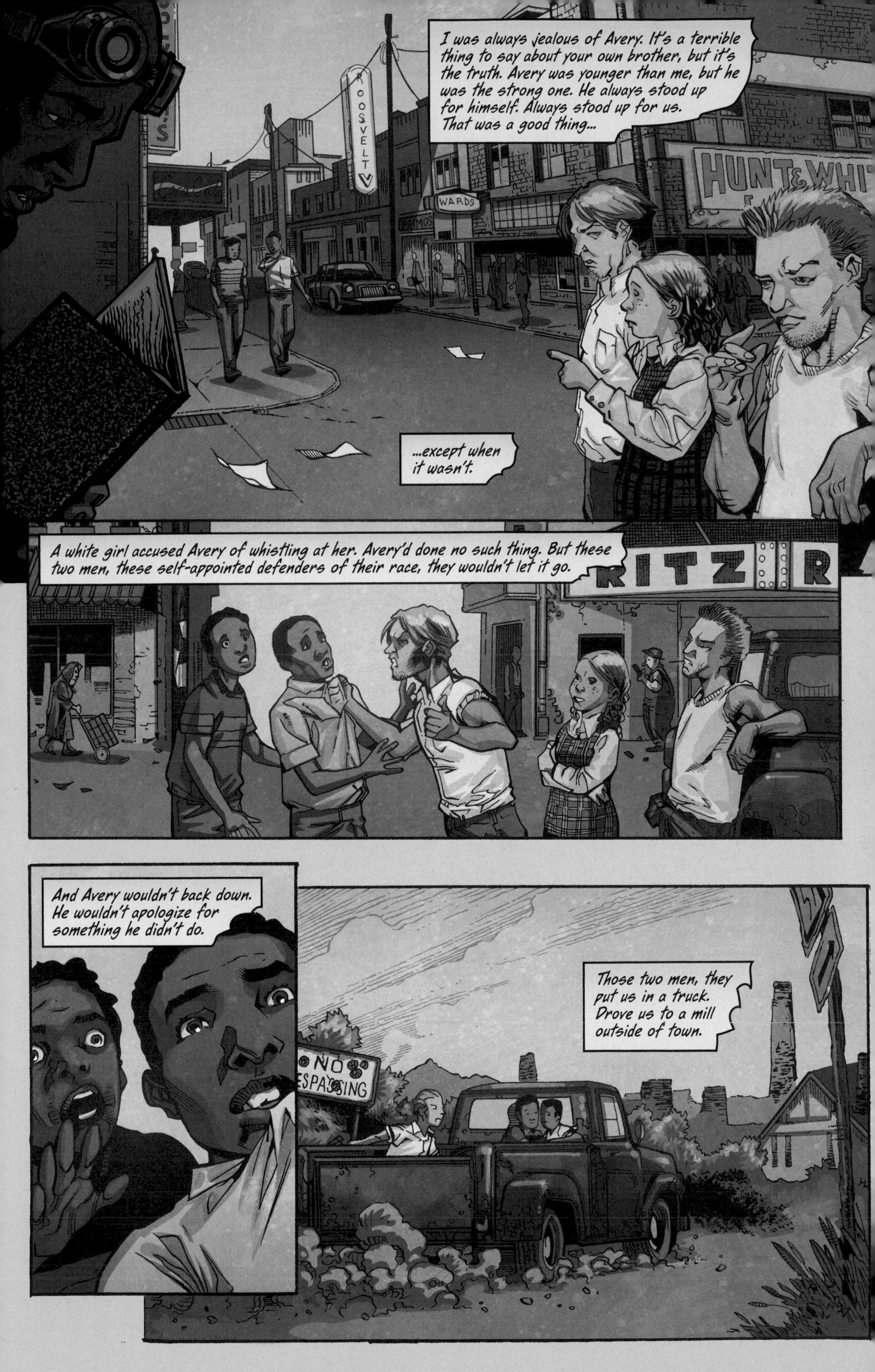
I was always jealous of Avery. It's a terrible thing to say about your own brother, but it's the truth. Avery was younger than me, but he was the strong one. He always stood up for himself. Always stood up for us. That was a good thing...
ROOSVELT
WARDS
HUNT&WHIT
...except when it wasn't.
A white girl accused Avery of whistling at her. Avery'd done no such thing. But these two men, these self-appointed defenders of their race, they wouldn't let it go.
RITZ
And Avery wouldn't back down. He wouldn't apologize for something he didn't do.
Those two men, they put us in a truck. Drove us to a mill outside of town.
NO

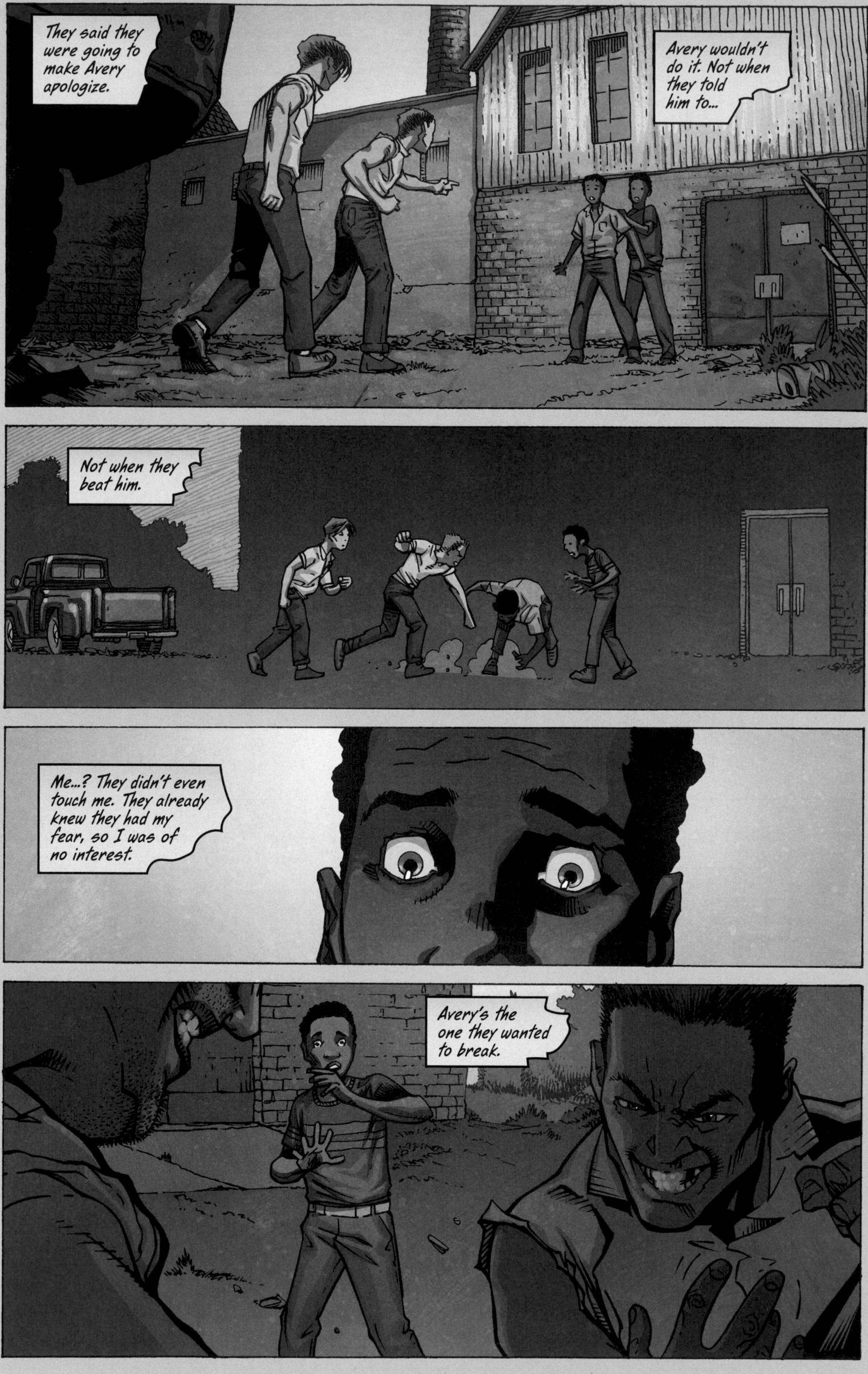
They said they were going to make Avery apologize.
Avery wouldn't do it. Not when they told him to...
Not when they beat him.
Me...? They didn't even touch me. They already knew they had my fear, so I was of no interest.
Avery's the one they wanted to break.

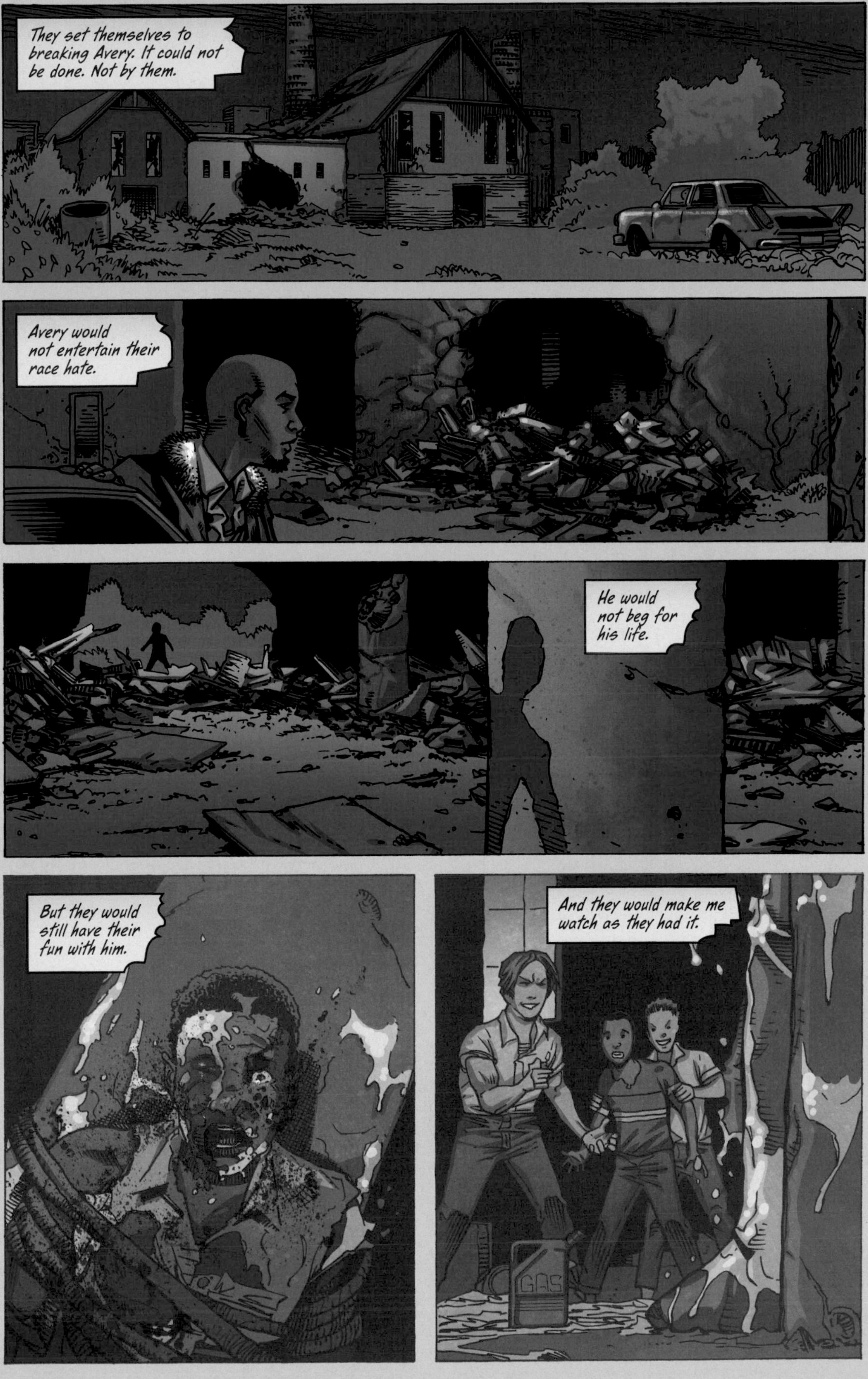
They set themselves to breaking Avery. It could not be done. Not by them.
Avery would not entertain their race hate.
He would not beg for his life.
But they would still have their fun with him.
And they would make me watch as they had it.
GAS

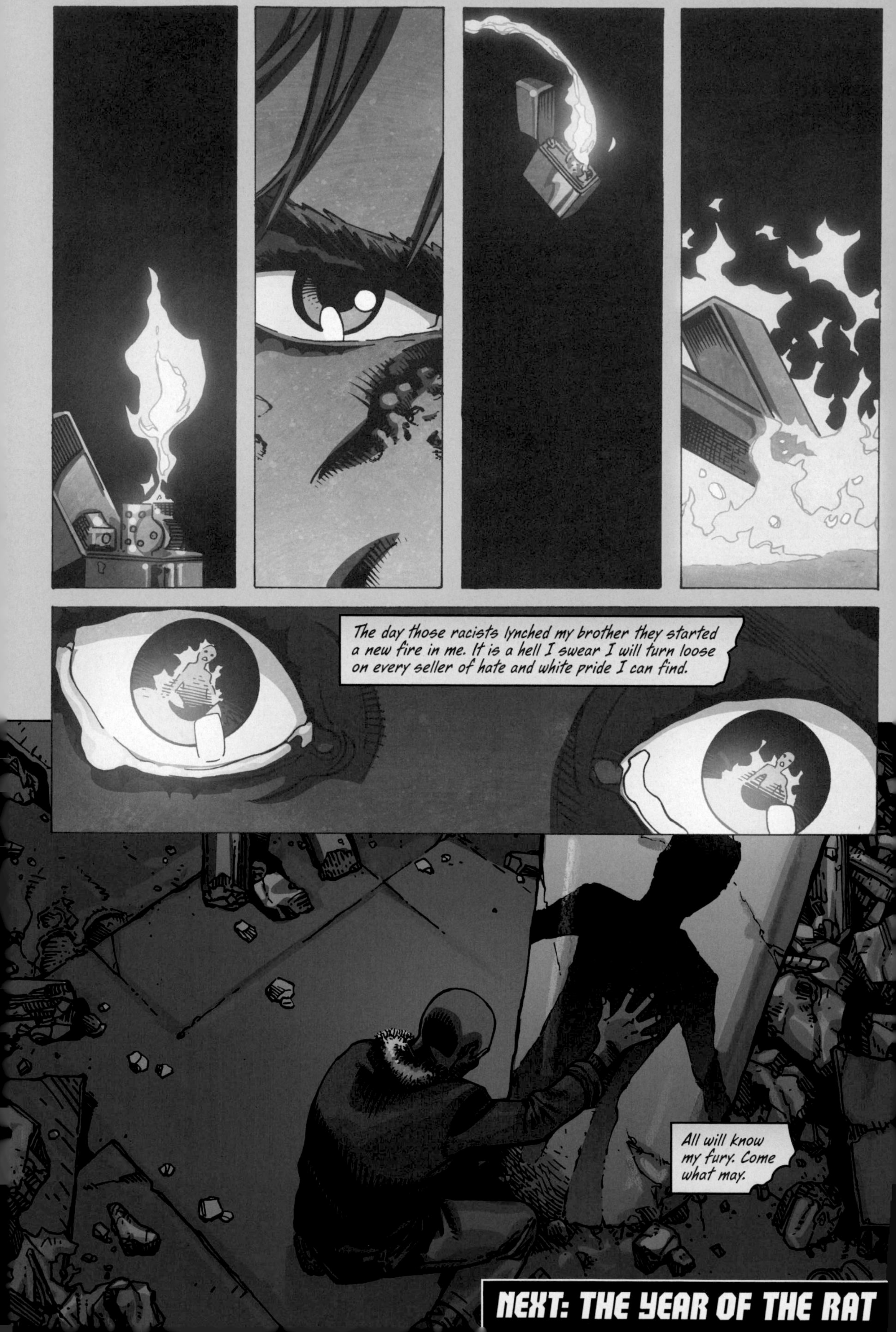

The day those racists lynched my brother they started a new fire in me. It is a hell I swear I will turn loose on every seller of hate and white pride I can find.
All will know my fury. Come what may.
NEXT: THE YEAR OF THE RAT

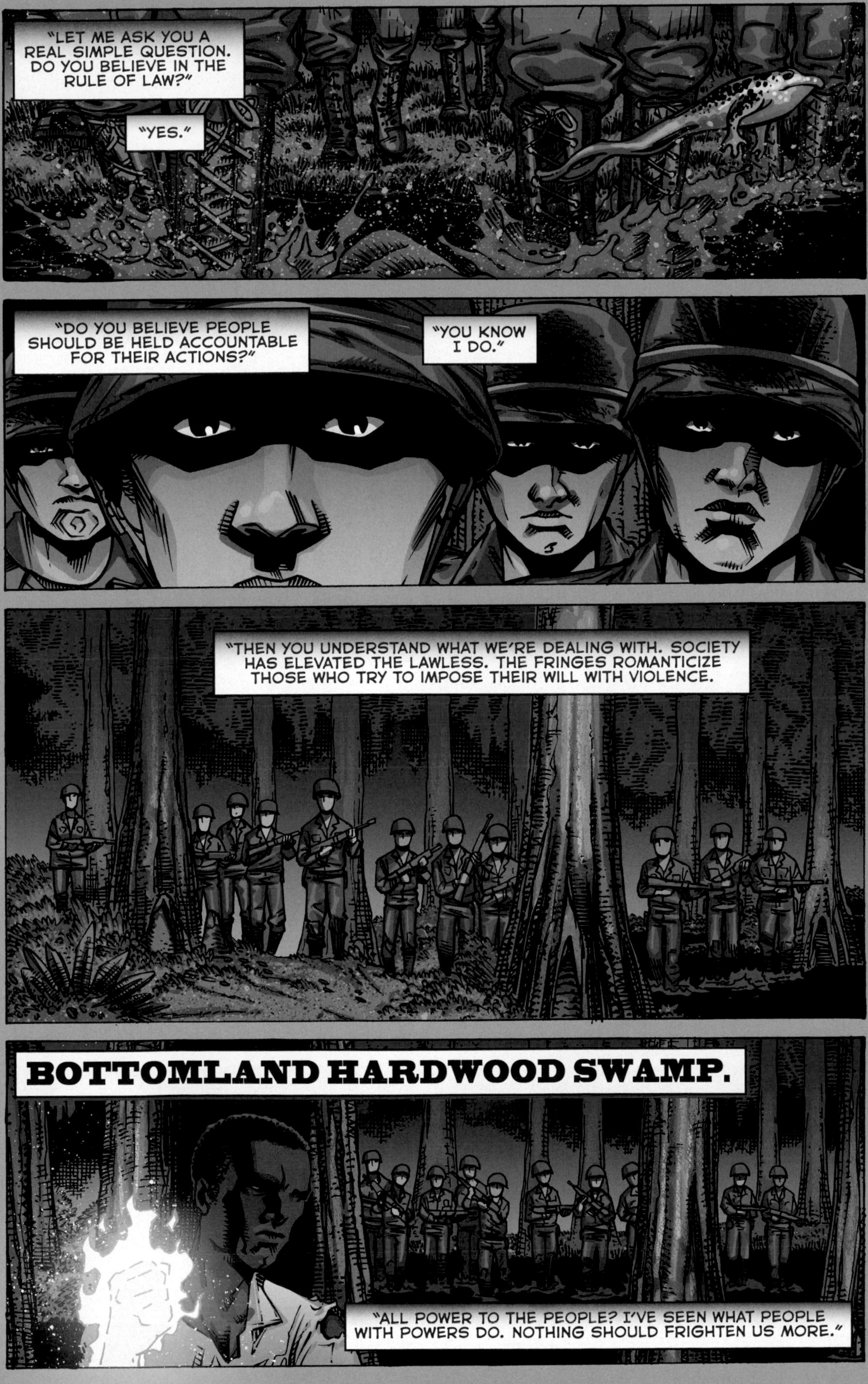
"LET ME ASK YOU A REAL SIMPLE QUESTION. DO YOU BELIEVE IN THE RULE OF LAW?"
"YES."
"DO YOU BELIEVE PEOPLE SHOULD BE HELD ACCOUNTABLE FOR THEIR ACTIONS?"
"YOU KNOW I DO."
"THEN YOU UNDERSTAND WHAT WE'RE DEALING WITH. SOCIETY HAS ELEVATED THE LAWLESS. THE FRINGES ROMANTICIZE THOSE WHO TRY TO IMPOSE THEIR WILL WITH VIOLENCE.
BOTTOMLAND HARDWOOD SWAMP.
"ALL POWER TO THE PEOPLE? I'VE SEEN WHAT PEOPLE WITH POWERS DO. NOTHING SHOULD FRIGHTEN US MORE."

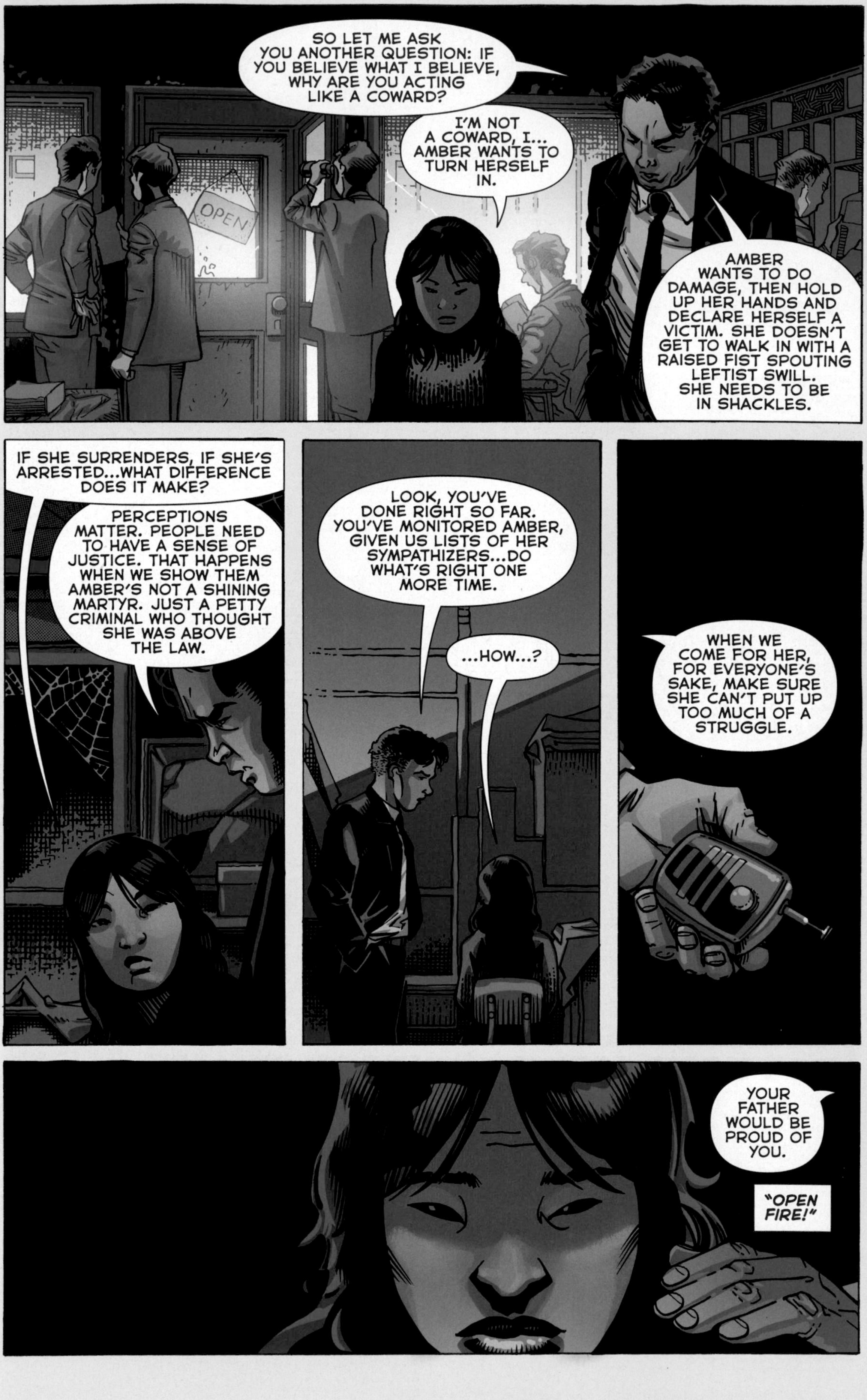
SO LET ME ASK YOU ANOTHER QUESTION: IF YOU BELIEVE WHAT I BELIEVE, WHY ARE YOU ACTING LIKE A COWARD?
I'M NOT A COWARD, I... AMBER WANTS TO TURN HERSELF IN.
OPEN
AMBER WANTS TO DO DAMAGE, THEN HOLD UP HER HANDS AND DECLARE HERSELF A VICTIM. SHE DOESN'T GET TO WALK IN WITH A RAISED FIST SPOUTING LEFTIST SWILL. SHE NEEDS TO BE IN SHACKLES.
IF SHE SURRENDERS, IF SHE'S ARRESTED...WHAT DIFFERENCE DOES IT MAKE?
PERCEPTIONS MATTER. PEOPLE NEED TO HAVE A SENSE OF JUSTICE. THAT HAPPENS WHEN WE SHOW THEM AMBER'S NOT A SHINING MARTYR. JUST A PETTY CRIMINAL WHO THOUGHT SHE WAS ABOVE THE LAW.
LOOK, YOU'VE DONE RIGHT SO FAR. YOU'VE MONITORED AMBER, GIVEN US LISTS OF HER SYMPATHIZERS...DO WHAT'S RIGHT ONE MORE TIME.
...HOW...?
WHEN WE COME FOR HER, FOR EVERYONE'S SAKE, MAKE SURE SHE CAN'T PUT UP TOO MUCH OF A STRUGGLE.
YOUR FATHER WOULD BE PROUD OF YOU.
"OPEN FIRE!"

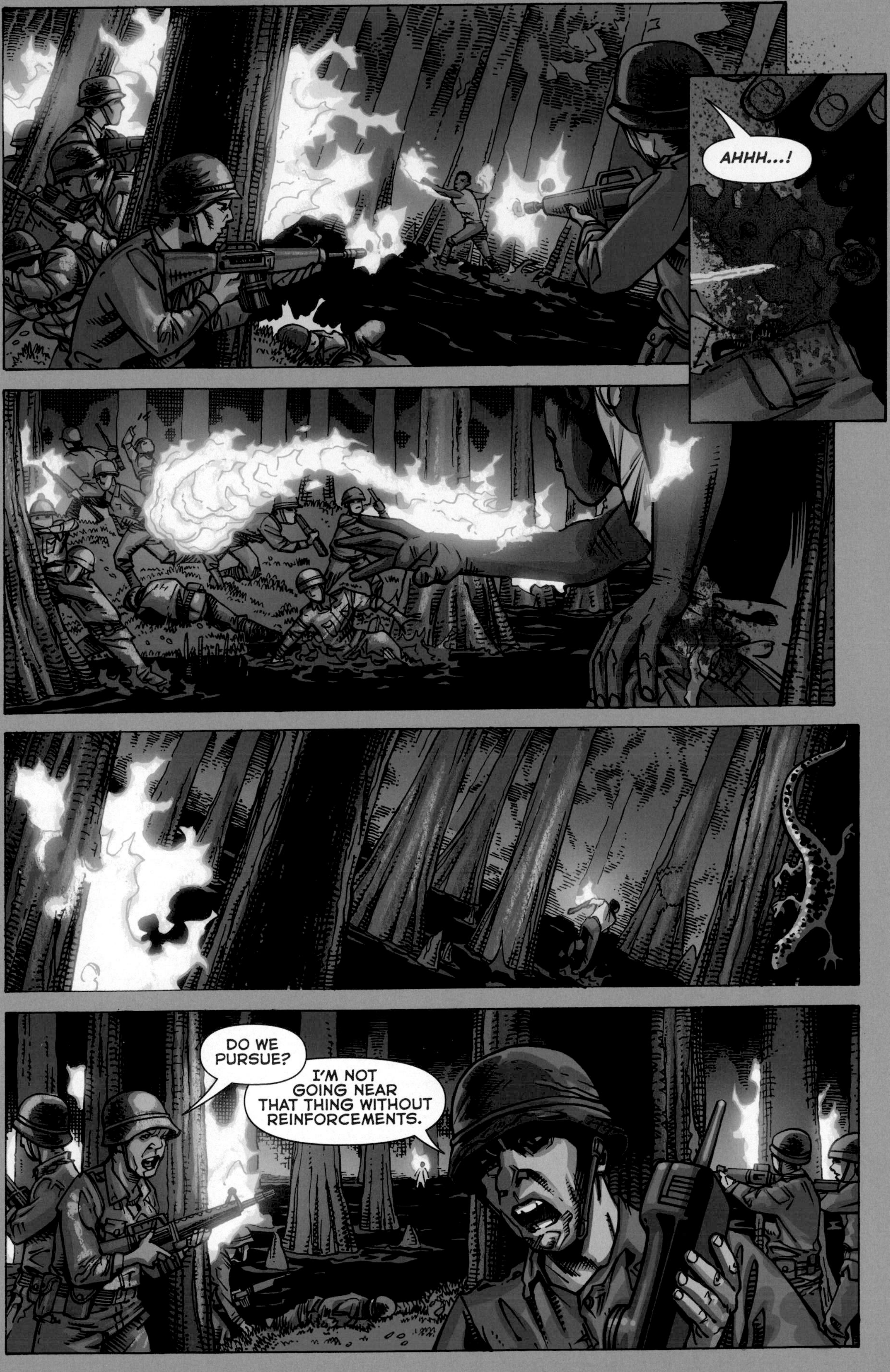
AHHH...!
DO WE PURSUE?
I'M NOT GOING NEAR THAT THING WITHOUT REINFORCEMENTS.

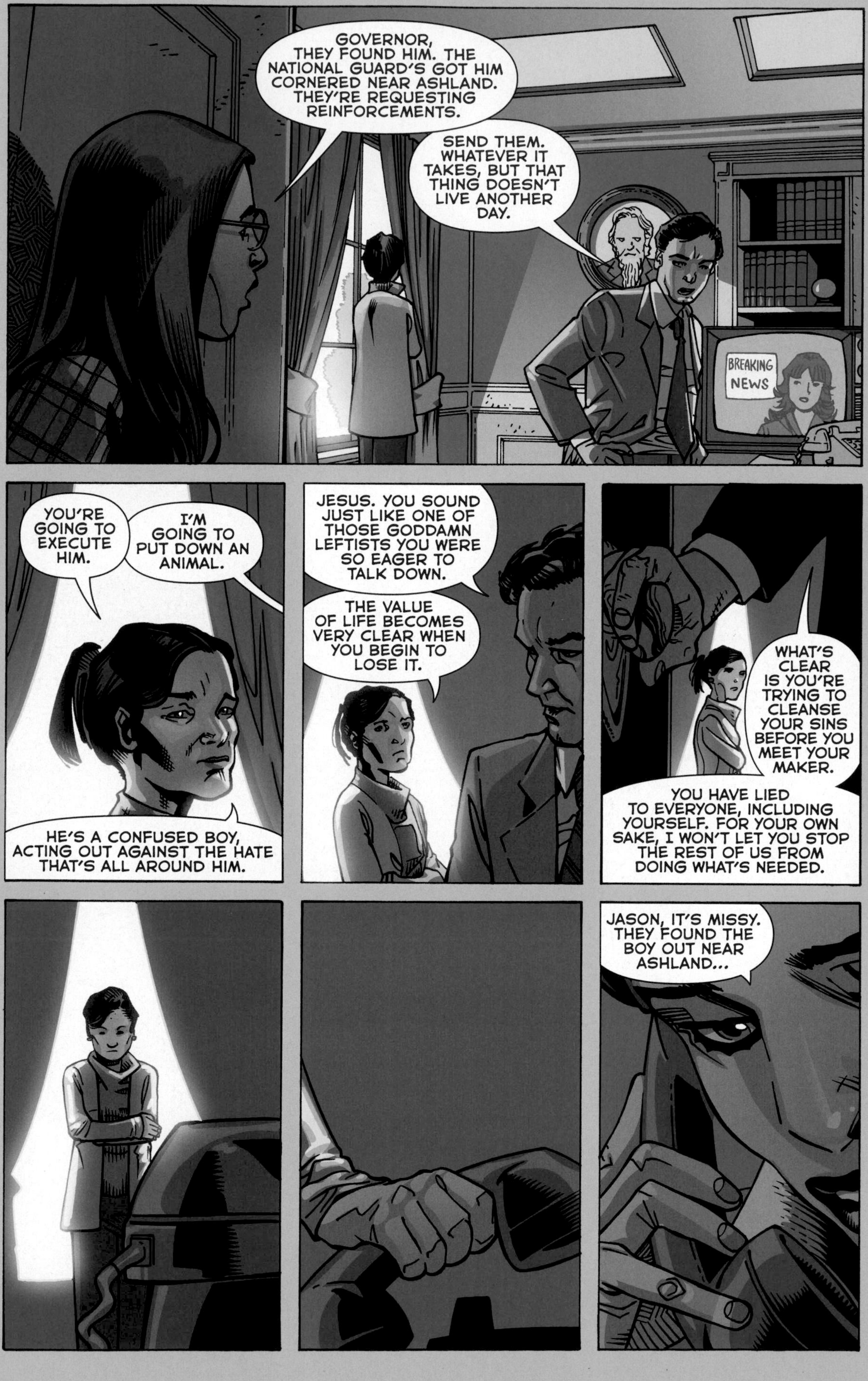
GOVERNOR, THEY FOUND HIM. THE NATIONAL GUARD'S GOT HIM CORNERED NEAR ASHLAND. THEY'RE REQUESTING REINFORCEMENTS.
SEND THEM. WHATEVER IT TAKES, BUT THAT THING DOESN'T LIVE ANOTHER DAY.
BREAKING NEWS
YOU'RE GOING TO EXECUTE HIM.
I'M GOING TO PUT DOWN AN ANIMAL.
HE'S A CONFUSED BOY, ACTING OUT AGAINST THE HATE THAT'S ALL AROUND HIM.
JESUS. YOU SOUND JUST LIKE ONE OF THOSE GODDAMN LEFTISTS YOU WERE SO EAGER TO TALK DOWN.
THE VALUE OF LIFE BECOMES VERY CLEAR WHEN YOU BEGIN TO LOSE IT.
WHAT'S CLEAR IS YOU'RE TRYING TO CLEANSE YOUR SINS BEFORE YOU MEET YOUR MAKER.
YOU HAVE LIED TO EVERYONE, INCLUDING YOURSELF. FOR YOUR OWN SAKE, I WON'T LET YOU STOP THE REST OF US FROM DOING WHAT'S NEEDED.
JASON, IT'S MISSY. THEY FOUND THE BOY OUT NEAR ASHLAND...

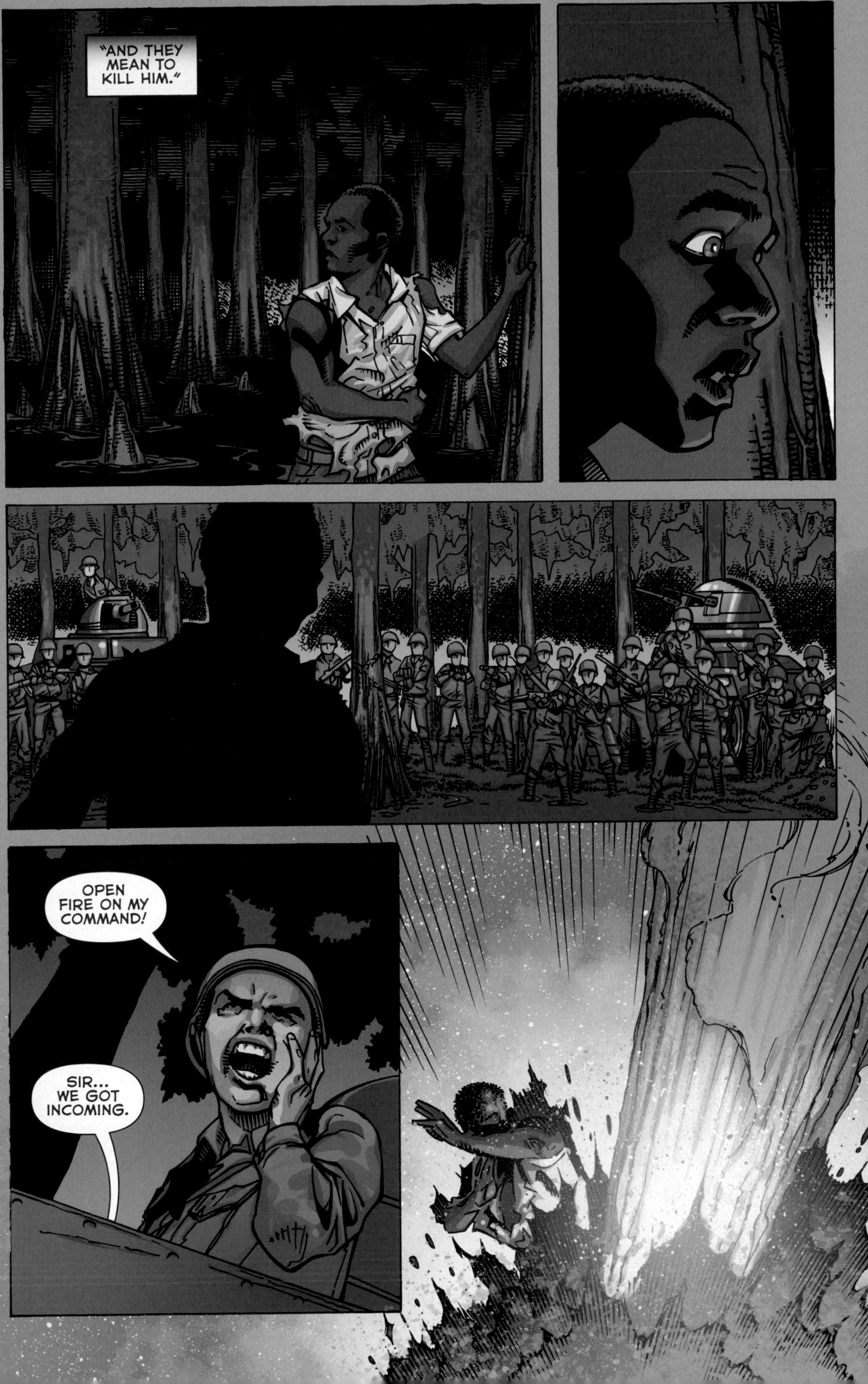
"AND THEY MEAN TO KILL HIM."
OPEN FIRE ON MY COMMAND!
SIR... WE GOT INCOMING.

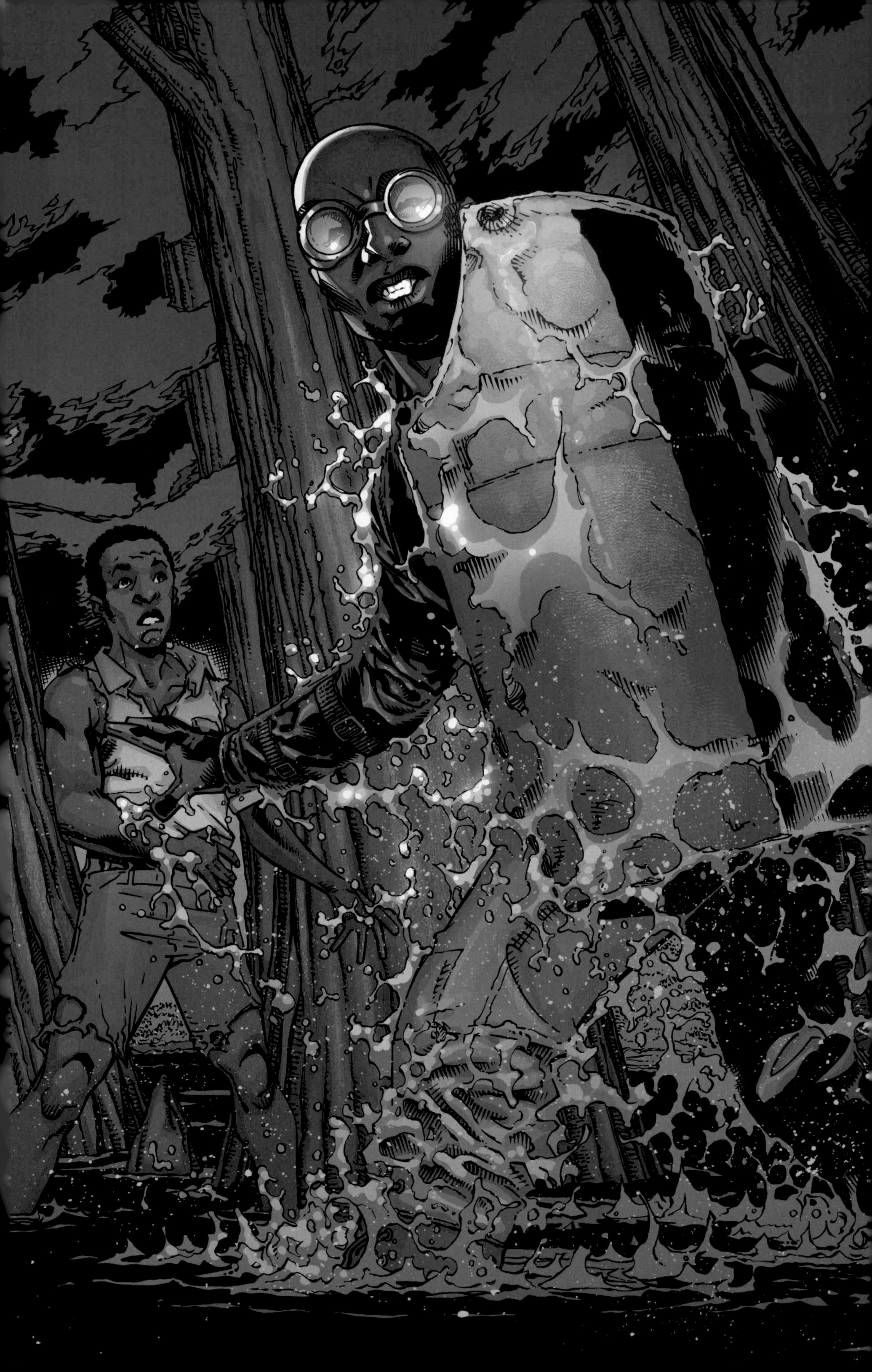

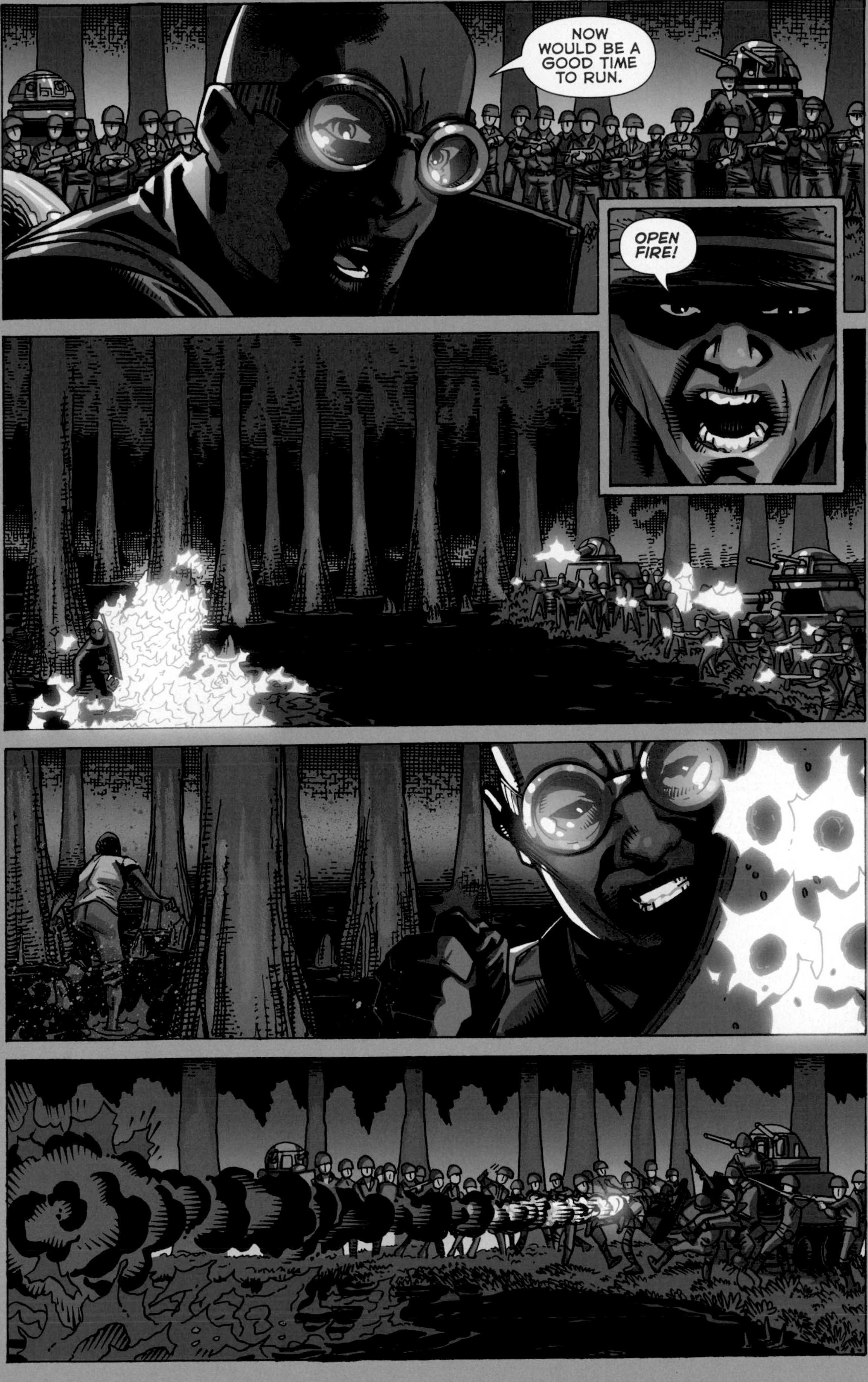
NOW WOULD BE A GOOD TIME TO RUN.
OPEN FIRE!

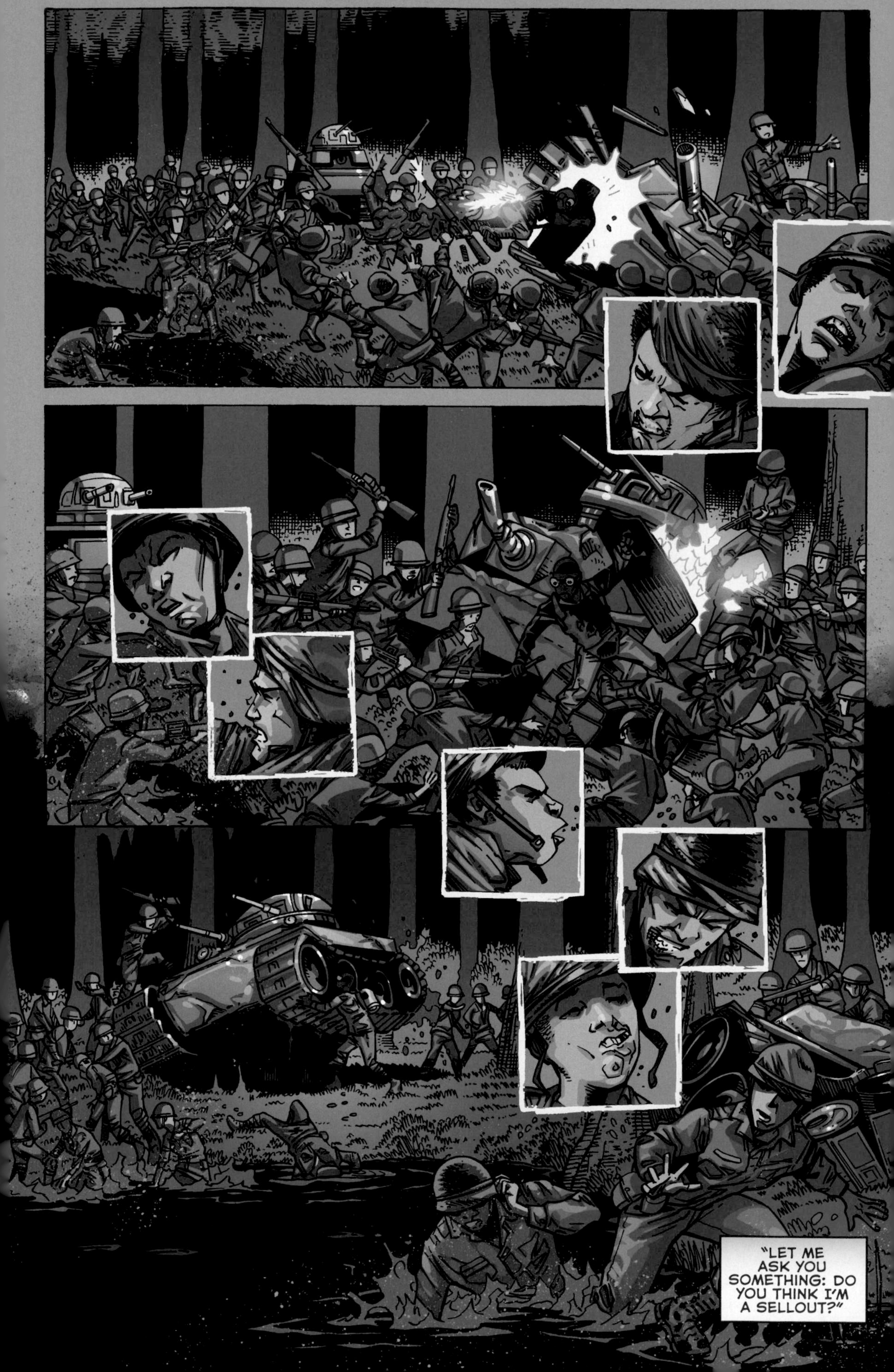
"LET ME ASK YOU SOMETHING: DO YOU THINK I'M A SELLOUT?"

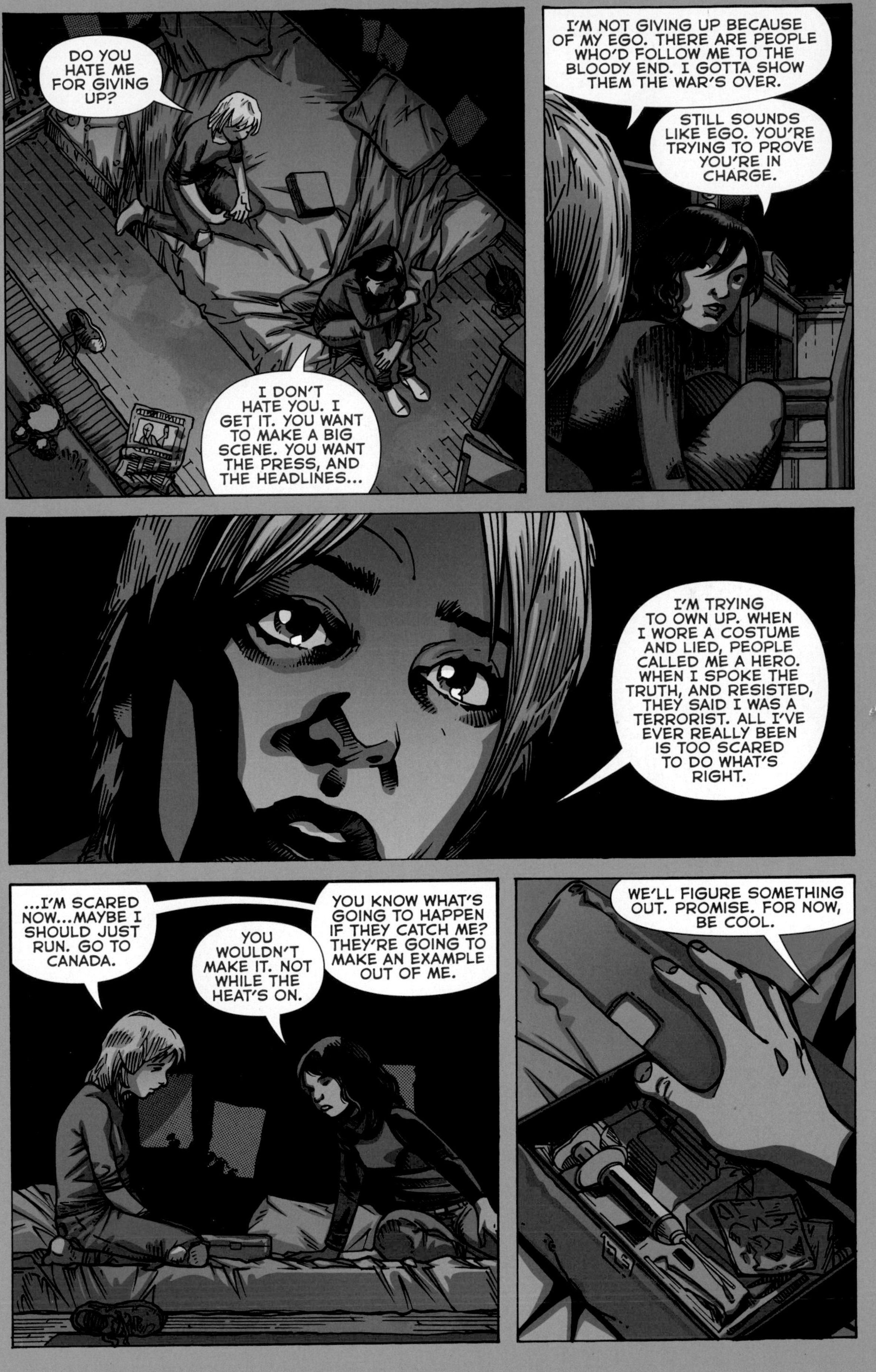
DO YOU HATE ME FOR GIVING UP?
I DON'T HATE YOU. I GET IT. YOU WANT TO MAKE A BIG SCENE. YOU WANT THE PRESS, AND THE HEADLINES...
I'M NOT GIVING UP BECAUSE OF MY EGO. THERE ARE PEOPLE WHO'D FOLLOW ME TO THE BLOODY END. I GOTTA SHOW THEM THE WAR'S OVER.
STILL SOUNDS LIKE EGO. YOU'RE TRYING TO PROVE YOU'RE IN CHARGE.
I'M TRYING TO OWN UP. WHEN I WORE A COSTUME AND LIED, PEOPLE CALLED ME A HERO. WHEN I SPOKE THE TRUTH, AND RESISTED, THEY SAID I WAS A TERRORIST. ALL I'VE EVER REALLY BEEN IS TOO SCARED TO DO WHAT'S RIGHT.
...I'M SCARED NOW...MAYBE I SHOULD JUST RUN. GO TO CANADA.
YOU WOULDN'T MAKE IT. NOT WHILE THE HEAT'S ON.
YOU KNOW WHAT'S GOING TO HAPPEN IF THEY CATCH ME? THEY'RE GOING TO MAKE AN EXAMPLE OUT OF ME.
WE'LL FIGURE SOMETHING OUT. PROMISE. FOR NOW, BE COOL.

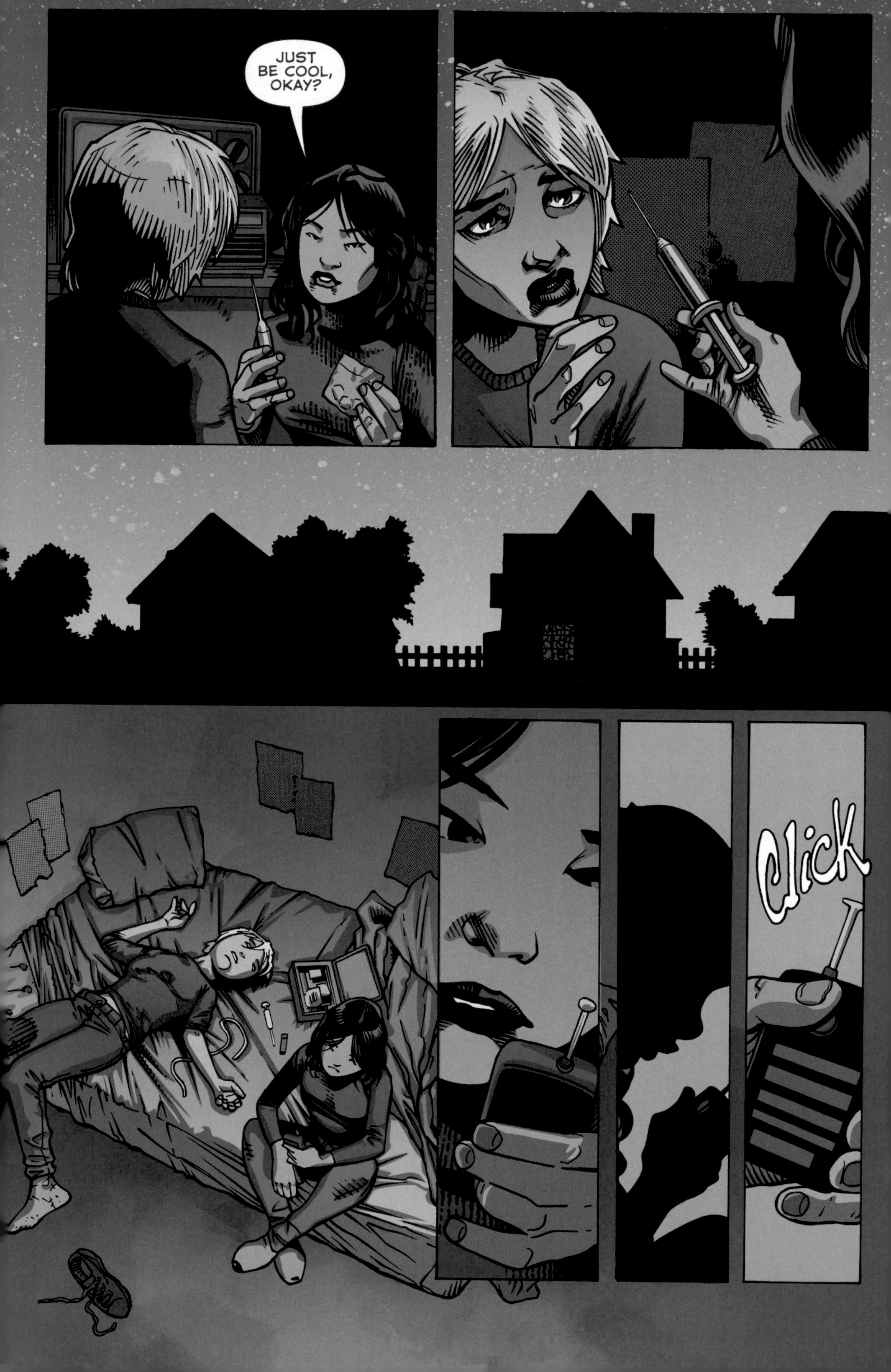
JUST BE COOL, OKAY?
CLICK

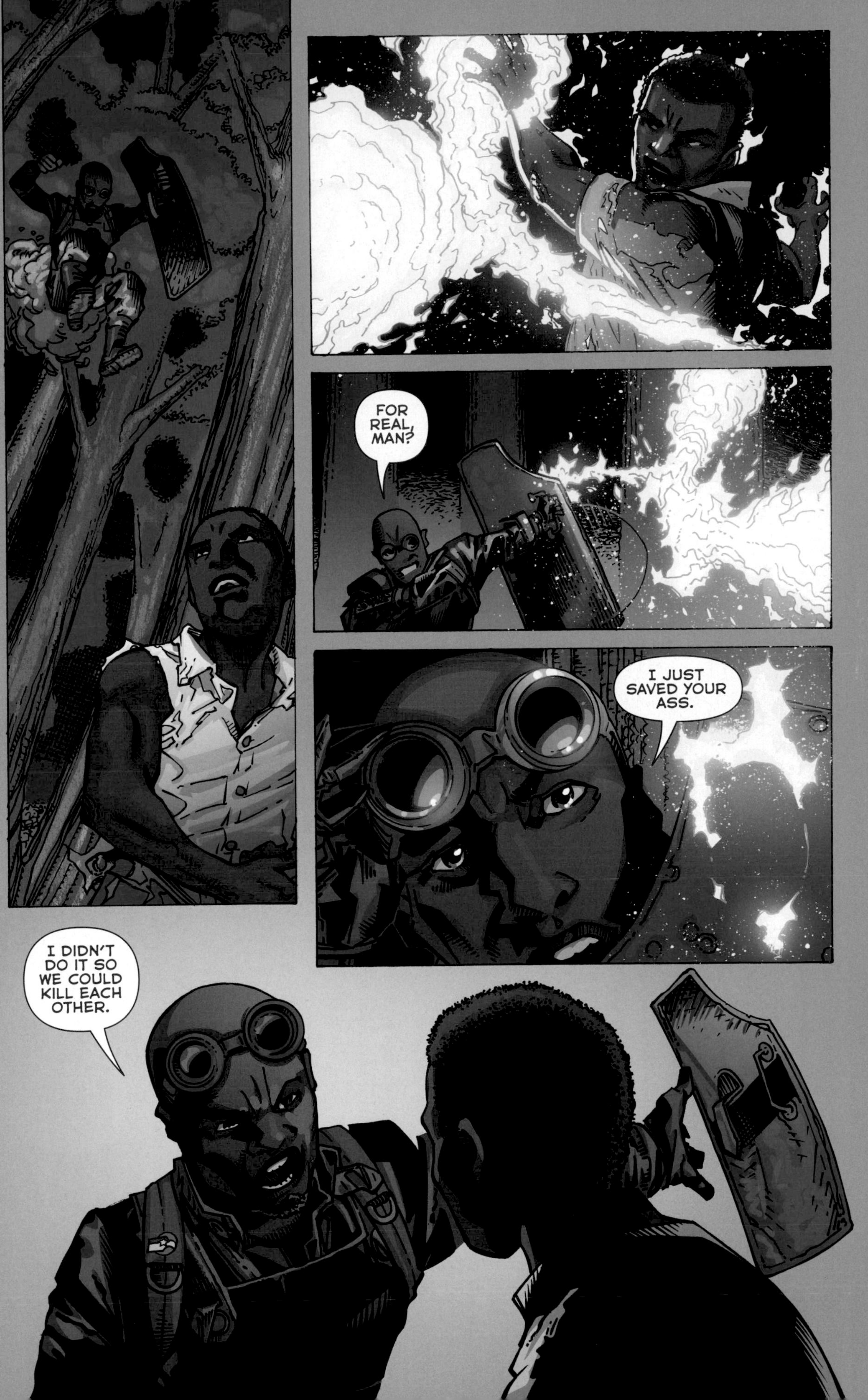
FOR REAL, MAN?
I JUST SAVED YOUR ASS.
I DIDN'T DO IT SO WE COULD KILL EACH OTHER.

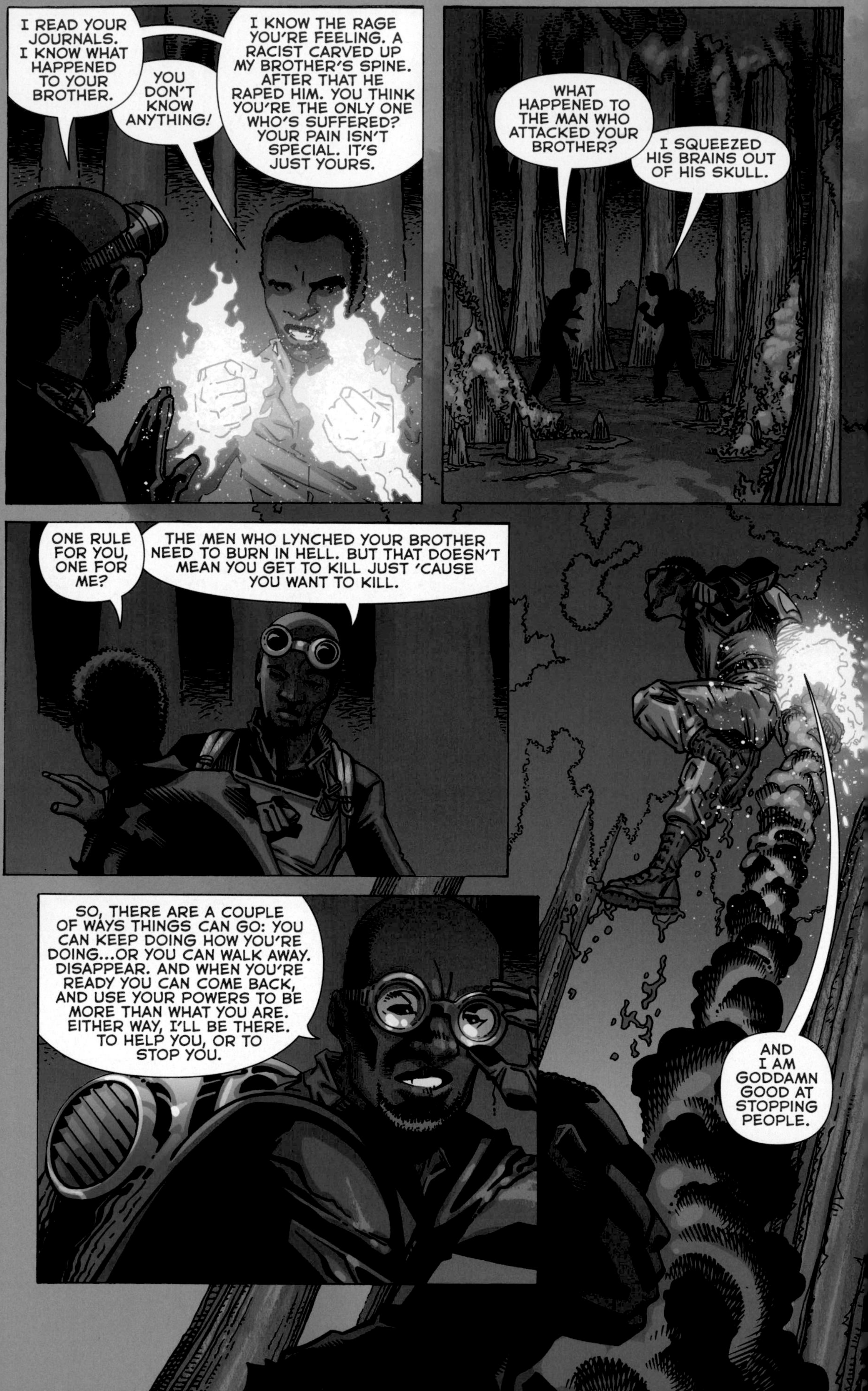
I READ YOUR JOURNALS. I KNOW WHAT HAPPENED TO YOUR BROTHER.
YOU DON'T KNOW ANYTHING!
I KNOW THE RAGE YOU'RE FEELING. A RACIST CARVED UP MY BROTHER'S SPINE. AFTER THAT HE RAPED HIM. YOU THINK YOU'RE THE ONLY ONE WHO'S SUFFERED? YOUR PAIN ISN'T SPECIAL. IT'S JUST YOURS.
WHAT HAPPENED TO THE MAN WHO ATTACKED YOUR BROTHER?
I SQUEEZED HIS BRAINS OUT OF HIS SKULL.
ONE RULE FOR YOU, ONE FOR ME?
THE MEN WHO LYNCHED YOUR BROTHER NEED TO BURN IN HELL. BUT THAT DOESN'T MEAN YOU GET TO KILL JUST 'CAUSE YOU WANT TO KILL.
SO, THERE ARE A COUPLE OF WAYS THINGS CAN GO: YOU CAN KEEP DOING HOW YOU'RE DOING...OR YOU CAN WALK AWAY. DISAPPEAR. AND WHEN YOU'RE READY YOU CAN COME BACK, AND USE YOUR POWERS TO BE MORE THAN WHAT YOU ARE. EITHER WAY, I'LL BE THERE. TO HELP YOU, OR TO STOP YOU.
AND I AM GODDAMN GOOD AT STOPPING PEOPLE.

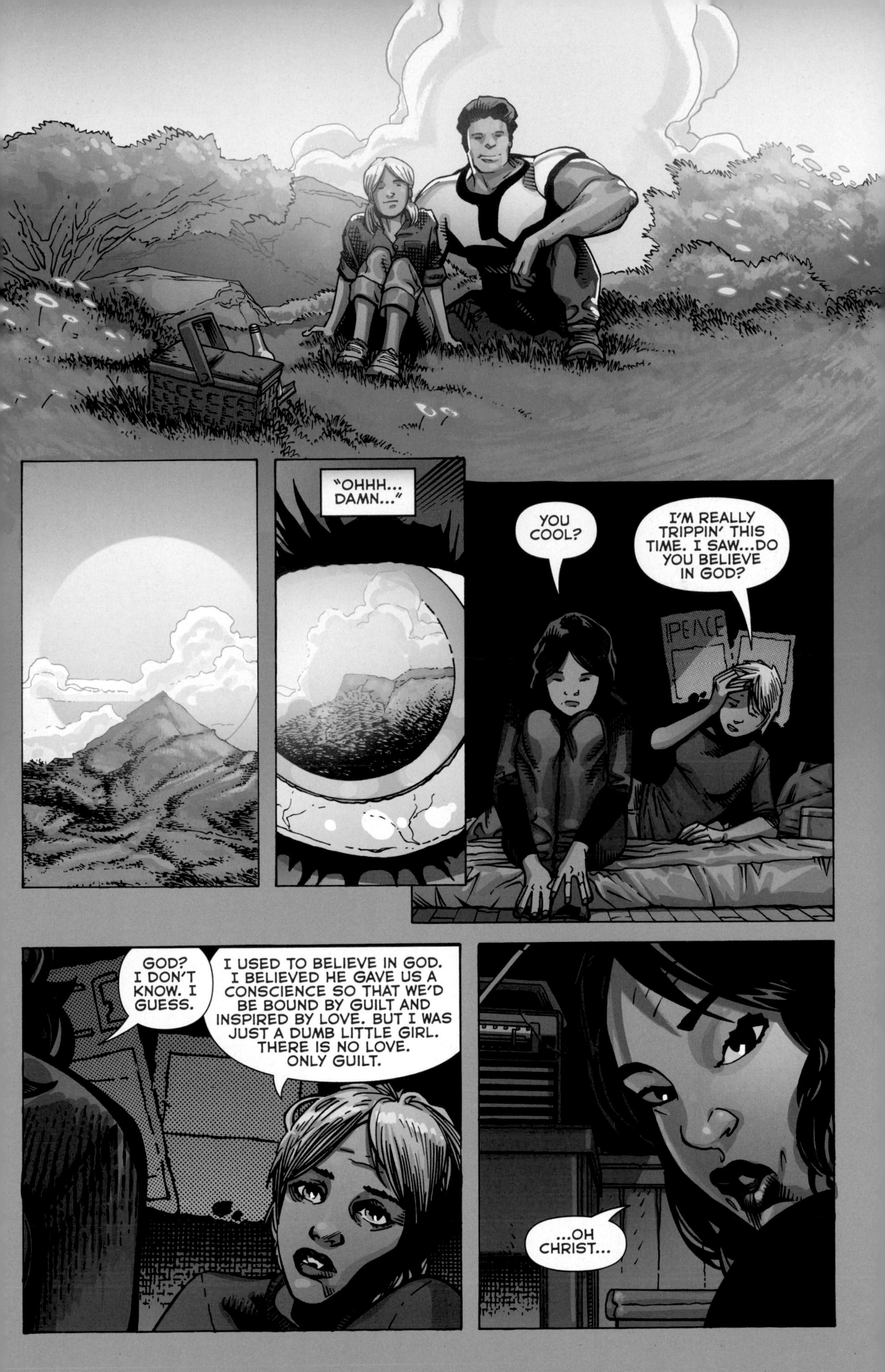
"OHHH... DAMN..."
YOU COOL?
I'M REALLY TRIPPIN' THIS TIME. I SAW...DO YOU BELIEVE IN GOD?
PEACE
GOD? I DON'T KNOW. I GUESS.
I USED TO BELIEVE IN GOD. I BELIEVED HE GAVE US A CONSCIENCE SO THAT WE'D BE BOUND BY GUILT AND INSPIRED BY LOVE. BUT I WAS JUST A DUMB LITTLE GIRL. THERE IS NO LOVE. ONLY GUILT.
...OH CHRIST...

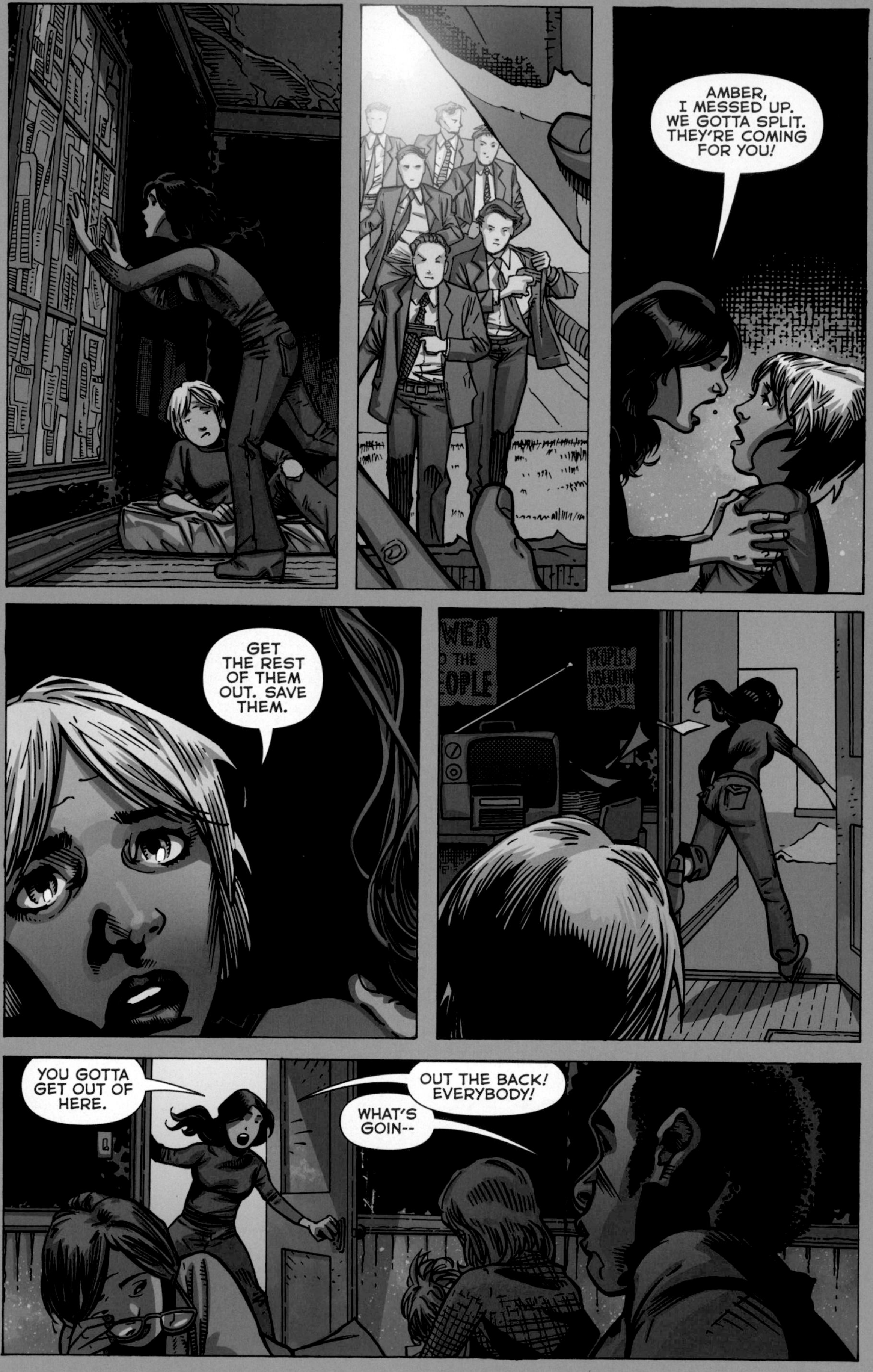
AMBER, I MESSED UP. WE GOTTA SPLIT. THEY'RE COMING FOR YOU!
GET THE REST OF THEM OUT. SAVE THEM.
PEOPLES LIBERATION FRONT
YOU GOTTA GET OUT OF HERE.
OUT THE BACK! EVERYBODY!
WHAT'S GOIN--

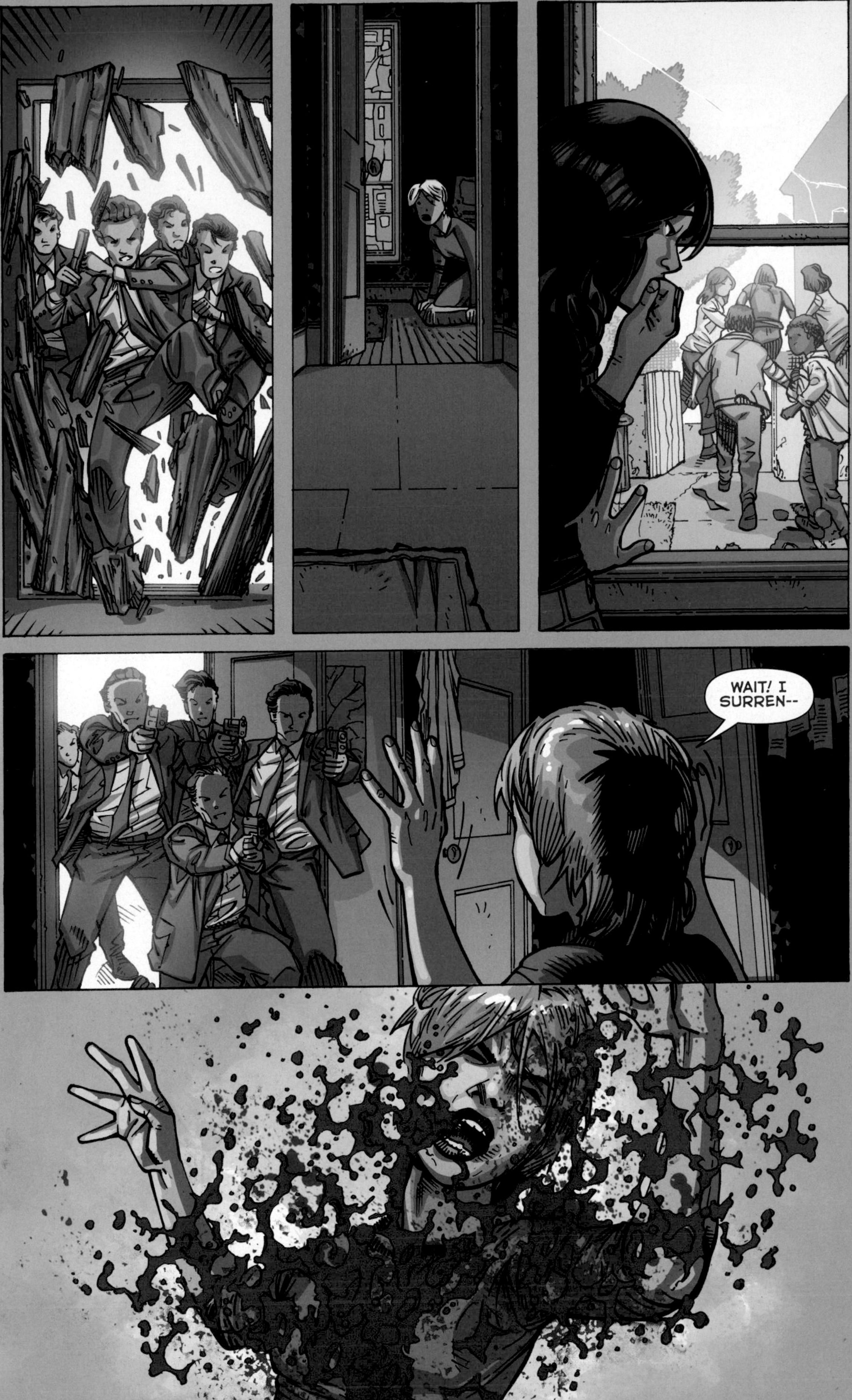
WAIT! I SURREN--

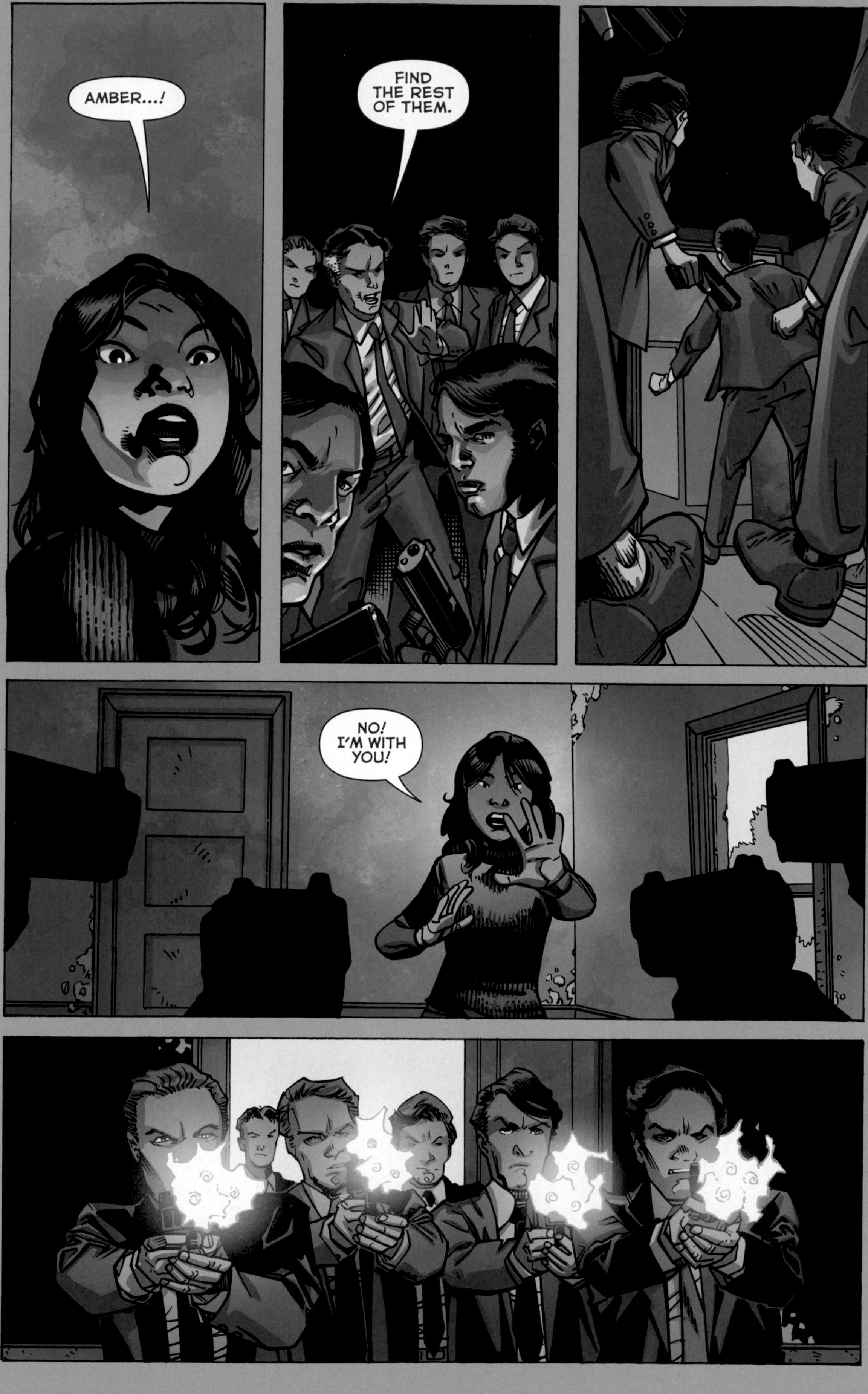
AMBER...!
FIND THE REST OF THEM.
NO! I'M WITH YOU!

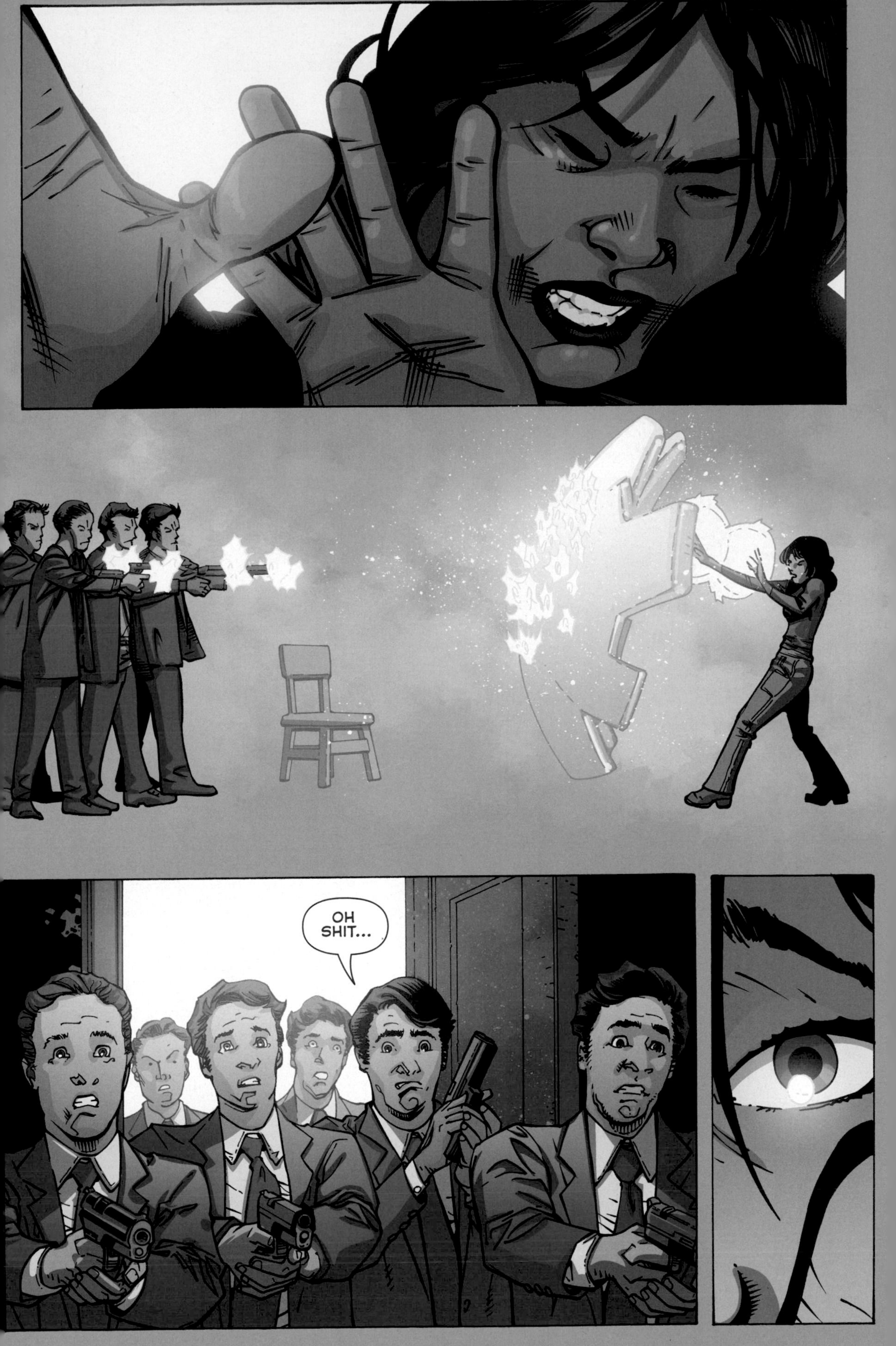
OH SHIT...

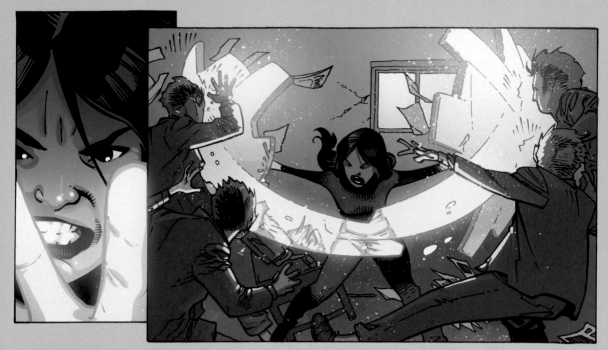

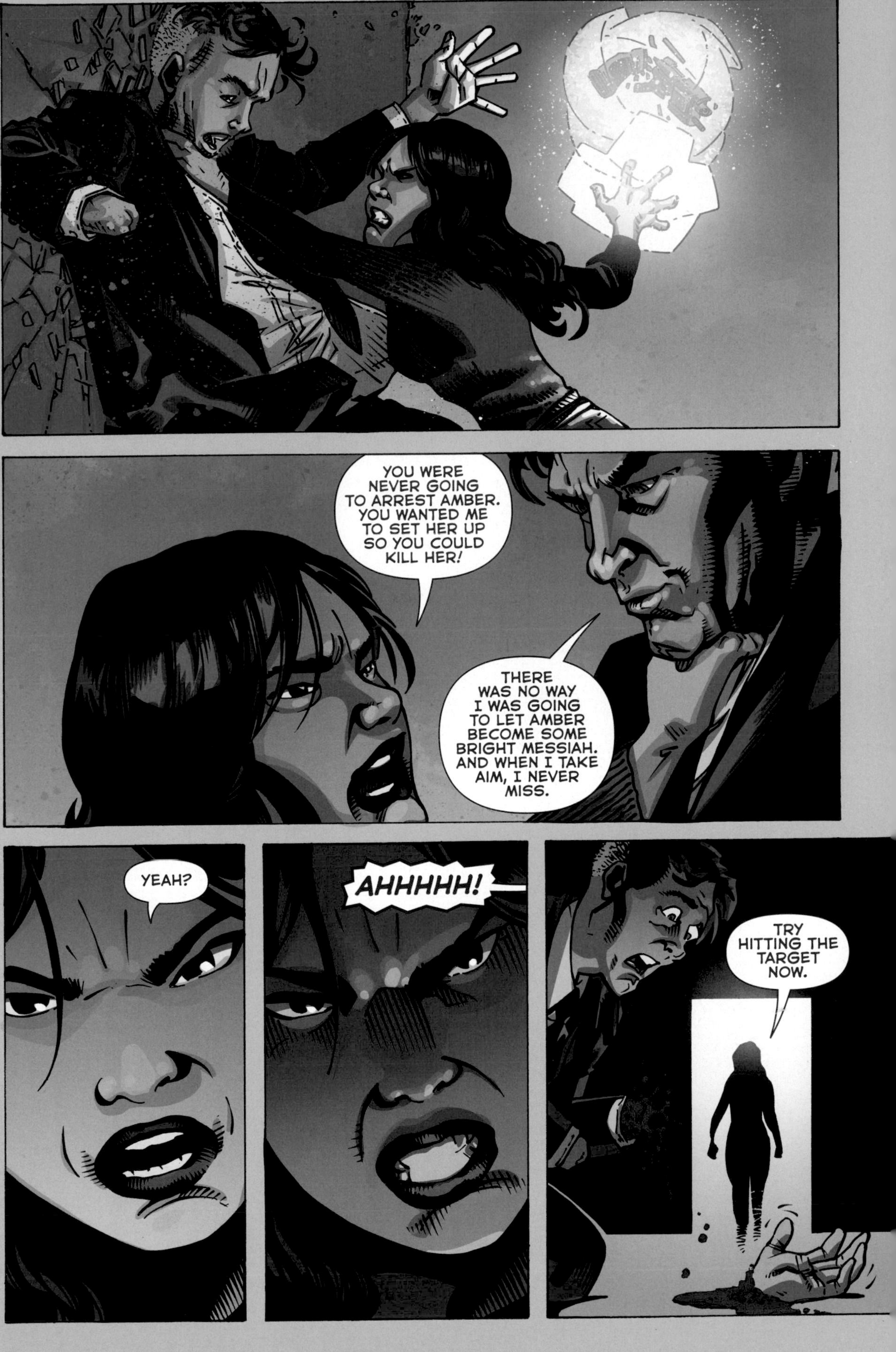

YOU WERE NEVER GOING TO ARREST AMBER. YOU WANTED ME TO SET HER UP SO YOU COULD KILL HER!
THERE WAS NO WAY I WAS GOING TO LET AMBER BECOME SOME BRIGHT MESSIAH. AND WHEN I TAKE AIM, I NEVER MISS.
YEAH?
AHHHHH!
TRY HITTING THE TARGET NOW.

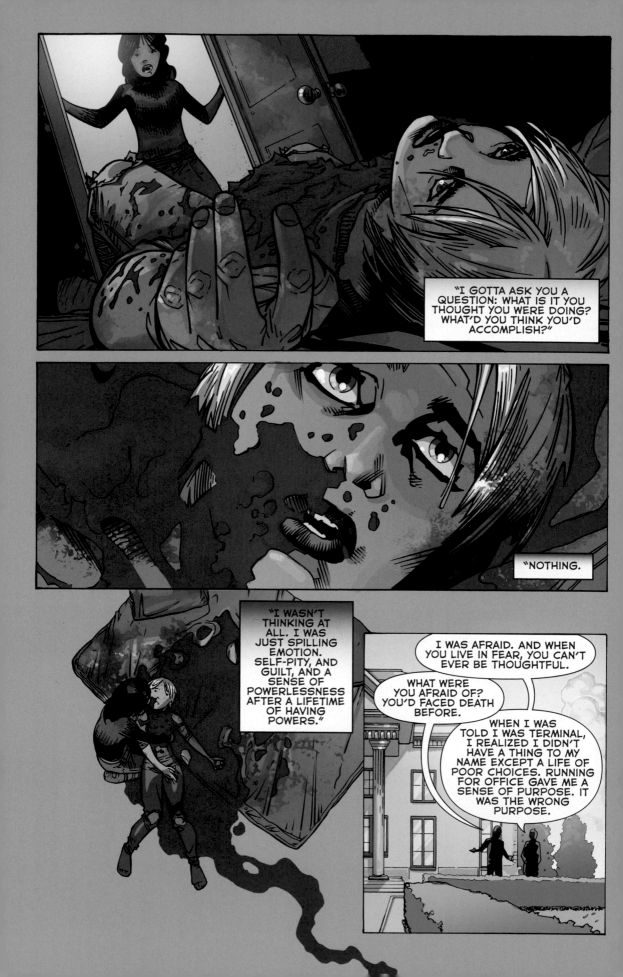

"I GOTTA ASK YOU A QUESTION: WHAT IS IT YOU THOUGHT YOU WERE DOING? WHAT'D YOU THINK YOU'D ACCOMPLISH?"

"NOTHING.

"I WASN'T THINKING AT ALL. I WAS JUST SPILLING EMOTION. SELF-PITY, AND GUILT, AND A SENSE OF POWERLESSNESS AFTER A LIFETIME OF HAVING POWERS."

I WAS AFRAID. AND WHEN YOU LIVE IN FEAR, YOU CAN'T EVER BE THOUGHTFUL.

WHAT WERE YOU AFRAID OF? YOU'D FACED DEATH BEFORE.

WHEN I WAS TOLD I WAS TERMINAL, I REALIZED I DIDN'T HAVE A THING TO MY NAME EXCEPT A LIFE OF POOR CHOICES. RUNNING FOR OFFICE GAVE ME A SENSE OF PURPOSE. IT WAS THE WRONG PURPOSE.

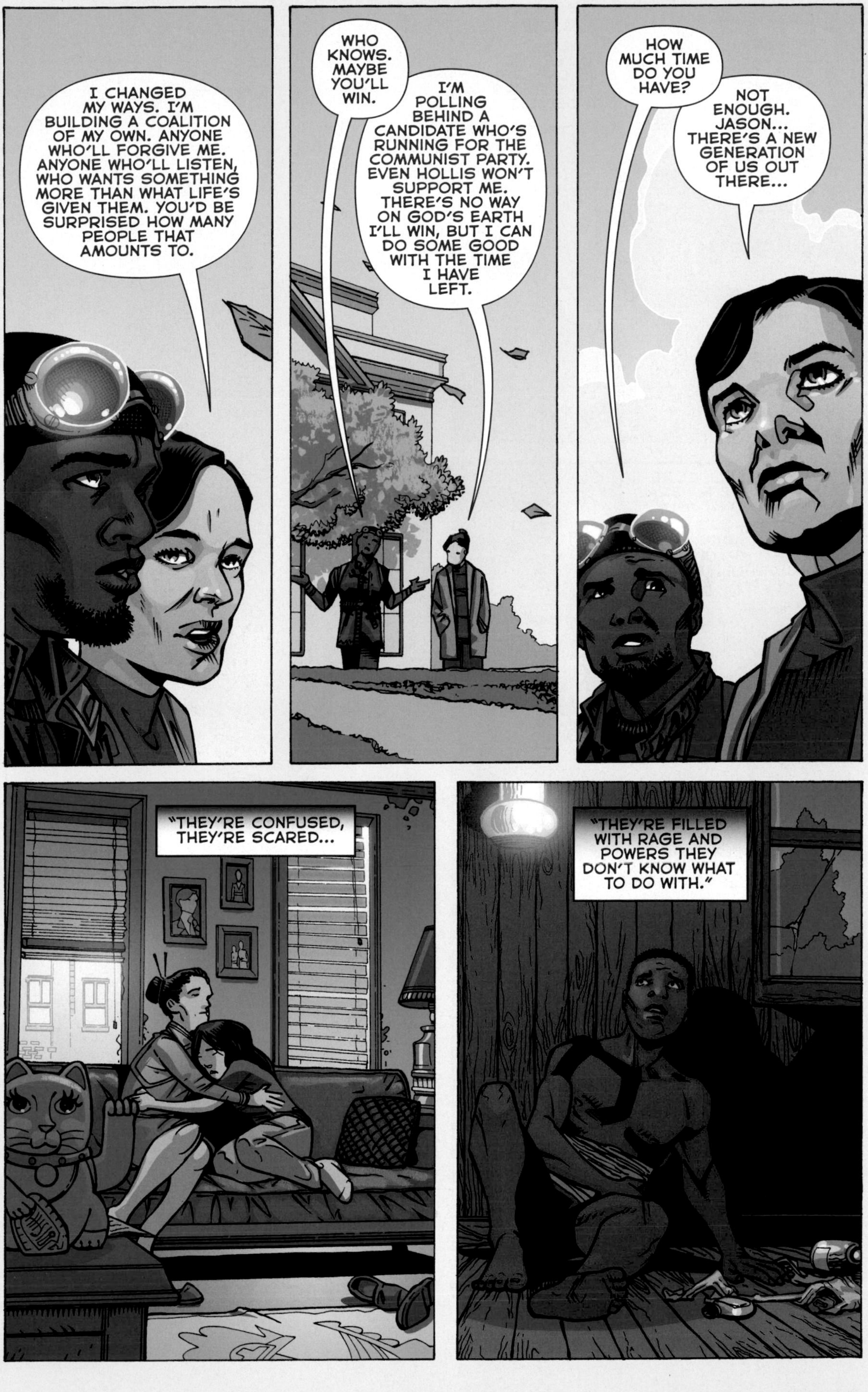
I CHANGED MY WAYS. I'M BUILDING A COALITION OF MY OWN. ANYONE WHO'LL FORGIVE ME. ANYONE WHO'LL LISTEN, WHO WANTS SOMETHING MORE THAN WHAT LIFE'S GIVEN THEM. YOU'D BE SURPRISED HOW MANY PEOPLE THAT AMOUNTS TO.
WHO KNOWS. MAYBE YOU'LL WIN.
I'M POLLING BEHIND A CANDIDATE WHO'S RUNNING FOR THE COMMUNIST PARTY. EVEN HOLLIS WON'T SUPPORT ME. THERE'S NO WAY ON GOD'S EARTH I'LL WIN, BUT I CAN DO SOME GOOD WITH THE TIME I HAVE LEFT.
HOW MUCH TIME DO YOU HAVE?
NOT ENOUGH. JASON... THERE'S A NEW GENERATION OF US OUT THERE...
"THEY'RE CONFUSED, THEY'RE SCARED...
"THEY'RE FILLED WITH RAGE AND POWERS THEY DON'T KNOW WHAT TO DO WITH."

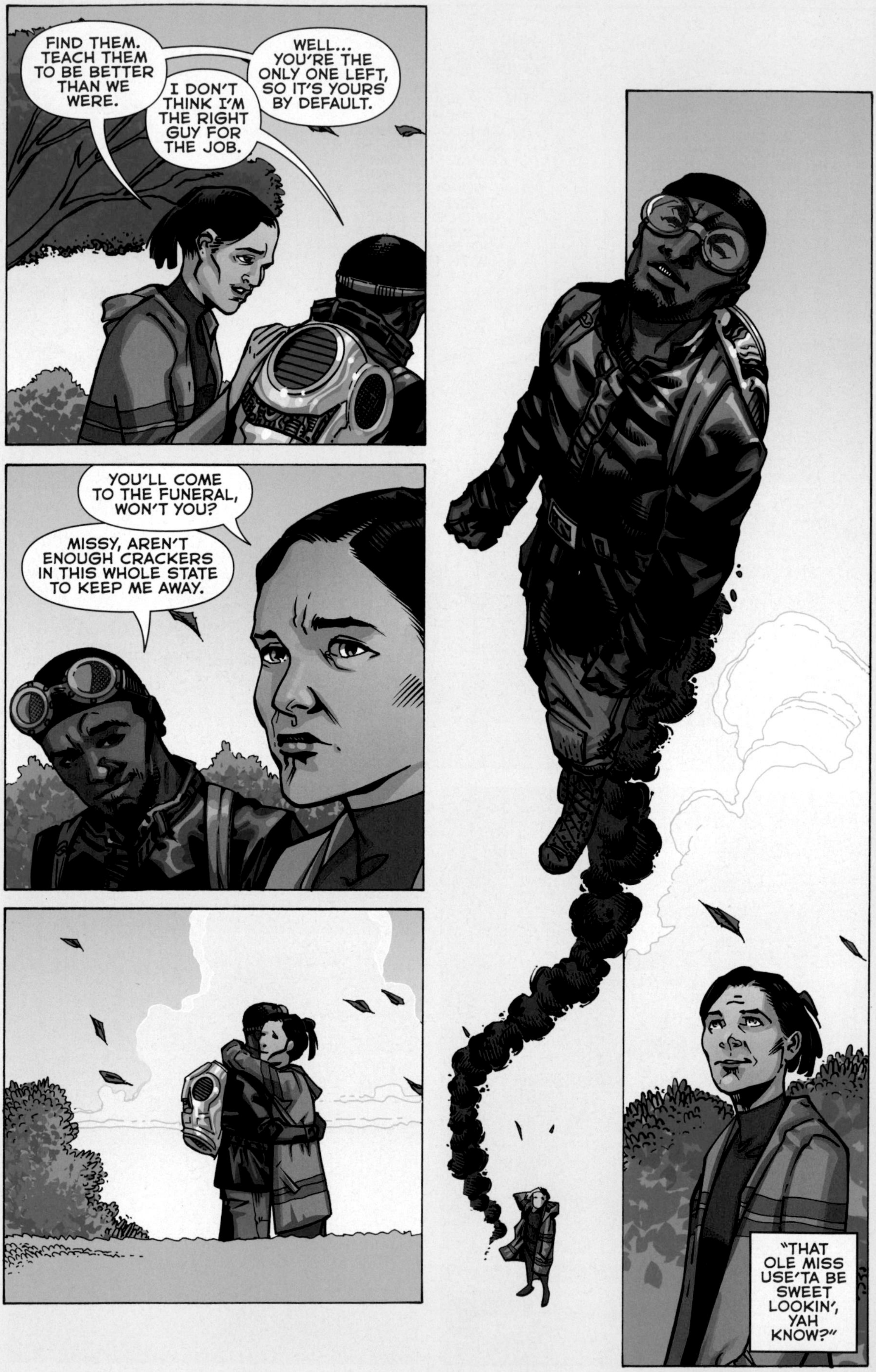
FIND THEM. TEACH THEM TO BE BETTER THAN WE WERE.
I DON'T THINK I'M THE RIGHT GUY FOR THE JOB.
WELL... YOU'RE THE ONLY ONE LEFT, SO IT'S YOURS BY DEFAULT.
YOU'LL COME TO THE FUNERAL, WON'T YOU?
MISSY, AREN'T ENOUGH CRACKERS IN THIS WHOLE STATE TO KEEP ME AWAY.
"THAT OLE MISS USE'TA BE SWEET LOOKIN', YAH KNOW?"

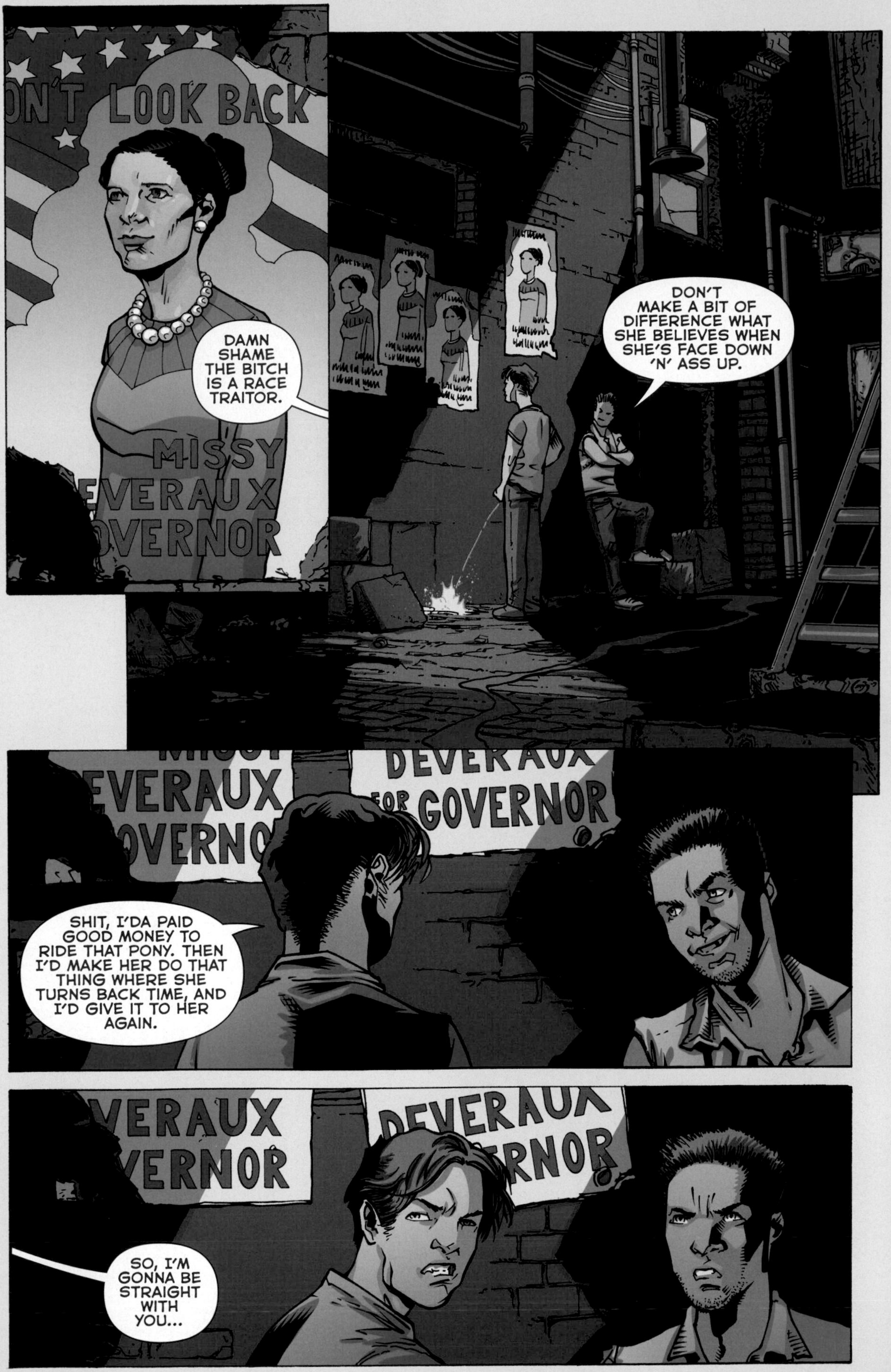

ON'T LOOK BACK
MISSY DEVERAUX GOVERNOR
DAMN SHAME THE BITCH IS A RACE TRAITOR.
DON'T MAKE A BIT OF DIFFERENCE WHAT SHE BELIEVES WHEN SHE'S FACE DOWN 'N' ASS UP.
DEVERAUX FOR GOVERNOR
SHIT, I'DA PAID GOOD MONEY TO RIDE THAT PONY. THEN I'D MAKE HER DO THAT THING WHERE SHE TURNS BACK TIME, AND I'D GIVE IT TO HER AGAIN.
SO, I'M GONNA BE STRAIGHT WITH YOU...

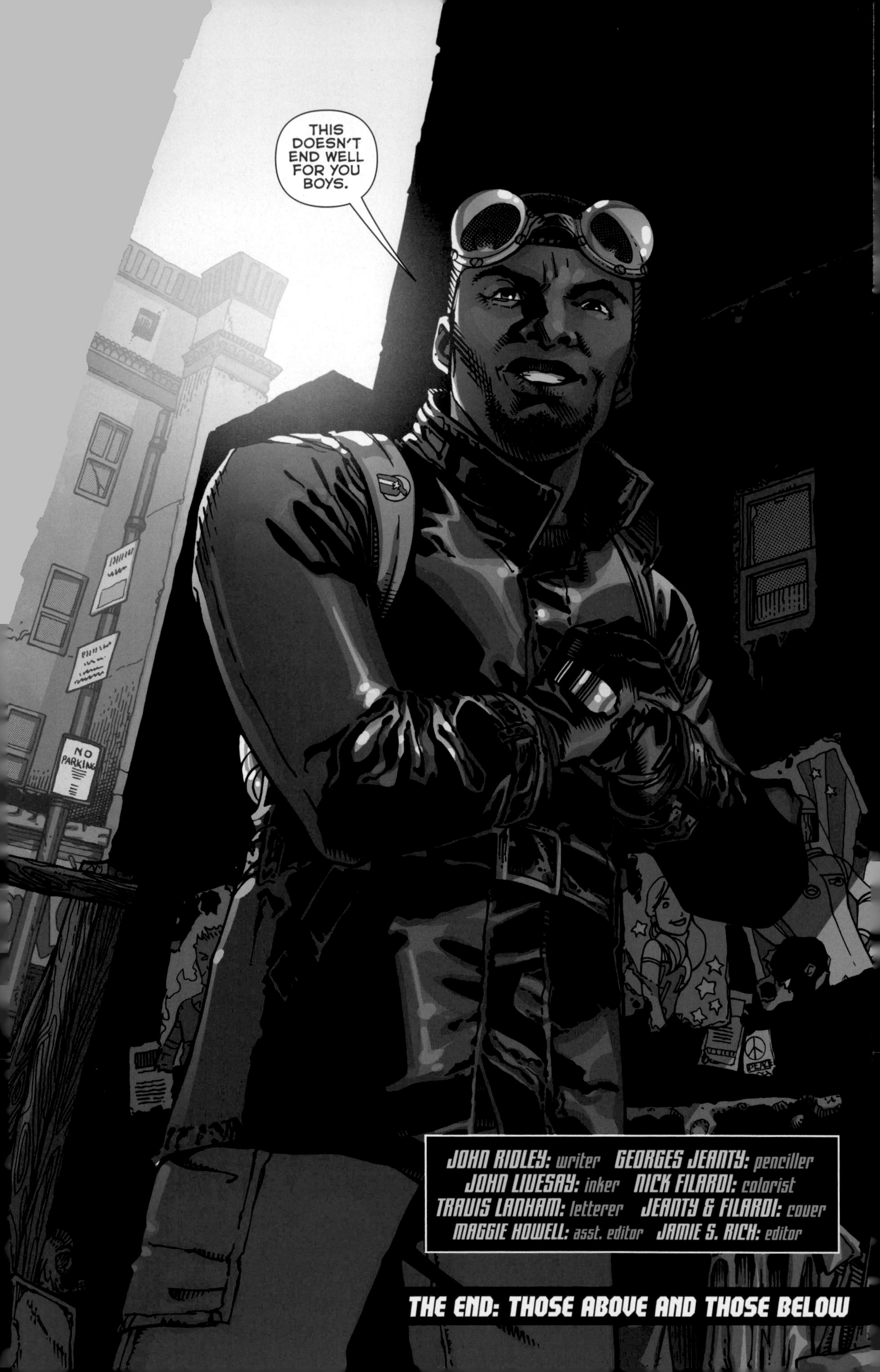
THIS DOESN'T END WELL FOR YOU BOYS.
NO PARKING
JOHN RIDLEY: writer GEORGES JEANTY: penciller
JOHN LIVESAY: inker NICK FILARDI: colorist
TRAVIS LANHAM: letterer JEANTY & FILARDI: cover
MAGGIE HOWELL: asst. editor JAMIE S. RICH: editor
THE END: THOSE ABOVE AND THOSE BELOW

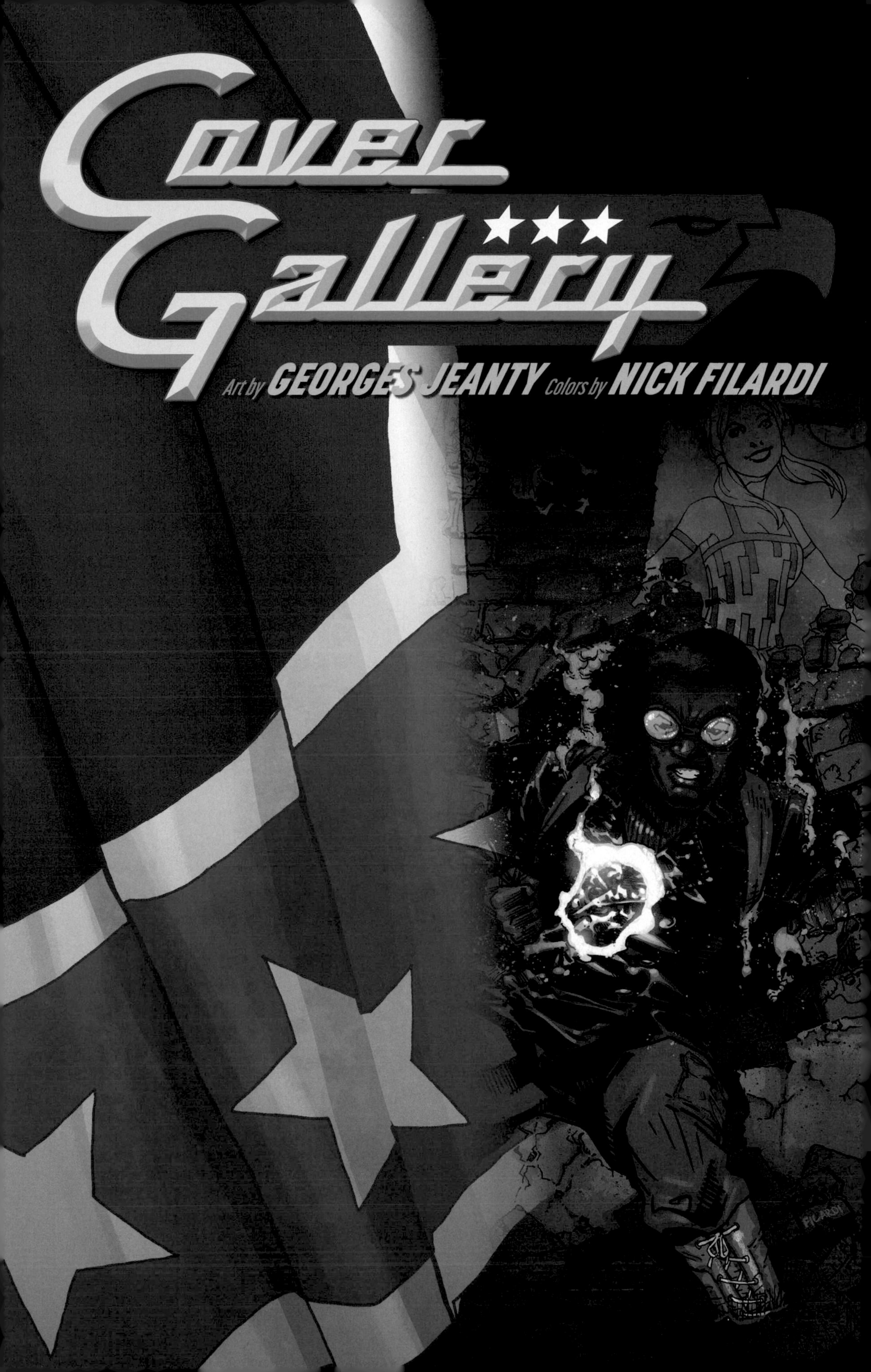
Cover Gallery
Art by GEORGES JEANTY Colors by NICK FILARDI
FILARDI

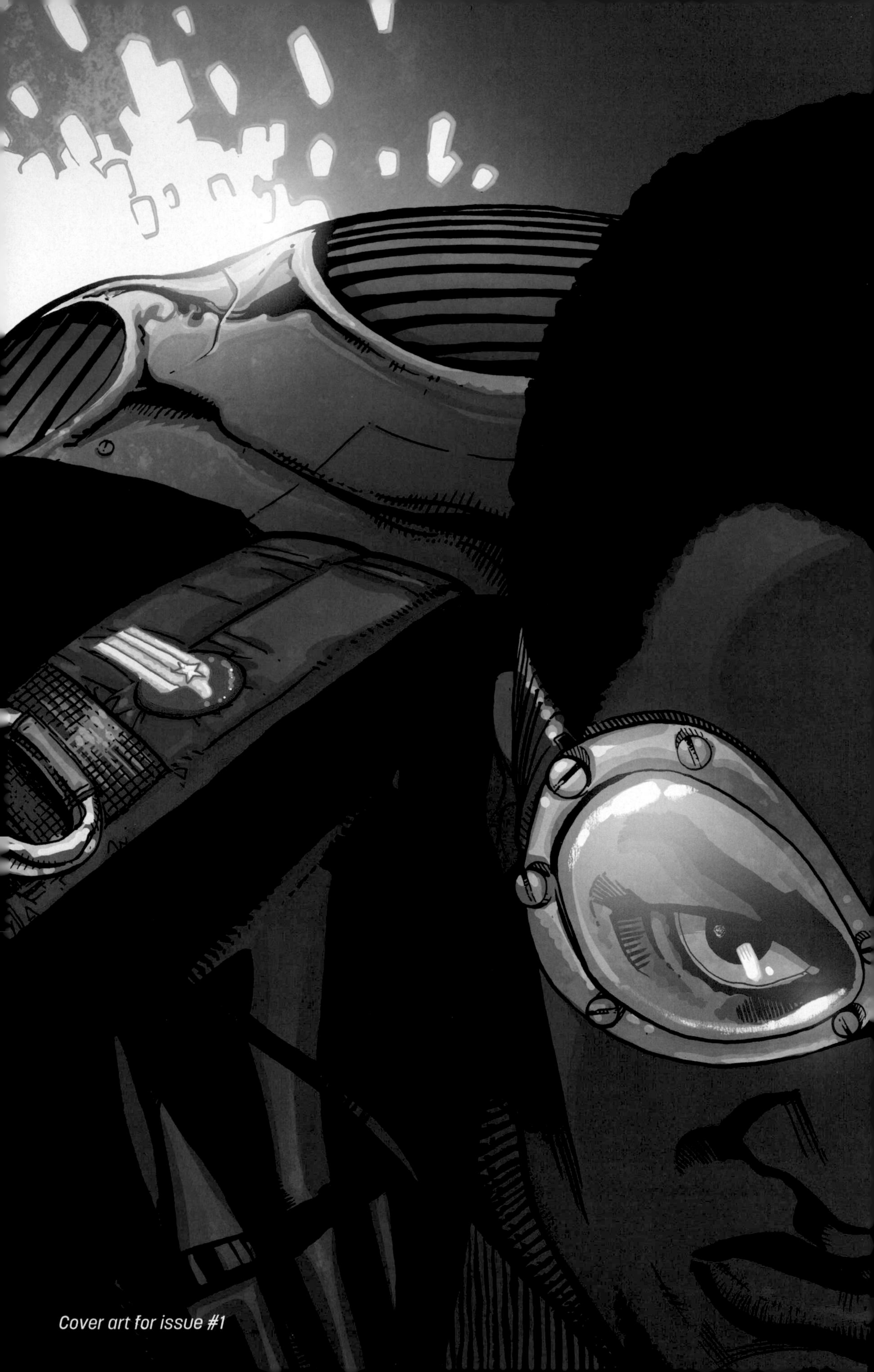

Cover art for issue #1

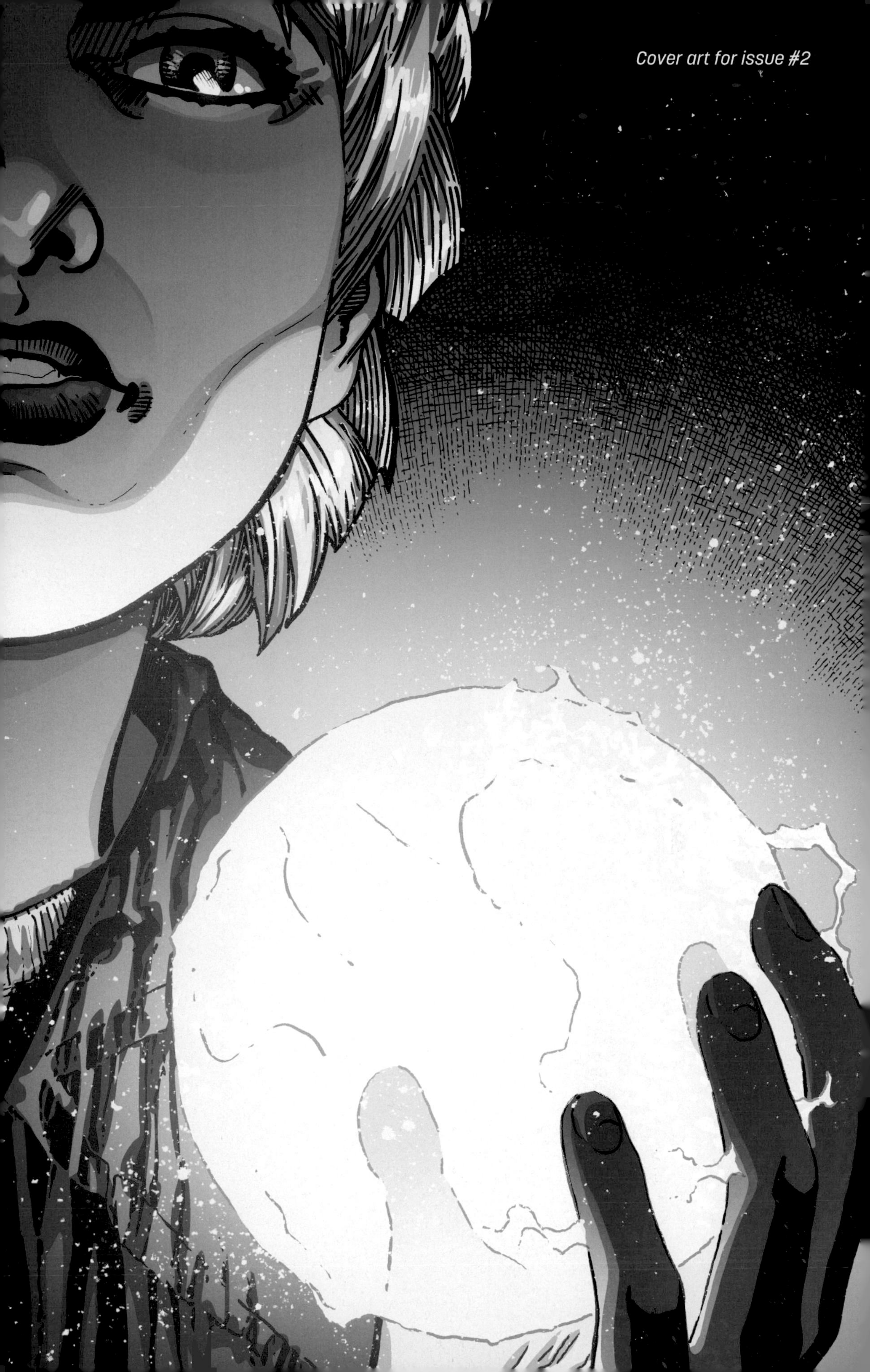

Cover art for issue #2

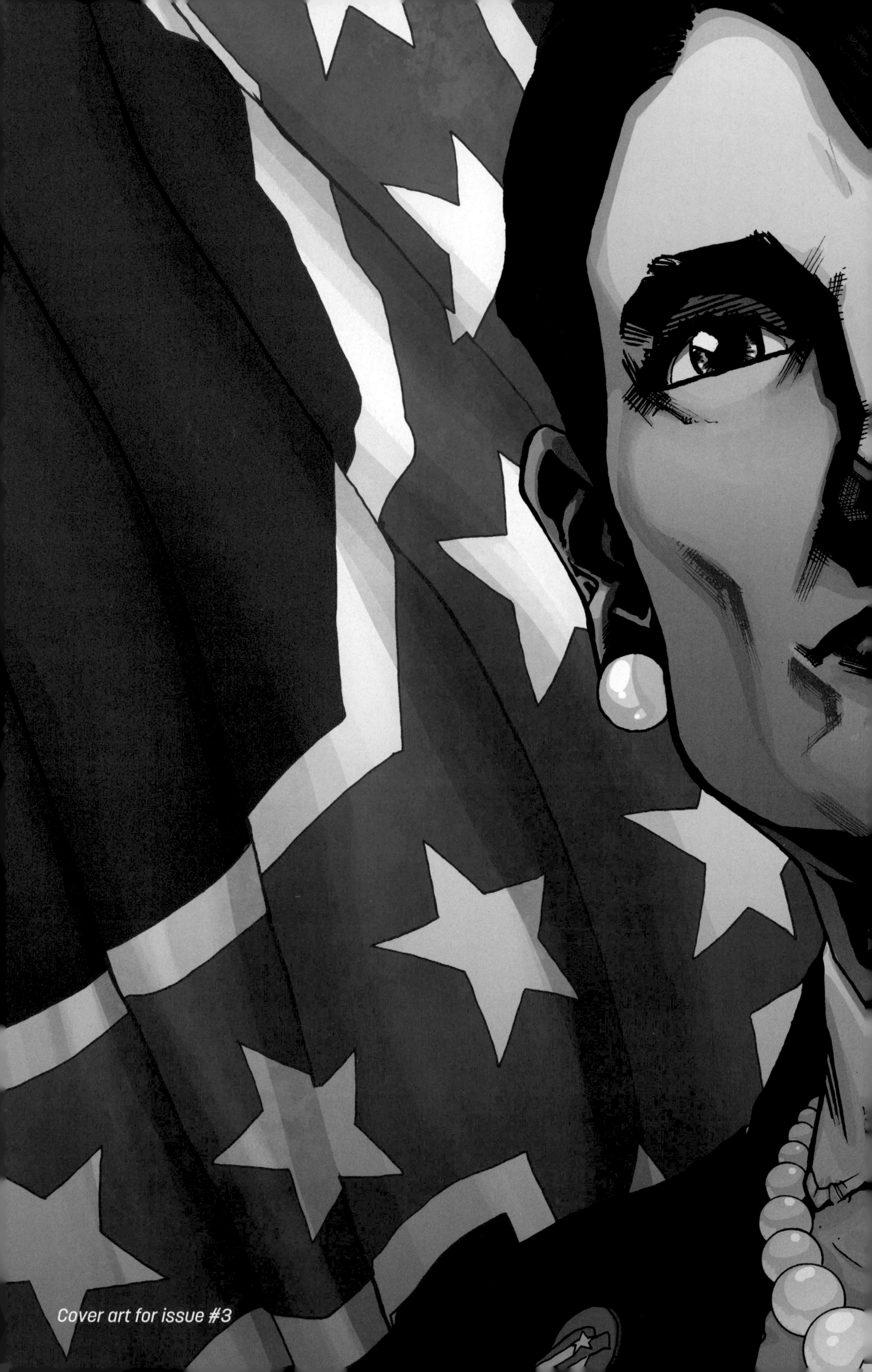

Cover art for issue #3

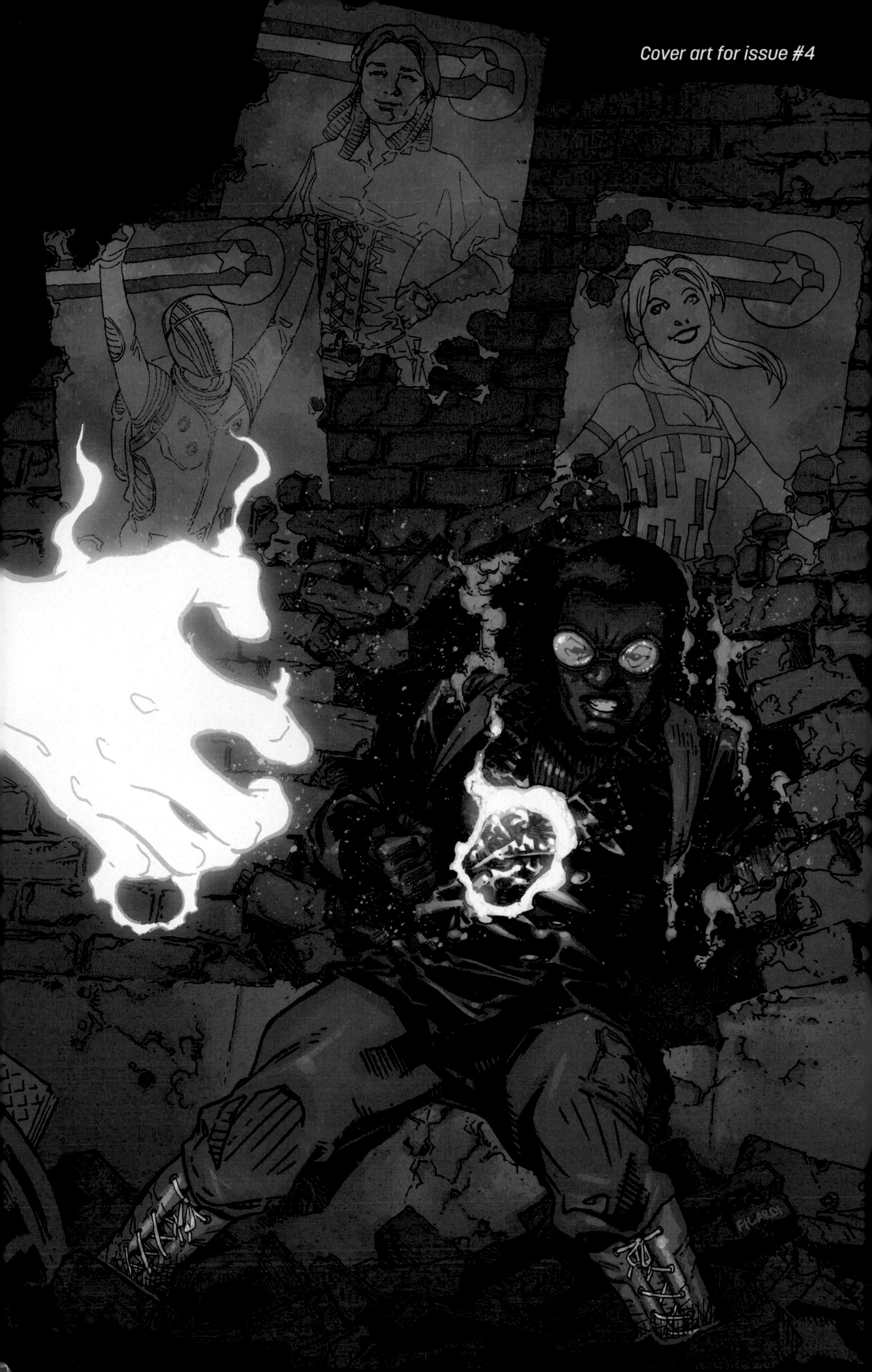

Cover art for issue #4

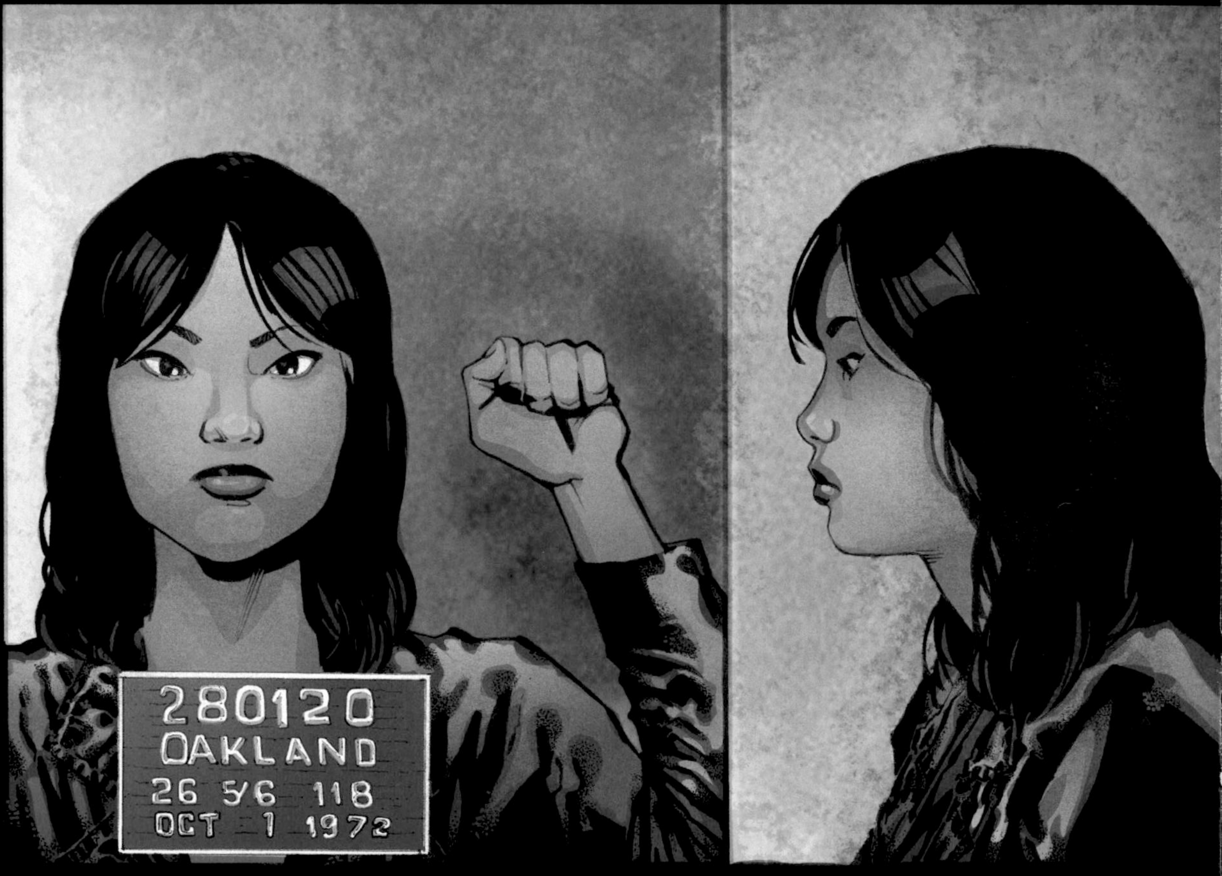
280120
OAKLAND
26 5/6 118
OCT 1 1972

Cover art for issue #6

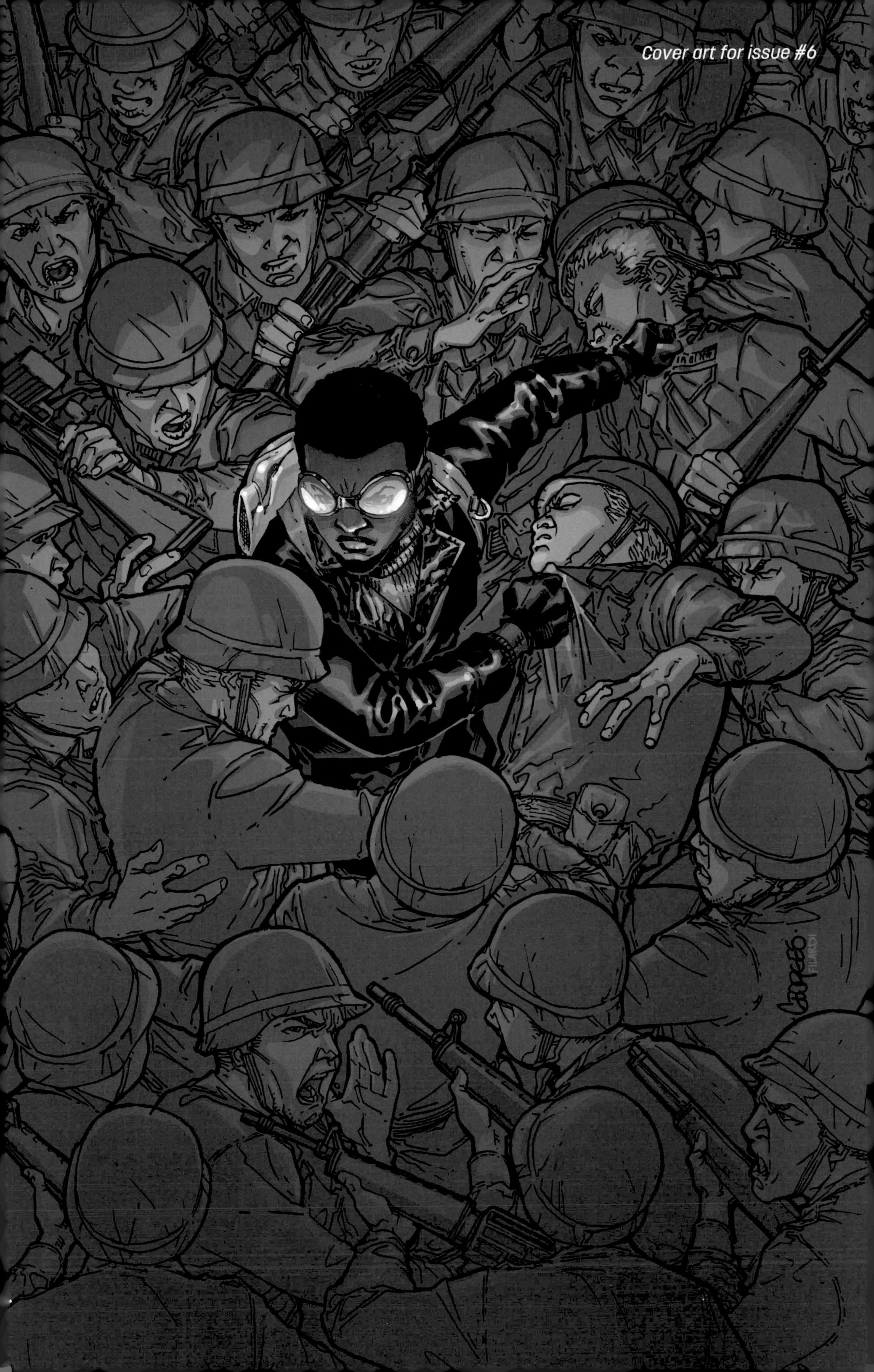

Promotional art

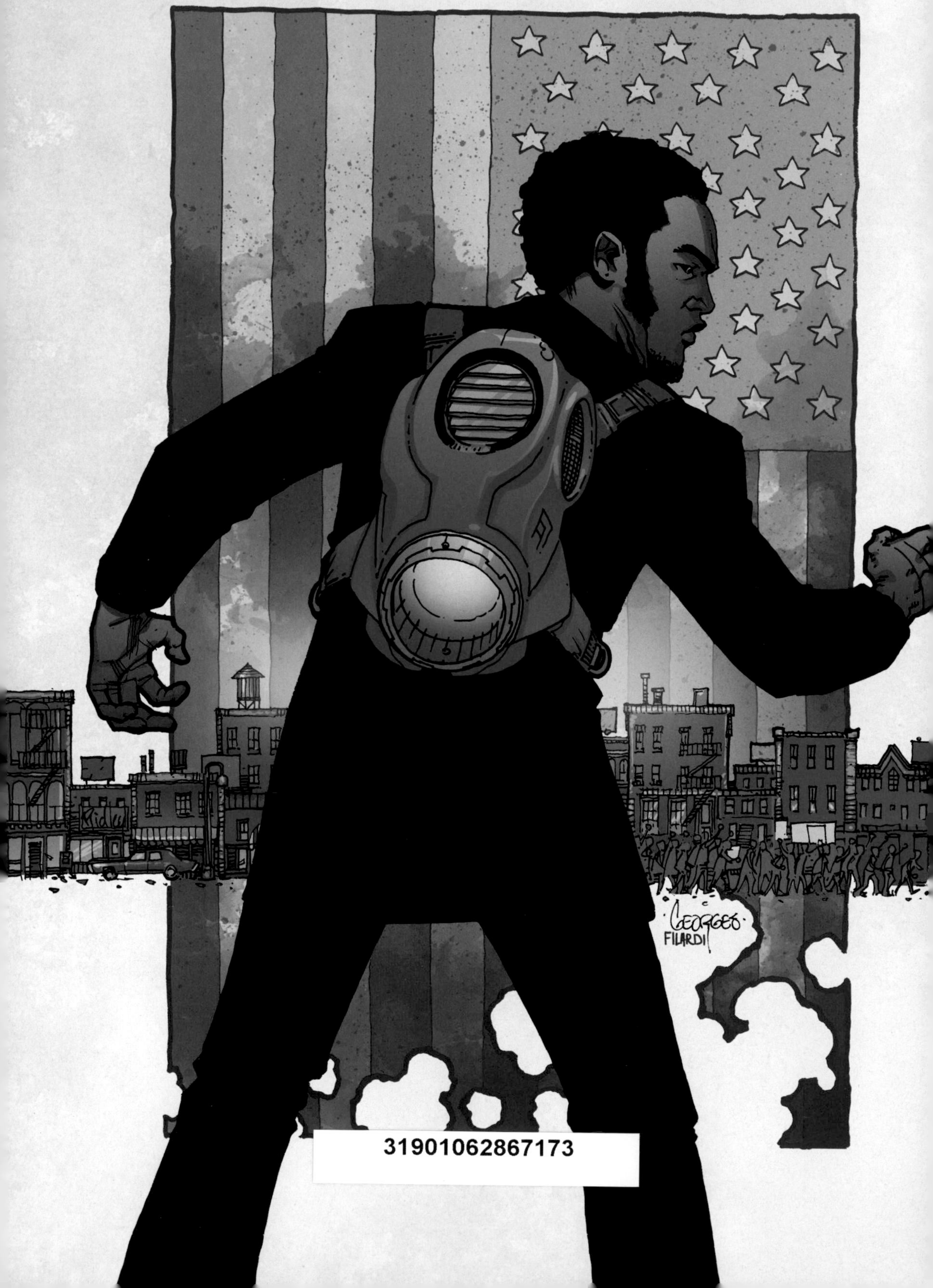
GEORGES FILARDI